COLLEY CIBBER

From a bust, probably by L. F. Roubiliac, in the possession of the National Portrait Gallery, London.

An Appreciation of Colley Cibber

Actor and Dramatist

Together with a Reprint of His Play

'The Careless Husband'

AN APPRECIATION
OF

Colley Cibber

ACTOR AND DRAMATIST

TOGETHER WITH
A REPRINT OF HIS PLAY

THE CARELESS HUSBAND

HASKELL HOUSE PUBLISHERS LTD.
Publishers of Scarce Scholarly Books
NEW YORK, N. Y. 10012
1967

First Published 1928

HASKELL HOUSE PUBLISHERS LTD.
Publishers of Scarce Scholarly Books
280 LAFAYETTE STREET
NEW YORK, N. Y. 10012

Library of Congress Catalog Card Number: 67-30815

Haskell House Catalogue Item # 716

Printed in the United States of America

Bij het beëindigen van mijn proefschrift, breng ik in de eerste plaats dank aan mijn Hooggeachten Promotor, Professor SWAEN, voor de vele en belangrijke hulp, mij steeds op de vriendelijkste wijze verleend. De voortreffelijke vingerwijzingen, die ik van Professor SWAEN mocht ontvangen, nadat deze mijn manuscript had doorgelezen, zijn tot even zoovele verbeteringen geworden voor mijn proefschrift.

Gaarne grijp ik ook deze gelegenheid aan om te getuigen van het vele, dat ik als Anglist en als mensch te danken heb, aan mijn hooggeachten oud-leermeester GRASÉ. Denk ik hierbij in de eerste plaats aan het onderricht dat ik van hem mocht ontvangen op de H. B. S. en daarna, dan vergeet ik toch ook niet dat het op zijn raad was, dat ik besloot tot een langdurig verblijf in Engeland en tot de studie der klassieke talen. In mijn oog is hij steeds gebleven, wat hij voor mij als jongen reeds was, de ideale leeraar.

Groote erkentelijkheid past mij ook jegens Dr. VAN DER GAAF, aan wiens uitnemende colleges ik zoo veel te danken heb en Professor FIJN VAN DRAAT en den Heer VAN NECK, wier lessen mede tot mijn aangenaamste herinneringen behooren.

Het is mij een behoefte een woord van eerbiedige hulde te brengen aan de nagedachtenis van Professor FRANTZEN, wiens colleges, die ik in den donkeren oorlogstijd, lang na de voltooiing mijner eigenlijke examenstudie, gedurende een jaar mocht volgen, mij tot een groote geestelijke verfrissching zijn geweest.

Allen persoonlijk te danken, die mij het werk hebben vergemakkelijkt, is mij onmogelijk. Ik moet een uitzondering maken voor mijn oom, den Heer VAN DER WAL, die de proeven heeft doorgelezen en van kantteekeningen voorzien en de beambten der Amsterdamsche Universiteitsbibliotheek, die met geduld en groote hoffelijkheid, mij hielpen, waar zij konden.

I cannot deny myself the pleasure of thanking my friend, Miss ISABEL M. RIBBANDS, of Norwich, for her untiring interest in my work, as well as for her invaluable assistance at the various stages.

I thank the Committee of the Garrick Club, London, for courteous permission to reproduce the portrait of Cibber as Lord Foppington, as well as the Secretary for his kind help in having the photograph taken.

In conclusion I have to acknowledge the courtesy of the officials of the British Museum Library and Reading-Room, of the Bodleian Library, and of the National Portrait Gallery.

CONTENTS

I

BIOGRAPHICAL NOTICE

Caius Gabriel Cibber was born at Flensburg in Holstein in 1630. His father was cabinet-maker to the king of Denmark. After being sent to Rome to prosecute studies in modelling, Caius became foreman to John Stone, the sculptor and accompanied the latter to Holland. There his master was seized with palsy and Cibber had to conduct him home to England. He established himself here and was twice married. On November 24, 1670, at St. Giles-in-the-Fields, he married his second wife Jane, daughter of William Colley of Glaston, Rutlandshire, and granddaughter of Sir Anthoney Colley, whose fortune was lost during the Civil War. She brought her husband a dowry of £ 6000.—

Cibber acquired a certain reputation as a sculptor. Among his works are the statues of the kings placed around the old Royal Exchange and the figures of *Melancholy* and *Raving Madness,*[1] originally set up over the entrance gate of Bethlehem Hospital,[2] and afterwards removed to the South Kensington Museum. Sir Christopher Wren commissioned Cibber to carve in bas-relief the phoenix, which is placed above the door of St. Paul's Cathedral, and he also executed the bas-relief on the western front of the pedestal of the Monument in 1672.

On November 6, 1671, in Southampton St., Bloomsbury, his wife gave birth to a son, whom they called Colley. Of Colley's early years little is known. In 1682 he was sent to the free school of Grantham in Lincolnshire, where he stayed for five years, but

[1] That these figures were very well-known at the time, may be inferred from the last sentence in *The Tatler* No. 125: "I will make him in a month's time as famous as ever Oliver's porter was". (One of the figures is said to represent Oliver Cromwell's porter, who was then confined in Bethlehem Hospital).

[2] Apology I, p. 4.

of these years few facts are recorded. The death of King Charles II (Feb. 6, 1685) was an event which he always remembered,[1] for his class were told to make the King's funeral oration, but, thinking this exercise too difficult, they refused to do it. Cibber was the only exception and, by way of reward, was put at the head of his form, becoming at the same time thoroughly unpopular with his schoolfellows.

After leaving Grantham he tried to gain admission to Winchester College, but failed.[2] Then he spent some time in London, where he acquired a taste for the stage. At the end of a few months he joined his father at Chatsworth, the residence of William Cavendish, then earl of Devonshire, where the sculptor had been engaged for some time executing various statues and monuments.

Arriving at Chatsworth, he found that his father was at Nottingham and had taken up arms in the following of the Earl of Devonshire, who had raised a number of troops, immediately after the landing of the Prince of Orange. Cibber himself was also accepted as a soldier and promised preferment as soon as more settled times came. He formed part of an escort, sent out to meet the Princess Anne, who had withdrawn from London, because she feared the King's resentment at the defection of the Prince of Denmark, who had gone over to the Prince of Orange. At the dinner, offered by the Earl of Devonshire to the Princess and Lady Churchill, who was in attendance, Cibber was appointed to wait upon the latter, a task which he evidently enjoyed.[3]

Having marched to Oxford with the troops of the Earl of Devonshire, he returned to Nottingham after the flight of James II. When he did not receive the promised commission, he went to London and for five months was a member of the Earl of Devonshire's household. At the end of that time he was tired of dancing attendance on the Earl without much prospect of the

[1] Apology I, p. p. 17 & 18.

[2] His brother (who died a Fellow of New College, Oxford, soon after he had been ordained) was admitted to Winchester College a few years after Colley's unsuccessful attempt, his father then having made a statue of the Founder and having presented it to the College.

[3] Apology I, p. 39.

promised preferment and, feeling much attracted to the stage, he joined the united companies of actors at the Theatre Royal in 1690.[1] For nine months he worked for no salary and at the end of that time he found himself in receipt of only ten shillings per week. His first appearance on record is as Sir Gentle's servant in Southerne's *Sir Anthony Love* in 1691. As his career as an actor will be traced in detail in the next chapter, it is not necessary to dwell upon the particulars here.

In 1693 he married a Miss Shore on an allowance of £ 20 a year, which he received from his father, and 20 shillings a week, which he received for his theatrical labours.[2] When in 1695 Betterton and his associates opened a new theatre in Little Lincoln's Inn Fields (April 30), Cibber, who stayed on at Drury Lane, saw his salary increased to 30 shillings.[3] The prologue, pronounced at the reopening of Drury Lane Theatre, was written by him, but Powel was instructed to speak it.[4] For several years his nominal income as an actor was very small, and of that meagre pittance he seldom received more than half. The patentees, the chief of whom was Christopher Rich (who received his share in the patent on March 24, 1691) were accustomed "never to pay their people when the money did not come in; nor then neither but in such proportions as suited their conveniency".[5] According to Cibber's assertion, it was the insufficiency of his income more than anything else that induced him to write plays for the support of his increasing family.[6]

At the beginning of the season 1706-1707 he joined the Haymarket Company, then under the management of Owen Swiney.

[1] The King's Company and the Duke's Company were united in 1684. See Apology I, p. 54. Stephen Jones, however, says the junction took place in 1682. (*Biographia Dramatica,* Introduction, xxv.)

[2] The increase of salary from fifteen to twenty shillings a week he owed to the personal intercession of Congreve.

[3] Apology I, p. 105. [4] Apology I, p. 106. [5] Apology I, p. 125.

[6] Apology I, p. 144. "It may be observable, too, that my muse and my spouse were equally prolifick; that the one was seldom the mother of a child but in the same year the other made me the father of a play: I think we had a dozen of each sort between us; of both which kinds some died in their infancy, and near an equal number of each were alive when I quitted the theatre."

Early in 1708 the two theatrical companies united, the Haymarket Theatre being made over to Swiney for opera, while Cibber joined the Drury Lane Theatre Company. His friend, Colonel Brett, was then in possession of a share in the patent, but on March 31, 1708, he assigned this share to Sir Thomas Skipwith, from whom he had received it a short time previously.

The actors laid their grievances before the Lord Chamberlain, who in 1709, ordered Rich to satisfy their demands. When Rich refused, Drury Lane Theatre was closed on June 6, 1709 by order of the Queen. William Collier, M. P. for Dover, now obtained for himself a license and a second lease from the proprietors, and Rich was turned out of Drury Lane Theatre.[1] By the close of the season 1709-1710 Cibber was the virtual manager, Collier having withdrawn from the management in view of a payment of £700. a year. At the death of Queen Anne, the three actors, resenting Collier's behaviour, applied to the Duke of Marlborough to have Sir Richard Steele's name substituted for that of Collier. From this moment the managers enjoyed a period of almost uninterrupted prosperity, till 1733, when Cibber retired[2] and set himself to writing his Apology, although he made several reappearances on the stage.

In the morning of Dec. 12, 1757, he died at the age of 86 and was buried in the vault of the Danish Church, where his father had been interred before him.

"Bays, form'd by nature Stage and Town to bless,
And act, and be, a Coxcomb with success."

(The Dunciad, Bk. I).

[1] A humorous description of the evacuation of the theatre by Rich, is to be found in No. 99 of *The Tatler*.

[2] See page 18. [3] Now the British and Foreign Sailors' Church.

II

CIBBER AS AN ACTOR

After his first recorded appearance, it was a long time before Cibber made any progress worth mentioning in the profession he had chosen.[1] Nor is this at all surprising, when one reads the candid description of his own natural disabilities,[2] which he gives in the *Apology*.

The first part in which he appeared with any sign of success was that of the chaplain in *The Orphan* by Otway. On this occasion he received his first applause. Goodman, a retired actor, having attended a rehearsal of this play, asked one of the principal actors, who the new young fellow was whom he had seen as the chaplain. On being introduced to Cibber, he clapped him on the back and predicted his ultimate success as an actor, which praise, as Cibber tells us "fairly drew tears from his eyes".[3]

In 1793 he replaced Kynaston, who was ill, in *The Double Dealer,* which Queen Mary had ordered to be acted. Congreve, the author, was so pleased with his performance, which he had had to undertake at a day's notice, that he procured him an increase of salary.[4] In 1795 he was still too insignificant to be taken into the counsels of Betterton and his associates, but naturally his own relative importance rose with the departure from Drury Lane of so many of the best actors.[5] At the reopening of Drury Lane Theatre after the death of Queen Mary, Cibber

[1] See page 3.

[2] Apology I, p. 98 f. "The first thing that enters into the head of a young actor is that of being a hero: in this ambition I was soon snubbed, by the insufficiency of my voice; to which might be added an uninformed meagre person (though not then ill made) with a dismal pale complexion. Under these disadvantages I had but a melancholy prospect of ever playing a lover with Mrs. Bracegirdle, which had flattered my hopes that my youth might one day have recommended me to."

[3] Apology I, p. 99. [4] See Note 2 p. 3. [5] See Note 3, p. 3.

received another convincing proof of the low opinion people had of his ability as an actor, when he was not allowed to speak the prologue, composed by himself.

Betterton opened at Lincoln's Inn Fields with Congreve's *Love for Love* and from this moment began a very keen competition between the two playhouses.[1] For example one day, Powel, who was the leading actor at Drury Lane, announced a performance of *The Old Bachelor,* in which he himself was to take the part of the old bachelor and play it in imitation of Betterton's original personation. This was the occasion on which Cibber scored his next success. For want of a better actor they entrusted him with the part of Alderman Fondlewife. He so well imitated Doggett's interpretation of this part, that many of the spectators thought it was Doggett himself that they saw.[2] All this, however, had very little effect upon his career, for no other important part was intrusted to him. Instead of being disheartened, however, he set to work to write a part for himself and in '94 he produced *Love's Last Shift.* The play might never have been staged, however, but for the intervention of Southerne, who allowed Cibber to read the play to him and immediately recommended it to the patentees. It was decided that the play was to be acted in January 1795. When Southerne heard that Cibber had given himself the part of Sir Novelty Fashion, he said to him: "Young man! I pronounce thy play a good one! I will answer for its success, if thou dost not spoil it by thy own action".

His fears proved to be unfounded, if we are to judge by the opinion expressed by Lord Dorset (then Lord Chamberlain), after he had witnessed the performance, "that it was the best first play that any author in his memory had produced; and that for a young fellow to shew himself such an actor and such a writer, in one day, was something extraordinary."[3] The next year, Sir John Vanbrugh wrote *The Relapse* as a sequel to *Love's Last*

[1] According to Cibber, Dryden at one time undertook to write two plays a year for the King's Company; in the same way Congreve now promised to write one play a year for Betterton's Company, in consideration of his receiving a whole share in the theatre. The promise was not kept, for there was a three years' interval between: *Love for Love* and *The Mourning Bride* and another 3 years between this and *The Way of the World.*

[2] Apology I, p. 112. [3] Apology I, p. 115.

Shift and entrusted the part of the chief character in that play, whom he had styled Baron of Foppington, to Cibber. Cibber's performance in this play finally established his reputation. Many are the parts he played successfully after this, both in tragedy and in comedy, though contemporary evidence all points to the fact that, although to the last Cibber persisted in taking tragical parts as well, his attempts in that direction were not nearly so much appreciated as his portrayal of humorous characters.

In 1719 the management of Drury-Lane Theatre were ordered by the Duke of Newcastle, the then Lord Chamberlain, to suspend Cibber. This order was obeyed by Steele, Wilks and Booth, who at that time were joint managers with him. The theatre itself was closed for three days:[1] January 25th, 26th and 27th. In connection with this action on the part of the Lord Chamberlain, there appeared an article in *The Theatre,* Jan. 23, 1719, in which the writer (Steele) enumerates the following parts taken by Cibber:

Sir Foplin Flutter and Sir Courtley Nice, in the plays so-called.

Sir Novelty Fashion	in *Love's Last Shift.*
Lord Foppington	in *The Relapse.*
Sparkish	in *The Country Wife.*
Witwould	in *The Way of the World.*
Attall	in *The Double Gallant.*
Brazen	in *The Recruiting Officer.*
Cibbet	in *The Stratagem.*
Richard III	in the play so-called.
Iago	in *Othello.*
Syphax	in *Cato.*
Burleigh	in *The Earl of Essex.*
Cardinal Wolsey	in *Henry VIII.*

After this enumeration Steele adds the following comment:

"I have at first view been much astonished to observe a strong inclination and propensity of the Town to receive with pleasure anything that tends to the personal mortification of Mr.

[1] Genest attributes the fact that in his *Apology* Cibber was silent on this head to the Duke of Newcastle's being instrumental in obtaining the Laureateship for him at a later date.

Cibber, who with much address and capacity has pleased them in all these characters". The writer then accounts for it by the fact that Cibber had always personated vices and imperfections and illustrates this point by means of the following anecdote: A country gentleman at Bury in Suffolk, inviting all the players of a strolling company to his house, excepted the actress of greatest merit, because she happened to have performed that week before his worship the part of the Countess of Nottingham in *The Earl of Essex.* He said "he did not care who laughed at him for it, but that false hussey should never come under his roof".[1] Steele then goes on to remark that "the hardship done to Cibber by the Lord Chamberlain was pushed farther than that, because the country gentleman did not order the Countess of Nottingham to starve in general, but was contented she should not eat at his house, whereas Cibber was for some time forbidden to perform".[2]

[1] In his appreciation of Sandford (Apology I, p. 74 ff.) Cibber gives a good illustration of the same phenomenon. "Sandford was not the Stage-villain by choice, but from necessity; he had a low and crooked person. The less comely the actor's person, the fitter he is to perform a hateful or mischievous character. The spectator, too, by not being misled by a tempting form, may be less inclined to excuse the wicked or immoral sentiments of them...

In a new play, Sandford, who generally acted the wicked parts, happened to perform the part of an honest statesman. The pit, expecting that the well-dissembled honesty of Sandford would soon be unmasked, but finding themselves dissappointed, damned the play, as if the author had imposed the most incredible absurdity upon them."

Because of the parts he took, Sandford got very little applause. "We may honestly style him a theatrical martyr to poetical justice: for in making vice odious, or virtue amiable, where does the merit differ?" (Apology I, p. 77).

[2] In estimating the value of Steele's opinion in this particular respect, it should be borne in mind that Cibber and himself were partners at the time. The same fact probably accounts for Cibber's reference to the relations between Addison and Steele in his dedication to *Ximena,* or *The Heroic Daughter,* Sept. 29, 1719, when he quoted Dryden (Mark Anthony speaking of Octavius):

> "Fool that I was! Upon my Eagle's wings,
> I bore this Wren, till I was tired with soaring,
> And now, he mounts above me."

Mist's Journal of Oct. 31, 1719, contained the following comment on the above:

Thomas Davies in various passages of his *Dramatic Miscellanies* bestows high praise on Cibber as a comic actor. According to this authority his greatest perfection as an actor was in the rôle of the coxcomb of quality, and especially his Lord Foppington in *The Careless Husband,* which Davies calls a very fine draught of a man of good parts stepping beyond the bounds of sense, as shown by peculiarity and excess both in dress and behaviour.[1] Cibber appears to have been very successful as Sir John Brute in Vanbrugh's *The Provok'd Wife,* which part Davies saw him act with great and deserved applause. In this, however, he was surpassed at a later date by Garrick, who considered it as one of his great parts.[2]

Of Cibber's pretensions to the buskin Davies speaks in quite a different manner. "Cibber had two passions", he informs us, "which constantly exposed him to severe censure and sometimes to the highest ridicule: his writing tragedy and acting tragic characters. Iago he acted in a style so drawing and hypocritical, and wore the mask of honesty so loosely, that Othello, who is not drawn a fool, must have seen the villain through his thin disguises. The truth is, Cibber was endured in this and other tragic parts, on account of his general merit in comedy".[3] We should take this explanation of Cibber's moderate success in certain tragic parts for what it is worth; there were no doubt a great many natural disadvantages Cibber had to struggle against and he was evidently better suited for personating comic characters. On the one hand we read that no audience was ever

"Thus Colley Cibber greets his Partner Steele,
"See here, Sir Knight? how I've outdone Corneille!
"See here, how I, my patrons to inveigle,
"Make Addison a Wren, and you an Eagle!
"Safe to their silent Shades we bid defiance,
"For living Dogs are better than Dead Lions."

[1] *Dramatic Miscellanies*, p. 453.

[2] *Dram. Misc.*, p. 457.

On March 26, 1765, Horace Walpole, compares Garrick to Cibber in the character of Bayes in *The Rehearsal,* and considers the latter's performance superior. "Indeed, his (Garrick's) Bayes was original, but not the true part. Cibber was the burlesque of a great poet, as the part was designed, but Garrick made it a Garetteer!"

Dram. Misc., p. 469.

more fixed in deep attention, at Cibber's first appearance as Justice Shallow, or more shaken with laughter during the progress of the scene; on the other hand he represented Cardinal Wolsey in *Henry VIII* "not unsuitably", although he was lacking in dignity.[1]

In reading what he says about himself and his suggestive criticism and praise of the performance of others, we cannot help feeling sure that in many respects Cibber must have made up for his natural deficiencies by a careful and intelligent study of the parts entrusted to him. That he was not always so well prepared for his comic parts need not astonish us. There he was in his element and we can well imagine him dexterously supplying the deficiency of his memory by prolonging his ceremonious bow to the lady he was saluting, and drawling out "Your humble servant, madam", to an extraordinary length; then gravely taking a pinch of snuff, and strutting deliberately across the stage, to ask the prompter: "What is next?"

John Downes, bookkeeper[2] and prompter to the theatre in Lincoln's Inn Fields from its opening in 1662 until October 1706, testifies to Cibber's all-round perfection as an actor in the following terms: "Mr Cyber has arriv'd to an exceeding Perfection, in hitting justly the Humour of a starcht Beau, or Fop; as the Lord Foppington, Sir Fopling and Sir Courtly, equalling in the last, the late Eminent Mr. Mountfort, not much inferior in Tragedy, had Nature given him Lungs Strenuous to his finisht Judgment." The value of this opinion is greatly enhanced by the fact that Downes, who was an old man when he wrote this, naturally felt most admiration for the great actors of his younger days and was in no way dependent on Cibber, who, in fact, during the greater part of his theatrical career belonged to a rival theatre.

Another very valuable and interesting testimony is found in Horace Walpole's Letters (Vol. IV, p. 335). Writing of Garrick in 1765, Walpole has this remark: "Cibber and O'Brien were

[1] *Dram. Misc.*, p. 306.

[2] *Bookkeeper* here means *bookholder,* the person, who holds the manuscript or book of the play. This meaning is not recorded in the N. E. D. See Induction to *Cynthia's Revels;* Everyman's Library: Ben Jonson I, p. 152. Cf. *Nomenclator,* 1585: He that telleth the players their part when they are out, and have forgotten; the prompter or bookeholder. (T. Wright, Dictionary of Obsolete and Provincial English).

what Garrick could never reach, coxcombs and men of fashion".[1] In this respect Cibber was privileged beyond most actors. When we glance over the list of his intimates,[2] we see that all through his life Cibber had the inestimable advantage of conversing with the best people. We have referred to the post assigned to him at the reception of the Princess Anne by the Earl of Devonshire; the detailed description of the same event by himself fifty years after proves sufficiently that he was a close observer, when his interest was aroused. We receive the clearest proofs of this in reading his biography, from which we infer at the same time that a man, who could write like that, would not be restricted to mere observation, and we can quite believe that Stephen Jones or rather, David Erskine Baker (for it was he, who originally compiled the *Biographica Dramatica,* to the year 1764) was right in informing us that, even in the latter years of his life, when amidst a circle of persons, not one of whom perhaps had attained to the third part of his age, Cibber by his easy good-humour, liveliness of conversation and a peculiar happiness he had in telling a story, was often the very life of the company.

Dr Johnson appears to have been of a different opinion, for when, on one occasion, Boswell asked him if he had read Cibber's *Apology,* he answered: "Yes, it is very entertaining. But as for Cibber himself, taking from his conversation all that he ought not to have said,[3] he was a poor creature."[4] On another occasion, we read, Dr. Johnson, as usual, spoke contemptuously of Colley Cibber in the following terms: "It is wonderful that a man, who for forty years had lived with the great and the witty, should have acquired so ill the talents of conversation: and he had but half to furnish: for one half of what he said was oaths."[5]

[1] G. Birkbeck Hill: *Boswell's Life of Johnson;* Vol. IV, p. 243, Note 6.

[2] On March 4, 1755, Walpole wrote: "Cibber is within a few days of eighty-four, still hearty, and clear, and well. I told him that I was glad to see him look so well: "Faith", said he, "it is very well that I look at all".

[3] Referring to Cibber's habit of swearing.

[4] Birkbeck Hill, Vol. II, p. 92.

[5] We ought to bear in mind, however, that Johnson was a man of strong resentments and that he probably thought he had a reason to dislike Cibber, as appears from the following incident, recorded by Boswell (Birkbeck Hill,

There are numerous references in contemporary literature to comic parts of minor importance played by Cibber, and he appears to have remained successful up to the time of leaving the stage and even after.[1] After 1733 he made more than one reappearance on the stage, his last signal success being the part of Randolph in his version of Shakespeare's *King John,* called *Papal Tyranny in the Reign of King John,* which he played in 1745. Writing of those boisterous elements among the spectators, who were in the habit of creating disturbances at theatrical performances, Cibber says: "they have done me this involuntary service, that it has driven me a year or two sooner into a quiet life, than otherwise my own want of judgment might have led me: I left the Stage, before my strength left me; and though I came to it again for some few days a year or two after, my reception not only returned to my account, but seemed a fair invitation that I would make my visits more frequent; but to give over a winner, can be no very imprudent resolution."

Vol. I, p. 256): "A sudden disgust was taken by Johnson upon occasion of his having been one day kept long in waiting in his Lordship's ante-chamber, for which the reason assigned was, that he had company with him; and that at last, when the door opened, out walked Colley Cibber; Dr. Johnson was so violently provoked when he found for whom he had been so long excluded, that he went away in a passion, and never would return." (The Lord referred to was Lord Chesterfield, to whom Johnson had paid the high compliment of addressing the Plan of his Dictionary. Johnson said afterwards that Lord Chesterfield had behaved to him (Johnson) in such a manner as to excite his contempt and indignation.)

[1] On Dec. 3, 1741, Walpole wrote "Old Cibber plays to-night and all the world will be there."

OLD DRURY LANE THEATRE

III

CIBBER AS A THEATRICAL MANAGER

We saw in a preceding chapter that the patentees of Drury Lane Theatre were very irregular in paying their actors. The profit derived from the theatrical management grew less and less and for several years Mr. Rich was the sole managing patentee. Sir Thomas Skipwith, who had a share in the patent equal to that of Mr. Rich, actually made a present of his share to Colonel Brett, telling him at the same time that he had never succeeded in making any profit out of it. This Colonel Brett happened to be a friend of Cibber's and that is the reason why he applied to him for advice as to what he should do with his newly acquired theatrical authority. In pursuance of the advice he had received, Colonel Brett had an interview with Mr. Rich, produced his deeds and claimed a share in the management. At this time there was another company of actors, those who performed at the Haymarket Theatre. [1] Mr. Rich had some influence at court and soon received permission to amalgamate the two companies of actors. It so happened that just then there was a growing desire among the theatre-going public for foreign operas. When Owen Swiney, the director of Haymarket Theatre, was offered the sole right for the performance of operas at the Haymarket, he closed with the proposal at once, thinking that his profits from the opera would be ample compensation for his giving up several of his actors. This matter having been adjusted to the satisfaction of all parties concerned, the actors were all ordered to return to Drury-Lane, there to remain (under patentees) her Majesty's only company of comedians.

This reunion of the actor companies naturally had a favourable influence on the performances; moreover, Mr Brett proving a capable manager, soon became popular with the actors and the

[1] See p. 3.

first year of his management was a decided financial success. Mr. Rich, of course, shared in the general prosperity, but this did not reconcile him to the fact that he saw his own influence dwindle and that of Mr. Brett increase, so that he began to think of a way to get rid of his partner. He found an unexpected ally in Sir Thomas Skipwith, who repented of his former generosity and applied to the Court of Chancery to have his property restored. Mr. Brett, disgusted at this treatment on the part of his friend, did not defend the case and withdrew from the management, leaving Mr. Rich in possession of the full powers of the patent. The immediate consequence was that several of the actors found themselves reduced in their pay and threatened, moreover, with a further attack on their incomes. Ever since 1695, when the existing company divided into two, the patentees had been in the habit of paying their actors half in good words and half in ready money, while the actors were kept from revolting by the promise that they should be given a chance to make up the arrears by the profits of a benefit play at the end of the season. In course of time these benefits grew so advantageous, that they became the chief article in the agreements.

Unfortunately these agreements were only verbal at the time, so that the actors had no immediate remedy when, in 1708, Mr. Rich claimed one third of the profit of every benefit for himself. No actor could have the date of his benefit fixed till he had signed a paper, signifying his acceptance of this condition. If one refused to sign, the next in rank was offered his benefit before that of the refuser, on the same condition. This mode of treatment proved effectual at last; the actors felt forced to comply, but resentment rankled in their hearts and the next year they laid their grievances before the Lord Chamberlain. The result of this action was described above.[1] The actors, who were now free to do as they liked, entered into an agreement with Swiney, who admitted Wilks, Dogget, Cibber, and Mrs. Oldfield as joint managers with himself. Dogget being of opinion that their business would not be on a sure foundation if the other sex was admitted to the management, Mrs. Oldfield was easily induced to accept £ 200 a year and a benefit performance instead of a share,

[1] See p. 4.

at the same time being exempted from any responsibility in the management. It is an ill wind that blows nobody any good. The prolonged mismanagement of Mr. Rich at last gave Cibber the chance of showing his own skill in theatrical management.

Unfortunately the first year opened unpropitiously. First of all the joint managers had to have the Haymarket Theatre altered, the accoustics of which were very poor; secondly the long trial of Dr. Sacheverell in Westminster Hall provided so much entertainment to the people of quality that they did not feel the need of any other; and lastly Collier, after obtaining a new license, had set up for himself in Drury-Lane Theatre. At the end of the season, Collier found himself disappointed in his hopes of considerable financial success and, once more availing himself of the influence he had at court, succeeded in obtaining the Lord Chamberlain's support for a new scheme, that of putting himself in possession of the Haymarket Theatre with all the singers, scenes and clothes and thus becoming sole director of the opera. In consideration of this, Swiney and his partners were to return to Drury-Lane Theatre, at the same time receiving the promise that no other company should be allowed to act plays against them. In this the actors had very little cause for complaint: their operas had been less successful than their plays, and the prospect of having a monopoly for the acting of plays would well have reconciled them to their loss of the operatic entertainments, if it had not been for two very hard conditions imposed on them, which they could do nothing but comply with; the first was, that, because the sole license for acting plays was considered to be more advantageous than that for acting operas, Collier was to receive two hundred pounds a year from them; the second was that on every Wednesday, on which an opera was performed, there should be no performance at Drury-Lane, in order to give the opera a better chance of a full house.

These absolutely arbitrary advantages, Collier received only because he was a Member of Parliament and had some influence at Court. The next year he once more had recourse to the same Court interest. The fact was that the season at Drury-Lane had been excellent, while the opera soon appeared to be in a sinking condition. Therefore, at the end of the year, he meditated an exchange of posts with Swiney. The latter remonstrated, but his friend, Sir John Vanbrugh, advised him to accept the change, because he knew for certain that the only alternative would be Swiney's exclusion from any post in either theatre. Collier cut the matter short by obtaining a new license for himself, Wilks, Dogget, and Cibber, with the exclusion of Swiney, who was thus forced to return to the Haymarket. In 1712 he found his losses on the opera so great that, in order to avoid imprisonment for debt, he was forced to leave the country. In the meantime, Collier, who had found by this time that the theatre was a rather precarious source of income, offered to withdraw from the management in consideration of an annual sum of £ 700. It was a hard bargain, but the actors, who had learned from Swiney's fate that they were up against a formidable power, with which they could not contend, resolved to close with it, although they first tried to persuade Collier to accept an equal share with themselves. Collier refused to accept this offer and, as Cibber remarks triumphantly, thus cheated himself of about three hundred pounds a year, for the other managers never made less than £ 1000 each annually till the death of Queen Anne in 1714.

From this moment Wilks, Dogget and Cibber were acting managers of Drury Lane Theatre and very soon Cibber proved to be the real leader, which position he owed to his undoubted capacity and to the fact that, from the very beginning, he had to act as mediator between Wilks and Dogget. The latter, being somewhat of an economical disposition, was inclined to look askance at the great expenditure on scenery and especially on dress, to which Wilks committed them. For this actor, who in this respect had a real artistic temperament, was more interested in a liberal applause than in ample receipts, and was inclined to spend money indiscriminately. Cibber indulged him as much as was at all consistent with a business-like management, but had to be continually on the alert to avoid any likelihood of a rupture between his two colleagues. In the course of the next few years

[1] Apology II, p. 88.

Wilks' temper became more and more difficult, but Cibber managed to remain on good terms with him for full twenty years.[1]

In 1712, Addison's *Cato*[2] was put on the stage and acted daily, with the exception of Monday, for a month at a stretch, to a crowded house. The chief part was acted by Booth, who up to that time had held a subordinate position in the theatre, but who now, owing to the high favour in which he was held by the public and the support of some influential person at Court, was in a position to claim a share in the management. Cibber immediately recognised that it would be impossible for himself and his friends to refuse Booth's demand, as this might lead to the license being withdrawn altogether, and advised his colleagues to make the best of a bad job and try to come to some sort of an agreement with Booth, by which he might be obliged to pay them a sum of money, in consideration of his receiving a share in the theatrical property. He experienced no difficulty in convincing Wilks, who, as a matter of fact, did not care much who was admitted to a share in the profits, as long as the acting could go on as usual. With Dogget it proved to be a different matter. He told Cibber and Wilks they might do as they liked, but that nothing but the law would make him part with his legitimate property. He refused to take any further part in the discussions and left the theatre for good.

Booth was now admitted to a share of the management and together the three actors offered Dogget half a share, if he was willing to leave the stage altogether and thus make his position a sinecure. Dogget refused and preferred a bill in Chancery against the joint managers, who entrusted Cibber with the conduct of their cause. He immediately directed his solicitor to use all delay the law would admit of, a direction lawyers are not slow to follow. It is not necessary to dwell on the details of the case here: the result of it all was that at the end of over two years Dogget was awarded six hundred pounds with 15 % interest.

[1] Cibber observes (Apology II, p. 90.): "Dogget could not hold it so long; but as he had more money than I, he had not occasion for so much philosophy."

[2] As early as 1703, Cibber had read the first four acts privately with Sir Richard Steele. The 5th Act was not added till early in 1712.

Upon the death of Queen Anne, the actors, who had not yet forgotten the unfair treatment they had received at the hands of Collier, applied to Sir Richard Steele to use his interest at court to have their license renewed, and to have his own name substituted for that of Collier. Steele received the patent and from that moment he was one of the partners and shared the profits with the three actors. After some years, however, Steele ceased taking any active part in the work and from that time Cibber and his friends reduced Steele's income from the theatre by £1. 13 s. 4d. per acting day during his absence. Steele, who was a notoriously bad financier, on being informed of this, replied that he had always taken a delight in making his friends easy and had no reason to doubt that they would do him justice. When, however, a couple of years later, Steele became insolvent and his affairs passed into the hands of trustees, a bill in Chancery was filed against the actors by the administrators of Sir Richard Steele's estate. It came to a hearing before the Master of the Rolls in the year 1726, when Cibber made an excellent speech to defend his cause. It is rendered at full length in his *Apology* and he is evidently, and we may add, justly proud of his success on that occasion. [1]

In 1729 Steele died and, according to the terms of the license, this had to be renewed three years after Steele's death. This was done accordingly in 1732. By this time Booth had sold his share in the patent to Mr. John Highmore, while after Wilks's death, Mrs. Wilks had deputed Mr. Ellis to attend to the conduct of the Theatre on her behalf. The two new managers appear to have been totally unqualified for the offices they had to fill. Cibber therefore made up his mind to withdraw and authorised his son Theophilus to act for him as far as his interest was concerned. Mr. Highmore, who was very rich, was soon offended by the impertinence of young Cibber, and, in order to get rid of him, bought Colley's share, too, for the sum of three thousand guineas. [2]

In the preceding pages Cibber's career as a theatrical manager has been traced chiefly from data, provided by himself in his

[1] Apology II, p. 130 ff.
[2] *Biographica Dramatica,* Introduction, p. 34.

Apology. That the account given by Cibber in his autobiography is not always fully confirmed by contemporary writings on the same subject, stands to reason. One anonymous author even went so far as to say that the way in which Cibber and the other actors obtained the license for the Drury-Lane Theatre was not in the least like his own statement of the transaction. This writer declares that Cibber and his friends proved themselves to be great scoundrels by taking advantage of a serious illness of the patentee and therefore proposes to write an essay on the art of Fibbing. He adds that "if the *Fibbers* usually get their way in a court of justice, why not the *Fibbers* (or *-bbers*) in a Theatre. [1] I have not been able to find this insinuation confirmed, so that it may safely be assumed to be on a level with the rest of the paper, which is little more than a personal attack on Colley Cibber and his son. [2] Speaking in general, we may say that the actual facts were fairly accurately recorded by Cibber. It is only when he starts to draw conclusions or assign causes that a critical attitude becomes necessary.

One thing is absolutely certain, namely that Cibber was a most capable manager, with a great insight into human nature and that he understood from the very beginning that his success, and eventually his prosperity, depended on the way in which he treated his actors. A very good instance of this is afforded by the treatment the actors received during a visit the company paid to Oxford in 1712. On former occasions it had been usual for them to give two performances a day, while there; one in the morning, ending before the hour for dinner and another in the evening, which was never allowed to extend to a later hour than the customary time of shutting the college-gates. When the actors had to perform twice a day, they received double pay, even when Mr. Rich was in authority. The present managers, however, considering that the actors could hardly be at their

[1] *An Apology for the Life of Mr. The' Cibber,* p. 159.

[2] This appears very clearly from the conclusion, where the author compares the characters of Colley Cibber and his son in the following terms: "The father was the greater Hypocrite, the Son was the greater Madman—Colley had rather *be* immoral than be esteem'd so; He thought it more Glory, the more he acquired the Character of being so."

best under these conditions, reduced the number of performances by having only one daily, but left the actors' payment intact. The idea of the managers, according to Cibber, was, rather than let their fraternity suffer, to get nothing for themselves by the expedition. Thus they laid an obligation upon their company by which, though they did not anticipate it, they were the gainers. In addition to Shakespeare and Jonson (for the University would not tolerate anything but the very best that was to be had), they played Addison's *Cato* with great success, perhaps partly due to the fact that Addison himself had been at Oxford. [1] On taking leave, Cibber and his company received the thanks of the Vice-Chancellor of the University for the decency and order observed by them. Their receipts enabled them, not only to double the pay of every actor, but also to contribute fifty pounds towards the repair of St. Mary's Church, and in addition, each of the managers had one hundred and fifty pounds, clear of all charges, as his share for twenty-one days' work. [2]

Cibber, to be sure, was too good a business-man to venture great sums upon "empty Projects, and Hopes of immoderate Gains", but we feel sure that, if he had been so inclined, he would not have made up the deficit out of the actors' salaries, as before him the patentees had been in the habit of doing. [3] The impression, however, which we get from his *Apology* that he was always kind and complaisant towards his inferiors, or to those with whom he had to deal in the way of business, is not borne out by the testimony of impartial contemporary judges. Thomas Davies, for example, who praises Cibber unstintingly, whenever he thinks he deserves it, states[4] that it is a matter of common knowledge that Cibber treated authors, who came to offer him their plays, with superciliousness and even accuses him of purloining from works that were left in his hands. It appears that he really felt he was "the Monarch of the Stage". [5]

[1] Cibber calls the play: "the flower of a plant raised in that learned garden."

[2] Apology II, p. 97.

[3] See: Dedication of *The Lady's Last Stake* or *The Wife's Resentment* to the Marquis of Kent.

[4] *Dram. Misc.*, Vol. III, p. 469.

[5] *A Hymn to the New Laureate by a Native of Grub-Street*, published

Whilst giving his opinion of a play, he always smoked a pipe and exasperated his visitors by treating the matter as a mere trifle. In several passages of the *Dramatic Miscellanies* the same statement is repeated. Notwithstanding the great improvement in their position, due to the work done by Cibber on behalf of the theatre and of themselves, he was not popular among the actors. His power over them was great and he knew it. His *Apology* is sufficient evidence that he knew how a play should be acted, even where he himself may have failed in the execution and we may be sure that he did not spare the members of his company, whenever he thought they deserved criticism. It is on record that, on one occasion, whilst talking about that part of *Love for Love,* where Scandal breaks out into the exclamation of: "Death and Hell! Where is Valentine?" Mills, remarking that Booth used to forget the "Death and Hell," was interrupted by Cibber, who with a contemptuous smile informed him that there was more beauty in Booth's forgetfulness than in all he (Mills) remembered.[1]

That remarks of this kind did not tend to increase his popularity with the actors stands to reason. He was a tyrant, there can be no doubt about that, and tyrants, however much they may be praised by those who appreciate the results of their actions, are rarely tolerated by their immediate dependants. When after the death of Queen Anne, the old patentee had completed the building of a new theatre, eight actors immediately deserted from Drury Lane and joined the new theatre in Lincoln's Inn Fields. Cibber and his partners were compelled to postpone several of their best plays, owing to this sudden desertion, with the result that, in that year, their profits were reduced to about

---

anonymously in London in 1731, contained the following satyrical address to:

"Cibber, darling of the
"Tuneful Nine! Whose Lays with most
"Celestial Splendor shine; Patron of Bards,
"Mild Monarch of the Stage, Thou Golden
"Laureat of this Golden Age! —
"To Mine and to my Country's deathless Praise,
"It may be said I liv'd when C....r wore the Bays."

[1] *Dram. Misc.,* Vol. III, p. 504.

one third of the usual amount. Although the actors were none of them leading players, their absence proved an almost insurmountable difficulty. [1] A short time after, when their hopes of quick preferment at Lincoln's Inn Fields had been disappointed, some of them, acting as spokesmen for the rest, told Cibber that their principal reason for leaving Drury-Lane had been the shocking temper of Wilks, which, to some extent, had also been responsible for Dogget leaving the theatre when he did. Cibber tells all this in detail in his autobiography and, although there is no doubt that there was a great deal of truth in this statement, it is equally sure that he himself had been to blame in the same way. [2]

As a man of business, Cibber was in every respect superior to his predecessor. In the first place there is not one instance in any of the books that treat of the history of the stage in the beginning of the eighteenth century that can lay claim to any authority, of Cibber's honesty being drawn in question. [3] During the twenty years in which he was one of the directors, they never had a creditor who had occasion to come twice for payment; every Monday morning all demands were discharged, before they took a shilling for their own use. That they were fully trusted by their actors is proved by the fact, that they were never asked for any written agreement; the salaries were entered upon the daily pay-roll, which plain record everybody looked upon as good city security. Cibber fully realised that

[1] Apology II, p. 115.

[2] In theory he is very moderate: "For though I allow actors in general, when they are too much indulged or governed by an unsteady head, to be as unruly a multitude as power can be plagued with; yet there is a medium, which, if cautiously observed by a candid use of power, making them always know, without feeling, their superior, neither suffering their encroachments nor invading their rights, with an immovable adherence to the accepted laws they are to walk by; such a regulation I say, has never failed in my observation to have made them a tractable & profitable society". (Apology II, p. 63.)

[3] In one passage, extremely unfavourable to Cibber as a manager and as a man, Davies expressly makes an exception to that effect: "As a manager, his behaviour to authors was illiberal and insolent; his treatment of actors unfriendly, if not tyrannical. A neglectful father, a confirmed gamester, but not a cheat. (*Dram. Misc.,* III, p. 506.)

mutual trust and confidence is the best basis for any business-transaction. [1]

Though as a rule economical, Cibber was not afraid on occasion to spend considerable amounts of money on the production of a play, in the hope of future gain. Six hundred pounds were laid out on the revival of Dryden's *All for Love.* About this time, it was rumoured that the walls and roof of Drury-Lane were liable to collapse. The partners knew that this rumour was unfounded, and Wilks immediately suggested finding the originator and prosecuting him. Cibber, however, held that it was of more importance to prove that the rumour was false, and therefore obtained an order from the King to have the theatre surveyed by Sir Thomas Hewet, who reported that it was in a safe and sound condition. This report was then duly published in the papers, with Sir Thomas's signature appended.

In all that referred to the mere business part of stage-management, Cibber was above reproach, but evidently he was more vulnerable in the matter of the quality of the entertainments he sometimes offered the public. It is said that in his desire to have full houses, he too often had recourse to performances, in which the acting was of very little importance, while music and dancing formed the principal attractions. However, it seems very unlikely that Cibber was to blame in this matter: there is not the slightest evidence to prove that Cibber actually promoted this sort of thing. Besides, it ought to be borne in mind that complaints of this kind had been made before and at a time also, when Cibber had no influence at all. For many years already music had formed a recognised and essential element of the theatrical program. In the *Historia Histrionica,* published in 1699, we read that "the present Plays can hardly draw an Audience, unless there be the additional Invitation of a *Signior Fidelé,* a *Monsieur L'Abbé,* or some such Foreign Regale exprest in the Bottom of the Bill." [2]

Cibber himself in the introduction to *The Lady's Last Stake,*

[1] "The severities and oppression we had suffered under our former masters, made us incapable of imposing them upon others; which gave our whole society the cheerful looks of a rescued people." (Apology II, p. 81.)

[2] *Historia Histrionica,* p. 56.

quoted above,[1] says that, but for the intervention of the Lord Chamberlain, the actors would have been almost entirely set aside, or at least, their former good work would have been discredited by the appreciation of the pretended merit of singing and dancing.[2] On the other hand, he could not offer the public plays that were too good for them. Before preparing his entertainment he consulted his list of guests, and he knew it would be useless to try and impose good plays on an audience that did not want them.[3] All through his career, he knew only too well that he was solely dependent on the judgment of his audience and that it was not to his interest to feed them on better fare than they asked for. While dancing and farce and music were the most profitable investments it is small wonder that, when real wit was not appreciated, the comedian should deal in that which would bring him most ready money and enable him to keep body and soul together.

In the *Apology* we read that many years before Cibber had any share in the management, it was the usual method of Mr. Rich to pay exceptionally high prices for singers and dancers, to balance which he reduced the salaries of his actors. The patentee's idea of what ought to be shown on the stage, appears to have been very much on a level with the taste of the multitude, whose opinion naturally weighed with him as much as, and even more than, that of the best judges. He meant to please the majority who can always more easily understand anything they see than the daintiest things that can be said,[6] which is a thing everybody realises in this twentieth century, when even the smallest town boasts a number of more or less gorgeously equipped cinemas, whereas theatres can hardly manage to pay their way.

[1] p. 20, N. 3.

[2] See also: E. Curll, *The Life of Robert Wilks,* p. 8.

[3] Preface to *Love's Last Shift.*

[4] Preface to *Woman's Wit.*

[6] Apology I, p. 47: "If people are permitted to buy it (i. e. folly), without blushing, the Theatrical merchant seems to have an equal right to the liberty of selling it, without Reproach."

[6] Apology II, p. 23.

Cibber's defence of his own policy in this matter is worth quoting and most of the things he says in it, we shall have no difficulty in applying to the state of affairs prevailing in the theatre of our own day. In page 120 of the second volume of the *Apology,* we read:

"I have upon several occasions already observed that when one company is too hard for another, the lower in reputation has always been forced to exhibit fine new-fangled foppery to draw the multitude after them: of these expedients, singing and dancing had formerly been the most effectual; but at the time I am speaking of, our English music had been so discountenanced since the taste of Italian operas prevailed, that it was to no purpose to pretend to it. Dancing therefore was now the only weight in the opposite scale, & as the new theatre sometimes found their account in it, it could not be safe for us wholly to neglect it.[1] To give even dancing therefore some improvement, & to make it something more than motion without meaning, the fable of *Mars and Venus* was formed into a connected presentation of dances in character, wherein the passions were so happily expressed and the whole story so intelligibly told by a mute narration of gestures only, that even thinking spectators allowed it both a pleasing and a rational entertainment; though at the same time, from our distrust of its reception, we durst not venture to decorate it with any extraordinary expense of scenes or habits; but upon the success of this attempt, it was rightly concluded that if a visible expense in both were added to something of the same nature, it could not fail of drawing the town proportionably after it. From this original hint, then (but in every way unequal to it), sprung forth that succession of monstrous medlies that have so long infested the Stage, & which arose upon one another, alternately at both houses, outvying in expense, like contending bribes on both sides at an election, to secure a majority of the multitude. But so it is, truth may com-

[1] Mr. A. W. Ward has the following note to *The First Epistle of the second Book of Horace II,* Pope's poetical Works, Globe-Edition, p. 314, l. 313: "Pantomimes were brought into the full blaze of public favour by Rich, manager of Covent Garden, in 1723; and Cibber, at Drury-Lane, was obliged to produce the same kind of entertainment in self-defence."

plain, and merit murmur with what justice it may, the few will never be a match for the many, unless authority should think fit to interpose and put down these poetical drams, these gin-shops of the Stage, that intoxicate its auditors and dishonour their understanding with a levity for which I want a name...

If I am asked (after my condemning these fooleries myself) how I came to assent, or continue my share of expense to them? I have no better excuse for my error than confessing it. I did it against my conscience! and had not virtue enough to starve, by opposing a multitude that would have been too hard for me...

Nothwithstanding, then, this our compliance with the vulgar taste, we generally made use of these pantomimes but as crutches to our weakest plays: nor were we so lost to all sense of what was valuable as to dishonour our best authors in such bad company: we had still a due respect to several select plays that were able to be their own support, & in which we found our constant account without painting and patching them out like prostitutes with these follies in fashion: if therefore we were not so strictly chaste in the other part of our conduct, let the error of it stand among the silly consequences of two Stages. Could the interest of both companies have been united in one only theatre, I had been one of the few that would have used my utmost endeavour of never admitting to the stage any spectacle that ought not to have been seen there; the errors of my own plays, which I could not see, excepted. And though probably the majority of the spectators would not have been so well pleased with a theatre so regulated, yet sense and reason cannot lose their intrinsick value, because the giddy and the ignorant are blind and deaf, or numerous: and I cannot help saying it is a reproach to a sensible people to let folly so publicly govern their pleasures."[1]

Now some may say that it was hypocrisy for a man like Cibber to write like that: he might pose as a champion of serious and decent performances, but his life proves that he was more attracted by what was light and frivolous than by what gave more sedate pleasures. But in this reasoning there is a funda-

[1] Apology II, p. 121 ff.

mental mistake. A man like Cibber might be addicted to gambling and a variety of other vices, and yet at the same time realise that a life like his own was not to be recommended. Many a man who knows that he has thrown away the splendid opportunities of his own youth and early manhood, becomes a most anxious and conscientious father. The famous *Confessions of an English Opium Eater* was written to warn others against the besetting sin of the author, if we may believe De Quincey's own words. But there is another point; whatever we may think of Cibber as a man, this need not affect our opinion of his policy as a theatrical manager and as an artist. This man, who often lost his last shilling at hazard or cards and was heard to call out: "Now I must go home and eat a child!" [1] was no more a bad man of business than he was a cannibal. He might be fond of gambling, but he did not allow it to interfere with his work.

His private life certainly was not exemplary, but that did not prevent him from taking theatrical art quite seriously. The excellent criticisms he wrote of the performance of so many of his contemporaries and the evident delight he took in dwelling on their excellencies give sufficient proof that he loved his art, and render it extremely unlikely that he did anything to degrade it, unless he was forced by circumstances to do so. Cibber, indeed, was a man who might have said of himself, in reference to his private life: "Video meliora proboque, deteriora sequor", but there was certainly no occasion for this humility on his part in connection with his conduct of the stage. His persistent attempts at tragedy, both as an actor and as an author, are there to prove that he was prepared to take any amount of trouble to achieve something in a branch of the histrionic art, for which he had no special aptitude, merely because he considered it to be more dignified than that in which he had already made his mark. [2]

Cibber's plea for the necessity of complying with the popular

[1] *Dram. Misc.,* II, p. 479.

[2] When Mr. Rich introduced a set of rope-dancers into his theatre as an additional attraction in 1707, Cibber, who had to play an important part in the play, made bold to go into the pit and announce to the spectators, that he declined to act upon the stage that was thus disgraced. His example inspired the other actors and Rich was forced to give up his plan. (Apology II, p. 24).

taste sounds both convincing and modern at the same time. In our own day many theatrical managers, who know exactly what sort of plays they would like to perform and can express their theories precisely, may occasionally produce something that answers to their own ideas of what a play ought to be, but as a general rule they have to adapt themselves to the vulgar taste. They find that ideals are inspiring, but cannot fill the house. Farcical and more or less indecent entertainments are required to keep the theatre afloat from a financial point of view. There are very few countries, in which it would not be possible to point to managers who, for a long time, held firm in their resolution to educate the public, but had in the end to give in to avoid disaster. [1]

Besides the desire of the people for light entertainments, there was in the 18th century the no less marked preference for foreign plays and players, a phenomenon that is just as familiar to us at the present day. It is a notorious fact that in many countries, where native actors do not succeed in getting full houses, foreign actors, often by no means superior, will draw large audiences. The reason is not far to seek; it lies in a desire for change, a relish for anything that is a bit out of the common, a particular appreciation for anything that has a foreign flavour, which is a characteristic, not of one particular nation at one particular period of its history, but of any nation at any time. This liking for all that is not familiar, for anything that takes people out of the ordinary routine accounts, too, for the fact that thousands of tourists, who travel abroad, whenever they get the chance, know very little about their own country. Travellers, who would not think of missing a single church or museum while abroad, in many cases know nothing beyond the exteriors of similar places of interest at home. [2]

During Cibber's management, he had continually to contend

[1] Dutchmen will remember the efforts made by Heijermans to raise the national theatre to a higher level, not only as an author by writing some of the best plays in the language, but also as a theatrical manager. They will remember too his dismal failure in the latter capacity.

[2] It is a notorious fact that in Holland, for example, an Italian Opera has been able to maintain itself for a great many years, while attempts at a national opera proved abortive.

with this competition from abroad. These foreign actors, besides being popular for the reasons indicated above, were also much freer in the matter of choice of plays. In England the Restoration period was over; Collier and other critics of the drama had had their way and the general tone of dramatic literature had become much purer from the moral point of view, several plays of the period, indeed, being in the nature of homilies rather than of anything else. Foreign players, on the contrary, were at liberty to present pieces of a different kind, which may well have come as a relief to those patrons of the stage who had had their theatrical tastes formed in the playhouses of the latter part of the seventeenth century.

In 1719, Steele published the following indignant criticism of the performances of a troupe of French players, that had visited London in February and March of that year. [1]

"The improvement we are to expect from them does not tend to instructing, but peopling the British Nation. Those who did not understand the language were, it seems, informed by the gesture of the Actor, of the main drift of the Play, which was no more nor less than to promote (as one of our own Prologues of King Charles's reign has it "the hopeful work of propagation" .... This is not to be spoken of with the least temper: to talk of learning, modesty, or politeness, would be ridiculous: it would be reading lectures to Savages. But if we are any longer to march on two legs, and not be quite prone, or on all four, like the other animals, let us assume manhood and indignation against so barbarous an affront. To acquaint women of honour with what is more filthy than could be seen at a brothel; to entertain our wives and daughters with what their whole education tended to make them abhor; is something more monstrous than I believed even this age of contradictions could ever produce."

As it appears from the same number of *The Theatre,* that the French performance was well attended, we ought, no doubt, to make some allowance for his natural pique at the success of a competitor, in which light Steele at that time could not help seeing the French company. That allowance being made, however,

[1] *The Theatre,* Number 21, Saturday, March 12, 1719.

we may be sure that the performance against which the diatribe is directed, had passed the bounds of decency and that Steele was honestly shocked at this prostitution of the London stage. [1]

We can well understand that Cibber commented rather bitterly on the ease with which the heirs of the old patentee succeeded in obtaining permission for the performance of plays in London. Besides the keen competition to which he was exposed on the part of operas, and especially foreign operas as well as foreign troupes of actors, a new and formidable rival now arose, one more permanent than they. The result, as he foresaw, could not but be a falling-off in his receipts as well as in the quality of performances in London in general. His ideal of one single company under the control of the authorities, he defends over and over again in his *Apology*. Formally, his principal grievance against this new competitor was the fact that for many years the managers of Drury Lane Theatre had been paying some six hundred pounds a year for a mere sinecure, in order to secure the same rights that were now so readily granted to the new rival at Lincoln's Inn Fields! [2]

Stage-setting and costuming [3] were becoming more and more important in all theatrical entertainments; in the opera, indeed, they were considered to be of more importance than the music, and certainly than the words. The *Spectator* held that it was essential for anything that was to be put to music, to be nonsense.

[1] John Dennis was very sceptical as to Steele's sincerity on this head. After referring to Steele's support of Cibber (see page 4, above) he addresses him in the following terms: "Have you really a mind to throw off the mask at last: and to own to the world, that all those plausible words, Religion, Honour, Conscience, Justice, Beneficence, Innocence, with *some* Nomenclators mean one and the same thing; and that is, Private Interest. Or are there some extraordinary qualities, which, being common to you both, cause this union of affections, and this sympathy of souls?"

[2] See page 21.

[3] The stage inventories of the time give evidence of poverty in this respect. Prof. Allardyce Nicoll *(Early 18th Cent. Drama)* draws attention to the fact that, whereas in the 18th century portraits of actresses we almost invariably see them represented in the usual eighteenth century garments, those of actors in many cases furnish the proof that some attempts at historical costuming had been made."

[4] *Spectator,* No. 18.

The opera itself had a serious rival in the so-called puppet-shows. In the *Spectator,* No 14, a comparison in made between the staging of the puppet-show by Mr. Powell (a dwarf, who made a fortune by entertainments of this kind) and of the opera at the Haymarket Theatre. From the description given it seems that the two performances were very much alike. At the Haymarket they played *Rinaldo and Armida,* an opera by Handel, at the puppet-show *Whittington and his Cat.* In the former the King of Jerusalem was obliged to come from the city on foot, instead of being drawn in a chariot with white horses, as had been promised in the programme. There was but a short allowance of thunder and lightning, but on the other hand the two dragons did their duty and spat fire and smoke. [1] The sparrows and chaffinches [2] were not very well trained and most of them flew into the galleries or put out the candles. At one time the scene-shifters forgot to change the side-scenes, so that the audience were treated to the unusual spectacle of an ocean in the midst of a delightful grove. In consequence of this, the spectator was not a little astonished to see a young man in a full-bottomed wig appear upon the ocean and take snuff without displaying the slightest concern. As to the mechanism of the stage and the scenery, the opera compared unfavourably with thc puppet-show, Mr. Powell introducing, among other novelties, a pig that was so well trained that in the first scene, the pig and Punch danced a minuet together. The wit of the two performances was about equal, for which reason, the writer thinks that the puppet-show deserved the preference, because it was in English and thus could at all events be understood by the audience.

The absurdity of a theatre full of people listening to a perfor-

[1] See also No. 3 of *The Adventurer.*

[2] In No. 5 of the *Spectator* occurs the following observation: As I was walking in the streets about a fortnight ago, I saw an ordinary fellow carrying a cage full of little birds upon his shoulder; and, as I was wondering with myself what use he would put them to, he was met very luckily by an acquaintance, who had the same curiosity. Upon his asking him what he had upon his shoulder, he told them he had been buying sparrows for the opera. "Sparrows for the opera," says his friend, licking his lips, "what, are they to be roasted?" "No, no," says the other, "they are to enter towards the end of the first act, and to fly about the stage."

mance, of which they did not understand a single word, is continually pointed out by Steele. According to him, this was merely a device on the part of the audience to save themselves the trouble of thinking. The result, he said, was that people could not understand the language upon their own stage, and were in danger of being abused to their faces by actors and singers, who felt quite safe in calling the spectators names in a language of which they knew nothing. The alternative of translating Italian operas into English was considered worse still. In No. 18 of the *Spectator,* an example is quoted of a speech in which an indignant lover reproached a woman for being untrue to him. The Italian speech was rendered in English by a very mild sort of lover's complaint, with the result that the audience was melting away and languishing to notes that were filled with fury and indignation. On other occasions when the translator had been better fitted for his task, the natural change in the word order would cause the music to be inappropriate to the English text, whereas it was perfectly all right in the original. An Italian verse that literally translated might run: "And turn'd my rage into pity," might be rendered in English by a different order, e.g.: "And into pity turned my rage", with the result that the soft notes adapted to the "pity" in the Italian, fell upon the word "rage" in the English. The *Spectator* proves himself to be a bad prophet, for he observes that he cannot forbear thinking that an historian two or three hundred years later will make the following reflection: "In the beginning of the 18th century, the Italian tongue was so well understood in England, that the operas were acted on the public stage in that language". [1]

[1] In another place *(The Spectator,* No. 29) this question of the position of the Italian Opera in London, is further considered. In the course of his essay, Steele has some highly interesting remarks on what he calls 'tone' or 'accent': "By the tone or accent I do not mean the pronunciation of each particular word, but the sound of the whole sentence," he observes. He goes on to say that English people often complain that French actors all speak in the same tone, and that French people have the same objection to the monotony of English speech. The notes of interrogation or admiration in Italian, he thinks so much alike the ordinary tone of voice of an Englishman in anger, that the audience often makes the mistake of expecting to see the hero knock down his messenger, when he is merely asking him

We can well understand that, at the death of Queen Anne, the actors wished to show Steele their gratitude for the benefits he had bestowed on them in the *Tatler* and *Spectator.* His articles had been one continual plea for a properly governed stage and his attacks on Mr. Rich, whom he used to call *Divito* were very numerous and must have been of great help to the actors in their struggle. Steele used to say that the impulses for good, he had received from theatrical representations, had been of more effect in his life than anything else. They never failed to send him home full of ideas that made him more courteous and kinder to his friends and acquaintances.

In his preference for one playhouse, even at a time when he was not personally concerned in the management, he was as conservative as Cibber. [1] "It has been within the observation of the youngest amongst us, that while there were two houses, they did not outvie each other by such representations as tended to the instruction and ornament of life, but by introducing mimical dances, and fulsome buffooneries. For when an excellent tragedy was to be acted in one house, the ladder-dancer carried the whole town to the other: and, indeed, such an evil as this must be the natural consequence of two theatres, as certainly as there are more that can see than can think. Every one is sensible of the danger of the fellow on the ladder, and can see his activity in coming down safe; but very few are judges of the distress of an hero in a play, or of his manner of behaviour in those circumstances. Thus to please the people, two houses must entertain them with what they can understand, and not with things which are designed to improve their understanding: and the readiest way to gain good audiences must be to offer such things as are most relished by the crowd; that is to say, immodest action, empty show, or impertinent activity." This criticism, published a considerable time before Cibber could have been at all responsible for the quality of the performances at Drury Lane, is another

a question, or fancying a man to be quarrelling with his friend, when he is only bidding him goodbye. Although not absolutely relevant in this connection these instructive remarks on what we should now call "intonation" are worth mentioning.

[1] *The Tatler,* No. 99.

conclusive proof, if that is necessary, that it will not do to blame him for the introduction of inferior elements into the entertainments offered to the public.

In the preceding pages it has been demonstrated that from the outside the theatre was threatened by competitors of various kinds; we shall now proceed to glance at the difficulties and dangers that threatened its prosperity from within. By this we do not mean the natural problems that anybody has to grapple with, whose duty it is to try and make a number of individuals co-operate to the same end; in other words, we are not referring to the many calls that must necessarily have been made upon his diplomatic powers in maintaining friendly, or at any rate peaceful relations among the actors, but the difficulties resulting from the nature and composition of the theatrical audiences of his time. One of the greatest menaces to an orderly and successful performance, was the fact that a great many of the *jeunesse dorée* were in the habit of having seats on the stage instead of in the body of the theatre. [1] The wish to be seen, which even at the present day accounts for the attendance at a great many public functions, here appeared in its crudest form. The presence of spectators on the stage, in addition to being an impediment to the freedom of action and movement, naturally had a good many undesirable consequences. It is a notorious fact that in a great many cases the presence of the actresses and the desire to be on a footing of familiarity with them, [2] formed the main attraction. But too often the attempts at familiarity were crowned with success, a fact that could not but lead to a general lessening of the esteem in which the theatrical profession as a whole was held. If, on the other hand, these attempts were repelled, the danger to the theatre, resulting from this, was still greater, for at that time, any rich

[1] *The Spectator,* No. 502 has the following remark: "It is ordinary for a cluster of coxcombs to take up the house to themselves, and equally insult both the actors and the company. These savages, who want all manner of regard and deference to the rest of mankind, come only to show themselves to us, without any other purpose than to let us know they despise us."

[2] Half a crown was the usual charge for access to the "tyring-room", where one might have a chat with the actresses.

young man, who had any grievance against an actor or actress, might take his revenge the very next time the person in question appeared on the stage.

The *Apology*[1] contains a very striking example, showing how completely actresses were at the mercy of these "unlicked cubs of condition", as Cibber calls them in another passage. An actress, who had refused to take any notice of the advances of a military man who sat near her, was at last treated by him in a manner so grossly insulting that she could endure it no longer, and turning upon him with an angry look told him she would not have anything to do with him. Some time after, when she was playing one of her best parts, he interrupted her performance with loud words of mockery and without paying any attention to the remarks of those who were sitting near him, he even went so far as to throw all sorts of things at her.

On another occasion, one of the actors, called Smith,[2] had the misfortune to receive a blow from one of the gentlemen behind the scenes. An account of what had happened was given to the King, who was so indignant at this behaviour on the part of one of his courtiers, that the offender was informed His Majesty did not wish to see him any more at Court. This punishment for assaulting a mere actor was considered so extreme that a party was formed to assert the right of a nobleman to treat an actor as he liked and consequently, the next time Smith made an appearance on the stage, he was received with a chorus of cat-calls that soon convinced him that he would not be allowed to proceed, and afterwards he found himself obliged to retire from the theatre altogether.

That the presence of spectators on the stage was felt to be objectionable also appears from the fact that on Nov. 13, 1711 an order of Queen Anne was published, worded as follows: "Whereas We are informed that the orders We have already given for the reformation of the Stage, by not permitting anything to be Acted contrary to Religion or good manners, have in great measure had the good effect We propos'd and being

[1] Vol I, p. 44.

[2] "Smith's character as a gentleman," Cibber bitterly observes, "could have been no way impeached, had he not degraded it, by being a celebrated actor."

further desirous to reform all other indecencies and disorders of the Stage, Our Will and Pleasure therefore is, And We do hereby Strictly Command that no person of what quality soever presume to stand behind the Scenes or come upon the Stage." A considerable time, however, before this order was published, Cibber and his partners had put a stop to that practice at Drury Lane. [1] As theatrical managers they realised that they were doing a very dangerous thing, but they saw no less clearly that they owed it to the dignity of their art and their profession to act in this way. [2]

At the time when the popularity of his theatre was at a particularly low ebb, Rich, considering that a good way to stand well with the people of quality was to be on good terms with their footmen, opened the upper gallery to the latter, free of charge. Before this time no footman had been supposed to enter the theatre before the fifth act of a play. This measure undoubtedly had the desired effect of filling the theatre, or at all events the gallery, but at the same time did away with the last vestige of quietude in the theatre. The new visitors were indeed liberal in their applause, but as they did not contribute in any way to the financial prosperity of the house, their indiscriminate applause soon proved to be a drawback instead of an advantage, because it was impossible to gauge the tastes of the paying part of the audience by the noise made by their footmen. This new privilege of free admittance was very soon regarded as a right, and, in course of time, became the occasion for some of the most disgraceful scenes in the playhouse. On May 5th, 1737, for example, the footmen, on account of their rudeness, were denied admission to the gallery. Three hundred of them broke open the door of Drury Lane Theatre, forced their way in, and wounded twenty-

[1] Apology I, p. 126: "which custom we found so intolerable when we had the stage in our hands, that at the hazard of our lives, we were forced to get rid of them; and our only expedient was, by refusing money from all persons, without distinction, at the stage door".

[2] When a second theatre was opened, it was imagined by Cibber's colleagues that "all those wo wished ill to (them), and particularly a great party who had been disobliged by (their) shutting them out from behind the scenes, even to the refusal of their money, would now exert themselves in any particular or extravagant measures that might either hurt (them) or support (their) competitors". Apology II, p. 119.

five persons, while the Prince and Princess of Wales, with some other members of the Royal Family were present. The Riot-Act was read and 30 footmen were sent to Newgate. Mr. Fleetwood, who was the manager at the time, after this received a letter, in which the footmen threatened to rase the theatre to the ground and consequently a guard of fifty soldiers was stationed near the theatre for several nights. [1]

In *The Lady's Last Stake,* Sir Friendly Moral says to Lord George Brilliant: "But the Sparks I observed you with, were Done-first the Jockey and Touch the Gamester; as infamous a Fellow as ever broke the Head of a Box-keeper". This suggestive remark gives us some idea of the treatment the officials of the theatre had to put up with on the part of this section of the audience. [2]

In the *Tatler,* No 1 for Tuesday, April 12th, 1709, we find a comparison made between the audience of Dryden's time and of Steele's own day. While songs, epigrams and satires used to be seen in the hands of every man one met, only packs of cards were in evidence in 1709. The old discussions about the style and the quality of the play and the performance were superseded by disputes as to the right of the game. On the particular occasion, described by Steele, the audience, however altered, gave no occasion for complaint. It was the night of Betterton's benefit and the attitude of the public in all parts of the house, proved, according to *The Tatler,* that "the true relish for manly entertainments and rational pleasures" was not yet wholly lost. On this occasion the presence of spectators on the stage was evidently considered a good sign for special mention is made of the fact that the stage itself was covered with ladies and gentlemen, and that the curtain, when drawn, disclosed a very splendid and distinguished audience there.

The actors also come in for a share of the praise: they were careful of their carriage, the parts were acted to perfection, and no one was guilty of the insertion of witticisms of their own. [3]

[1] Recorded by John Nichols in his edition of *The Theatre, &c.,* p. 19.

[2] *Cibber's Works,* London 1760: Vol II, p. 247.

[3] In *The Spectator* for Monday, Oct. 6th, 1712 the same practice is referred to. "The intolerable folly and confidence of players putting in words of their own, does in a great measure feed the absurd taste of the audience".

Another interesting and instructive description of the audience of this period is found in No. 502 of the *Spectator,* in which the theatrical public is divided into two categories: those who know no pleasure but that of the body and those who improve these mere animal enjoyments by means of mental activity. According to Steele the intelligent part of the audience was in every respect less influential than the other. "This is the reason," he says, "that when a scene tending to procreation is acted, you see the whole pit in such a chuckle and old letchers, with mouths open, stare at those loose gesticulations on the stage with shameful earnestness; when the justest pictures of human life in its calm dignity, and the properest sentiments for the conduct of it, pass by like mere narration, as conducing only to somewhat much better which is to come after. I have seen the whole house sometimes in so proper a disposition, that indeed I have trembled for the boxes, and feared the entertainment would end in the representation of the rape of the Sabines." His impression seems to be that really good acting was hardly appreciated for its own sake and that only humour of the nature referred to in the preceding passage and the roughest kind of horse-play and practical joking were admired. "The Spectator" feels sure that if a scene were written in which one of the actors broke his leg in a wrestling-match and a third came in it to set it, without anything being said, except what was absolutely necessary, the whole house would have been in a roar of applause at the dissembled pain of the victim and the cleverness and arch looks of the surgeon, and when we read it in our own day, we also feel sure that he was right.

In *The Theatre* for Jan. 9, 1719, Steele suggests a way of solving the difficulties of the actors, who find that every play they put on the bills, or propose to revive, is disliked by some of the spectators as much as it is approved of by others, even before it is actually played. He proposes therefore that a body of persons be selected, to be called "Auditors of the Drama." These persons, as representatives of the various classes of play-goers, to be elected by the public, on condition that no one is to have a free voice in these elections, unless he can produce a certificate, duly signed by the respective door-keepers of the theatre, to prove that he has never refused to pay for his seat. In the first place, the actors are to select two of their own society, viz. one male and one female, to look after their own interests, and also for the information of the other auditors with respect to matters immediately relating to the technical business of the stage. The next auditor, mentioned by the writer, is to represent, not the actors, but another group of persons, immediately interested in a proper choice of plays, namely the dramatic authors. This auditor, it is proposed, is to be elected by the tragic and comic writers: he will have to serve for the "Liberties of Parnassus." The other representatives, who are of more importance to us in this connection, as the manner of their election gives us a glimpse of the composition of the theatrical audiences at the time, are to be chosen by the spectators only.

In the first place the ladies are mentioned: "Three of the Fair Sex" shall represent the Front-Boxes. At this time it appears to have been the custom for the ladies to occupy the front, while the gentlemen were seated in the side-boxes. [1] The next members of the select committee are to be two "Gentlemen of Wit and Pleasure", to represent the side-boxes, and three "substantial Citizens" for the pit. The first gallery shall be represented by one lawyer's clerk and a valet-de-chambre and the upper gallery by a "Journeyman Baker". A footman that can write and read shall be "Mercury to the Board".

Now all this, which in *The Theatre* itself is followed by a description of the various types, who, according to the writer had already applied for a place on the body of auditors, is highly interesting and instructive. Not only are we in a position to infer from this by what class of people the various seats were taken, but also the relative importance of the several groups.

To begin with the actors; no mention is made of any business-

[1] See: Nichols' edition of *The Theatre, &c.*, p. 19.

Cf. *The Rape of the Lock*, canto V, l. 13 ff.:

Why round our coaches crowd the white-glov'd Beaux,
Why bows the side-box from its inmost rows:
How vain are all these glories, all our pains,
Unless good sense preserve what beauty gains:
That men may say, when we the front-box grace:
"Behold the first in virtue as in face!"

man being at the head of the theatrical business. The people of first-rate importance are actors, not managers and it is not surprising, that this should be Steele's idea. The management of the theatre by comparative outsiders, for the time being at least, was over; actors, in the case of Drury Lane Theatre at all events, having an author as a coadjutor, were their own masters.

Three ladies and two gentlemen of wit and pleasure on a total of fifteen members were to represent that part of the audience, which reigned supreme in the last quarter of the seventeenth century. If we may assume that Steele in his proposal, humorous as it is, observed those proportions, of which he, as a regular visitor of the theatre, was an excellent judge, it is clear that a great change had come about since the days of Dryden. Just as a change had come over the type of plays acted, so had a change come over the public and the influence of each, as we shall see in a following chapter, acted upon the other. No longer were ladies afraid to show their faces in the front boxes; the days when they used to come in masks were over; the dramatists no longer made "the undivided pursuit of lawless gallantry," as Lamb calls it, the business of their existence and Steele could safely give the ladies an important voice on his committee.

The only other group, to be allotted three seats were the substantial citizens. This again is a symptom of the change that had been effected in the theatre. At one time these substantial citizens, if they had any feeling of self-respect, would hardly go to the playhouse at all, the favourite theme presented to the public, being the successful intrigue of a nobleman with the wife of a merchant or tradesman and the discomfiture of the duped husband, who, in many cases was the laughing-stock of the play. The result had been that the "substantial citizens" had either imitated the nobility as far as they could do so, or had joined the extreme Puritans, as far as their attitude towards the stage was concerned. In 1719 they evidently were again to be counted among the respected patrons of the stage. Another sign of the democratic tendency of the time is provided by the fact that no fewer than four seats on the imaginary committee were to be reserved for the galleries. That much value would have been attached to their opinions does not seem very probable, but they certainly had to be considered, for, though not contributing much to the financial support of the theatre, they were in the habit of obtruding their views on the management in a most troublesome manner.

That nobody was to have a voice in the election of the auditors, if he failed to produce a testimonial to the effect that he had never refused to pay for admittance, sounds very strange now, and probably referred in the very first place to the footmen, who, as was mentioned above, had received the right to be admitted to the gallery without any payment being required of them. When Cibber became one of the managers, the old privilege, accorded to playgoers to see one act of a play without paying for admission, was no longer recognised;[1] but for a long time there were those who considered the payments they made to be rather in the nature of a favour bestowed, than a natural and necessary condition of visiting the theatre. Officially an end was put to the habit as far back as 1704, for on the 17th of January of that year, a proclamation of Queen Anne forbade women to wear masks in the theatre, and any spectator to have a seat for which the established price had not been paid. If we consider, however, that on the same occasion it was decreed that no one should be allowed to go behind the scenes, and that the same order had to be repeated as late as 1711,[2] we realise that the date of the official prohibition can hardly be looked upon as an indication of the time at which the practice was definitely dropped.

In one respect the audiences of our own day certainly show an improvement on those of Cibber's time; they are better-behaved. The descriptions of unruly audiences, given by Cibber and others, indicate this; such disgraceful scenes as were usual in those days would be impossible nowadays. When a play was not to the taste of the spectators, or at least some part of the spectators, the actors and the author received no mercy. "Every

[1] Pepys has it that on Jan 7. 1668, he went "to the two playhouses, in the pit, to gaze up and down, and there did by this means, for nothing, see an act in *The Schoole of Compliments* at the Duke of York's and *Henry the Fourth* at the King's House."

[2] See page 36.

fool", says Cibber, "the lowest member of the mob, becomes a wit, and will have a fling at him (viz. the author). They come now to a new play, like hounds to a carcase, and are all in full cry, sometimes for an hour together, before the curtain rises to throw it amongst them." [1] The remarkable part of it all was, that in many cases a play was often not given a chance; it was condemned beforehand and simply not allowed a hearing. Then, as now, the rowdy part of the crowd had it all their own way and those who were willing to hear the play and judge for themselves, frequently were not allowed to do so. On those occasions cat-calls would fill the air from the moment the first actor appeared upon the stage, and persist throughout the performance.

In 1729, John Gay wrote a sequel to the *Beggar's Opera,* called *Polly.* The presentation was forbidden by the Lord Chamberlain, no doubt through the influence of Walpole. [2] Somehow, Cibber was charged with having had a hand in this, and when, therefore, a short time after his play *Love in a Riddle* was going to be acted, a party was formed against it, and the play was received with all sorts of noises and cat-calls, so that it was impossible for the actors to make themselves understood. It so happened that Frederick, Prince of Wales, was in the theatre that evening, and the only way to appease the audience, that Cibber could think of, was to step forward to the pit and tell them that, since they would not allow the play to go forward he would give them his word of honour that it should not be acted again after that night; but he hoped they would consider in whose presence they were, and would at least for the present, suspend any further marks of the displeasure that they thought he had deserved. In this way, by sacrificing his own interests, he succeeded in calming the storm for that evening, and, according to Cibber's report, the play was fairly successful when a number of the more rowdy element in the audience had left the playhouse.

[1] Apology I, p. 96.

[2] Eventually, the suppression of the play proved to be a gain to Gay, and an advertisement for his play, which was published by private subscription in the same year, bringing its author more than £1000.

Another occasion, on which Cibber was singled out for similar treatment is recorded by Davies.[1] When the comedy of *The Provoked Husband* was performed, Cibber's enemies tried their utmost to get the play condemned by the audience. For some time it seemed as if their efforts would be crowned with success, but the reconciliation scene made such a good impression on the public that the conclusion was generously applauded. Mrs. Oldfield came forward to speak the epilogue, but no sooner had she begun the first verse: „Methinks I hear some powder'd critic say", than a man who was sitting near the orchestra, saluted her words with a loud hiss. This might have been the beginning of another attempt to spoil the success of the play, if Mrs. Oldfield had not immediately fixed her eye upon the spectator in question and saved the situation by saying: "Poor creature!", loud enough to be heard by the audience, and with such a look of pity and contempt, that—as Davies has it—"the poor reptile sunk down with fear and trembling", while the actress's conduct was rewarded with a thunderous applause.

This was the way in which a section of the audience turned against the actors, when they thought they had some reason to do so, but when this was not the case, they made other members of the audience their victims. In No. 268 of the *Spectator* there is a letter, the writer of which complains of the behaviour of the public in the following terms: "I do not wear a sword, but I often divert myself at the theatre, where I frequently see a set of fellows pull plain people, by way of humour or frolic, by the nose, upon frivolous or no occasion. A friend of mine the other night, applauding what a graceful exit Mr. Wilks made, one of those nose-wringers overhearing him, pinched him by the nose. I was in the pit the other night, when it was very much crowded; a gentleman leaning upon me, and very heavily, I very civilly requested him to remove his hand; for which he pulled me by the nose. I would not resent it in so public a place, because I was unwilling to create a disturbance; but have since reflected upon it as a thing that is unmanly and disengenuous, renders the nose-pullers odious, and makes the person pulled by

[1] *Dram. Misc.*, III, p. 466.

the nose look little and contemptible." That Cibber was able to make the theatre a paying concern and a very lucrative one at that, in circumstances of this nature, proves sufficiently that he was the right man in the right place, whatever his enemies may have had to say to the contrary.

IV

THE DRAMA BEFORE CIBBER

Austere morality and the fear of God, Macaulay tells us, characterised the men that gathered about Cromwell; the Commonwealth was founded on religion, by men, who firmly believed the principles they professed in public. As the Puritan movement grew in power and extent, its character changed; no longer did it attract only the chosen few as it had in the beginning, but thousands helped to swell its ranks who were inspired by no other ideal than the desire to show their allegiance to the party that seemed likely to be in power for good and all.[1] The godliness that had distinguished the original followers of Cromwell was required of everybody who wished to hold a position of any importance in the state; instead of being the result of a sincere conviction, it became a mere political badge, readily adopted by those who thought only of the immediate advantages accruing from it.

Even those who were averse to hypocrisy could not but realise that sincerity was dangerous, and the general atmosphere of life in the Commonwealth in course of time came to be one of pretended morality, the morality of appearances[2] and, towards the end of the life of Oliver Cromwell, a considerable part of the population had lost all sympathy with the governing classes and chafed at the unnatural restraint under which they were living. In this manner the way for the restoration of the Stuarts was being paved and it is small wonder that, when it did come, the tide of reaction for the time being, at least, swept away all that had been so carefully built up in the preceding years, till in the end not a trace seemed to be left of that religion and morality that had been so generally advocated and so rigidly imposed in the days of the Commonwealth. "The Restoration",

[1] See Appendix I.

[2] See also the article on Pope in *My Study Windows*, by J. Russell Lowell, pp. 342 ff.

Macaulay says, "placed supreme power in the hands of a libertine." .... "In London the outbreak of debauchery was appalling: and in London the places most deeply infected were the Palace, the quarters inhabited by the aristocracy and the Inns of Court". [1] From the compulsory saintship and cropped hair of the Puritans, men rushed or sneaked, as their temperaments dictated, to the opposite cant of sensuality and an extravagance of periwig. [2]

All this refers in the first place to the Court circles. [3] The people at large may have been glad to take up again some of their old "superstitions" for that was the name given by "the Lord's people" to the keeping of Christmas with decorations of holly and ivy, to dancing round the maypole and to all the other popular amusements and sports, [4] but their lives were not changed in any important respect. Religion was as essential to them as it had been in the preceding years; only the political enthusiasm, so closely connected with it in the first few years of the Commonwealth, had died with the Protector, and thousands were glad to return to their homes, realising that the war period was at an end, and resolved to have a good time in their own way. When Hettner, therefore, states [5] that, but for a few exceptions, the whole nation followed the example of the court, this statement, in its sweeping generality is not borne out by history. In a nation, wholly impregnated with the spirit of the Court of Charles II, the success of the *Pilgrim's Progress* [6] would hardly have been what it was, nor would so many thousands have flocked to the churches to hear the sermons of men like South, Barrow and Stillingfleet.

On the other hand, it is necessary to admit that it is easy to be misled in this particular point, for the literature of the time and the utterances of most of its public men certainly seem to confirm Hettner's statement. Another distinguished foreign

[1] Macaulay, *Comic Dramatists of the Restoration.* Tauchnitz, Vol. IV, p. 159.

[2] *My Study Windows*, p. 342.

[3] For the character of Charles II, see J. R. Green, *A Short History of the English People,* p. 630.

[4] Ibid. p. 606.

[5] H. Hettner, *Geschichte der Englischen Literatur,* 7th ed., p. 100 "Und wie der Hof war, so war mit wenigen Ausnahmen das ganze Volk."

[6] Before Bunyan's death, in 1688, ten editions had been sold.

critic, M. Beljame, makes the same sort of mistake, when he writes: "l'Angleterre, assujettie tout entière à la même discipline surhumaine par les Puritains, avait pendant plus de onze ans manqué d'air, étouffé. Au retour de Charles II, elle ouvrit les fenêtres, et toutes grandes. Elle les ouvrit trop. A l'exagération de la rigueur la Restauration répondit par l'exagération de la licence." [1] In this quotation there are two things that strike the careful reader, first that England is here represented as having been subjected to a very strict regimen by some outside force, called Puritanism; secondly that the nation, after having thrown off the yoke of Puritanism, indulged in unlimited licence.

Now there cannot be any doubt that Puritanism as a religious, and especially through Cromwell as a political force, was the outcome of the national character of the English and as such did not cease with the Restoration, but continued to exist as a living force throughout the country. It may be true that the Puritans imposed a "discipline surhumaine", but we ought not to forget that the original champions of Puritanism, imposed it on themselves in the first place, so that it would be almost as logical to speak of the priesthood throwing off the yoke of the church, as of England throwing off the yoke of Puritanism. Yet it was certainly true, as another critic observes, [2] that thc Puritans disposed of the power of the sword, a fact remarkable enough in itself, for during a long period before the Commonwealth the power of the sword had lain with the supporters of the Court only. It was the great spiritual force represented by Puritanism that attracted to its standards so many, who wanted to help in founding "the Kingdom of God on Earth". When, in the course of years, it was found that this high ideal could not be realised, they contented themselves with founding the supremacy of England in Europe, with the natural result that Puritanism, after forfeiting some of its religious force, lost a great deal of its attraction as a political system and the country as a whole was quite ready for the Restoration when it came. To say, however, that the nation turned from a life of

[1] A. Beljame, *Le public et les Hommes de Lettres en Angleterre au dix-huitième siècle.* Paris 1897.

[2] W. Heldt in *Neophilologus* VIII, I, p. 39.

"godliness", which in many cases had been imposed on people by their Puritan fellow-countrymen, to one of licentiousness, is evidently an overstatement.

Charles the Second and his followers, who had spent a great many years in enforced exile, did indeed return to their native country, resolved to have a good time and to make up for the pleasure they had missed during that absence, by one long continuous run of indulgence in all forms of sensual enjoyment. "Then came those days, never to be recalled without a blush, the days of servitude without loyalty and of sensuality without love, of dwarfish talents and gigantic vices, the paradise of cold hearts and narrow minds, the golden age of the coward, the bigot and the slave.... The caresses of harlots, and the jests of buffoons, regulated the policy of the state. The government had just ability enough to deceive, and just religion enough to persecute. The principles of religion were the scoff of every grinning courtier.... Crime succeeded to crime and disgrace to disgrace." In these words Macaulay describes some of the outstanding characteristics of the reign of Charles II and his observations are fully corroborated by evidence that may be gathered from contemporary witnesses.

"At court things are in a very ill condition, there being so much emulacion, poverty and the vices of drinking, swearing and loose amours, that I know not what will be the end of it, but confusion." [1]

"Mrs. Haselrigge, the great beauty, is now brought to bed, and lays it to the King or the Duke of York." [2]

"Captain Ferrers and W. Howe both have often, through my Lady Castlemaine's window, seen her go to bed, and Sir Charles Berkeley in the chamber." [3]

"Mr. Pickering tells me the story is very true of a child being dropped at a ball at Court; and that the King had it in his closet a week after." [4]

[1] Pepys, *Diary*. Everyman's Library, I, p. 188.

[2] Ibid. I, p. 336. [3] Ibid. I, p. 338.

[4] Ibid. II, p. 593. (These examples are taken from the excellent article: "A chronological and critical review of the apprecation and condemnation of the Comic Dramatists of the Restoration and Orange Periods" by W. Heldt, referred to above, page 47, note 2).

Many striking instances of the depth of immorality to which English nobility had descended at the time, may be gathered from the memoirs of Grammont, one of which may be recorded here.

"Le Comte d'Oxford devint amoureux d'une Comédienne de la troupe du Duc, belle, gracieuse .... Cette créature, pleine de vertu, de sagesse ou, si vous voulez, d'obstination, refusa fièrement les offres de service et les présens du Comte d'Oxford .... Dans cette extrémité, l'amour eut recours à l'Hymen.

Le Comte d'Oxford, premier Pair du Royaume, ... lui fit présenter une belle promesse de mariage, authentiquement signée de sa main .... Le mariage fut fait .... Vous croyez peut-être que la nouvelle Comtesse n'avoit plus qu'à se faire présenter à la Cour, y prendre son rang et arborer les armes d'Oxford? Point du tout. Quand il en fut question, on trouva qu'elle n'était point mariée, c'est-à-dire, on trouva que le prétendu Ministre était un Trompette du Mylord, et le témoin, son Timbalier ....

La pauvre créature eut beau prendre à parti les loix et la Religion, violées aussi bien qu'elle par cette supercherie; elle eut beau se jetter aux pieds du Roi; pour en demander justice: elle n'eut qu'à se relever heureuse d'avoir une pension de mille écus pour douaire, et de reprendre le nom de Roxelane au lieu de celui d'Oxford." [1]

The quotation is a long one, but at the same time it is well worth while, because it shows, in the first place, the all-powerfulness of the nobility from whom there was no appeal and, in the second place, because it is a sample not of loose-living, but of one of the most loathsome crimes imaginable, committed with impunity by one of the leaders of Society. If it is true that the comedy of any age is a faithful mirror of its morals, the character of Restoration Comedy could hardly have been anything but what it was. It is true, as was pointed out above, that the great body of Englishmen continued to live as decent lives as they had done during the Commonwealth, but, unfortunately, their lives, ethics and morals do not concern us here, for, educated in the Puritan tradition, they were enemies of the stage and the Theatre, which they considered as one of the most potent instruments

[1] Antoine Hamilton, *Mémoires du Comte de Grammont.* Histoire Amoureuse de la Cour d'Angleterre sous Charles II, p. 203.

of Satan. They turned their backs on the theatre, which, for some decades at least, had thus to depend exclusively on the patronage of the court and the higher classes, and consequently it is the morals and manners of the courtiers that we shall find reflected in the comedy of the Restoration period.

We are only concerned here to show that this comedy was bound to be what it was; the formulation of an opinion on its merits and quality is superfluous. Any opinion, expressed in our own day, would have to steer a middle course between the severity of Macauley's censure in his *Essay on the Comic Dramatists of the Restoration* on the one hand, and the unmixed praise of Hazlitt in his *Lectures on the English Comic Writers* on the other. The modern student of literature, however, will do well to allow himself to be guided by Professor Allardyce Nicoll, who in his admirable work on the *British Drama,* expresses himself as follows:[1] "On a first reading, therefore, the comedies of manners may strike many as being immoral and vulgar: but for students of literature a true historical perspective must be gained. There are many characteristics of the Elizabethan period which now seem to us brutal and unrefined, but we do not cease to read Shakespeare because these are reflected in his plays. One of the greatest secrets of the study of literature is to regard individual works not in the light of present-day theories and of present-day beliefs, but in the spirit of the age in which they were produced.[2] It would be almost as absurd to refuse to read Aeschylus because he was a pagan as to refuse to read Etherege because he was a courtier of the age of Charles II. There are, certainly, passages in the comedies of manners which overstep all bounds of decency and of good taste, where the dramatists have gone beyond even the excesses of the society of their time, and such passages can now be relished by none save a deliberate lover of pornographic literature".

[1] Allardyce Nicoll, *British Drama,* p. 251.

[2] Cf. John Palmer, *The Comedy of Manners,* pp. 293 & 294: "In so far as Restoration Comedy answers the severest test of imaginative sincerity it satisfies the severest test of morality. It is because Mr. Horner *(The Country Wife)* imaginatively expresses his period so well that he is morally immune from the censure of any other period."

Thus much for the stage immediately after the Restoration, on which, merely as the result of outward circumstances, the great undercurrent of decency and even Puritanism in the nation at large had very little influence. That it was there all the time, and remained a living force even in the reign of Charles II is certain, but for many years the stage remained so much apart from the life of the ordinary respectable citizen, that this latent force was unable to assert itself. Not before it was reinforced by an entirely new and outside influence, did it succeed in making itself felt, and was then reflected in the theatre; the influence referred to here was the expulsion of James II and the substitution of the court of William and Mary for that of the Stuarts. The result of this change was twofold: first the exemplary married life of the new King and Queen could not fail to influence the general moral atmosphere at Court; instead of being encouraged by the sovereign in their dissolute mode of life, as had been the case in the preceding reigns, courtiers now realised that they ran the risk of incurring the King's displeasure if they persisted in their evil ways; but in addition to this, there was another very important consequence, which concerned the stage in particular: during the preceding years the Court had been the mainstay of the theatre, but William III took no interest in the stage at all, which therefore had to look for support elsewhere. A gradual change in the composition of theatrical audiences made itself felt in the next few years, and these audiences, while becoming less brilliant, became more numerous and certainly more representative of the people.

Numerous, indeed, in the following years were the royal orders, proving that William and Mary were resolved to take a definite stand against the corruption of morals, as displayed on the stage and elsewhere. Before long, attempts at a reform of the stage were made from a different quarter: in 1692 the Society for the Reformation of Manners was founded and, at the instance of this body of reformers, actions were brought against several actors for expressions, *contra bonos mores,* uttered on the stage.

Summing up, we may say that after the Revolution, some sort of change in the theatre became inevitable as a natural result of the change in the general moral atmosphere.

V

CIBBER AS A DRAMATIC AUTHOR

In the last chapter we saw that the time was ripe for a change for the better in plays, a change for the better from the point of view of morality. After 1690 several protests against the nature of the stage-plays of the period were published, of which may be mentioned a sermon of Tillotson's, *Delight and Judgment* by Horneck, the *Country Conversations* by James Wright, Blackmore's preface to *Prince Arthur* and, last, but not least, Jeremy Collier's *A short View of the Immorality, and Profaneness of the English Stage, together with the Sense of Antiquity upon this Argument.*

The *Short View* has frequently been a subject for discussion; great praise has been bestowed upon it by some, while it has been severely criticised by others. [1] Some contemporary opinions about this paper will be referred to later on; there is no doubt that it had a great many good points as well as weak ones, the chief of the latter being the mixing up of cause and effect, or rather the substitution of the one for the other, for it ascribes the moral degeneration of the public to the obscenity of the stage. On the whole there has been a tendency to overrate the influence of the outspoken Non-Juror, who certainly was not lacking in moral courage, as he proved on more than one occasion. Dryden's *peccavi* is well-known and has been quoted a great many times, but then Dryden was at the end of his career. Every student of the literature of the early part of the eighteenth century, knows that the difference between that and the writings of the period before Cibber is not so striking as to render it plausible that the *Short View* [2] had that great influence, which has been attributed to it by many critics. It seems much more likely that Collier's outburst partly resulted from, partly coincided with that change in the general tone and opinions of the nation

[1] See: W. Heldt, *Neophilologus,* VIII, p. 44 ff.

[2] See Appendix II.

at large, referred to above, especially so, as at least one writer proves that he understood the tendency of the times a couple of years before the publication of the *Short View*. This author was Colley Cibber and the play in which he proves that he sensed the spirit of the times was *Love's Last Shift* or *The Fool in Fashion*. This play marked the definite beginning of a new style of play, in which considerations of morality and sentiment are substituted for the cynicism of the Restoration drama.

Of course Cibber was no more the first dramatist to catch the spirit of the age than Collier was the first to word the disapproval of theatrical performances. Professor Allardyce Nicoll, whose work would seem to have exhausted the general history of the periods covered by it, gives a list of works, varying in date of publication between the years 1663 and 1689, in all of which the new moral tendency begins to reveal itself. In that list occur: Tuke's *The Adventures of five Hours;* Stapylton's *The Slighted Maid* and *The Stepmother;* Porter's *Carnival;* Flecknoe's *Love's Kingdom;* Shadwell's *The Royal Shepherdess* and *The Sullen Lovers;* [1] Leanerd's *The Country Innocence* and *The Counterfeits;* Mrs. Behn's *The Amorous Prince, The Young King, The Forc'd Marriage, The Lucky Chance;* Ravenscroft's *Dame Dobson* (having in the prologue the characteristic verses:

"No Line in this will tempt your minds to Evil,
It's true, 't is dull, but then 't is very Civil");

Revet's *The Town Shifts;* Crowne's *The Country Wit, Sir Courtly Nice, The English Frier.*

In all these, according to Professor Nicoll, may be observed the growing power of sentimentalism, the encroaching of emotion upon the intellectualism of pure comedy, without that romantic flavour which gave to Shakespeare his exquisite humour. Cibber's *Love's Last Shift* was one of the final triumphs of the age. [2]

[1] In the preface to this play, Shadwell says: "But in the Plays, which have been wrote of late, there is no such thing as perfect Character, but the two chief Persons are commonly a Swearing, Drinking, Whoring, Ruffian for a lover, and an impudent ill bred Tomrig for a Mistress, and these are the fine People of the play; and almost anything is proper for them to say; but their chief subject is Bawdy, and Profaneness, which they call British Writing."

[2] Allardyce Nicoll, *Early Eighteenth Century Drama,* p. 126.

Some of these plays, though written in the worst days, were quite moral, indeed, far more so than Cibber's *Love's Last Shift.*

This comedy marks the beginning of a long series of similar dramas which may be described as "moral-immoral". It displays, that is to say, the ordinary licentious comic characters and themes of the day with a would-be moral ending, in which rapid conversions are attributed to those who had in the earlier acts been represented as sinners. Nothing shows better the hypocritical veneer which spreads over the age. The reformers were satisfied because virtue triumphs in the end; the pleasure-loving spectators were willing to witness the wholly artificial conversions for the sake of the careless intrigue and loose dialogue of the preceding scenes.[1]

The term "sentimental", technically applied to these dramas, has been the cause of some misunderstanding, partly owing to the modern more or less disparaging meaning of the word. The best definition is that given by Professor Nicoll,[2] and at the same time it is convenient to adopt the division of the development of sentimental comedy into three separate stages:[3]

1. The morals of comedy were purified and the new sentimental material intermixed with the old humorous material; this stage is represented by the work of Cibber.[4]
2. The sentimental theme is represented with very little comic entertainment; this stage is represented by *The Conscious Lovers* of Steele.[5]
3. The work becomes lifeless and artificial; this stage is represented by the work of Holcroft and his school.

[1] Allardyce Nicoll, *British Drama,* p. 281. [2] See above p. 53.

[3] Suggested by De Witt C. Croissant, *Studies in the work of Colley Cibber.*

[4] In Anglia XXX, Mr. Osborn Waterhouse states that English Sentimental Comedy embraces what has been called *Comédie larmoyante* and *Tragédie bourgeoise.* He considers Cibber's work in particular to belong to what Voltaire styled: *Comédie attendrissante.*

[5] "Sentimental comedy in its 2nd phase is comedy of manners in which the main action tends to inculcate a moral lesson, in which the incidents no longer deal with illicit intrigues, and in which the action is complicated by distressingly pathetic situations. The chief characters are serious and supersensitive in regard to such matters as filial duty, honour and the like. There is a great deal of extremely stilted moralizing and a notable absence of humour." (De Witt C. Croissant, p. 30).

In the literature of Cibber's own time, his merit in this respect was readily pointed out and admitted, but in modern literary history he has hardly received his due, until quite recently in the works mentioned above and some others.

Thomas Davies records that "the joy of unexpected reconcilement, spread such an uncommon rapture of pleasure in the audience that never were spectators more happy in easing their minds by uncommon and repeated plaudits and by honest tears".

The same authority tells us that John Dennis, who hated Cibber for obstructing, as he imagined, the progress of his tragedy called *The Invader of his Country,* in very passionate terms denies his (i.e. Cibber's) claim to this comedy. "When *The Fool in Fashion* (this is the sub-title of *Love's Last Shift*) was first acted", says the critic, "Cibber was hardly twenty-two years of age; how could he, at the age of twenty, write a comedy with a just design, distinguished characters, and a proper dialogue who now, at forty, treats us with Hibernian sense and Hibernian English?" [1]

Another unequivocal recognition of Cibber's merit may be gathered from the *Dramatic Miscellanies.* "To a player we are indebted for the reformation of the stage. The first Comedy, acted since the Restoration, in which were preferred purity of manners and decency of language, with a due respect to the honour of the marriage-bed was C. Cibber's *Love's Last Shift."* [2] "In his Narcissa, acted by Mrs. Mountford, Cibber drew an outline of a coquette in high life; of which character he afterwards made a finished picture in his Lady Betty Modish. Besides the honour of reforming the moral of comedy, Cibber was the first who introduced men and women of high quality on the stage, and gave them language and manners suitable to their rank and birth." [3]

In one of the later works on the subject we read as follows: "On an evening in January 1696, the usual audience at Drury Lane Theatre gathered to attend the first performance of a comedy by a new author.... They had no warning that they were to witness the beginning of a new epoch in English dramatic history.... They came, as usual, to laugh; they remained

[1] *Dram. Misc.,* III, p. 410. [2] Ibid. III, p. 436. [3] Ibid. III, p. 441.

to dissolve in tears.... The principal characters in *Love's Last Shift* were a sorely tried wife and a husband who, after being led astray into fashionable dissipation, sincerely repented and was reunited to her." [1]

There cannot be any doubt that Cibber's contemporaries admitted the fact that he had established an entirely new type of comedy; this does not mean that no author before him had made an effort in the same direction, but it does mean that he was the first to make his intention clear. Many writers before him had from time to time dropped expressions and voiced opinions that were not quite in the usual Restoration tradition, but no previous play could possibly be taken as the starting-point [2] of the sentimental comedy. No definite claim to that effect was ever made, unless Professor Saintsbury's observation in his preface to Shadwell in the Mermaid Series, that Shadwell in his old age was one of the fathers of sentimental comedy, may be considered as such.

More frequently has the honour been claimed for Steele, but if we compare the comedy of the Restoration with that of Steele, it is difficult to believe that one should be the immediate successor of the other, and the necessity of recognising a transition stage presents itself. This, then, is the first stage of the sentimental drama, as indicated above. [3]

It is necessary to consider the impression created by *Love's Last Shift* at some length for several reasons. The first is that it was Cibber's first play, and an original one at that; this is more than can be claimed for most of his works, which are, as a rule, adaptations of other plays. And then it was the first of a new form of comedy, the first for a long time to which Collier could not object that the evil-doer was rewarded, for before he

[1] Ernest Bernbaum, *The Drama of Sensibility*. For a definition of sensibility see page 10:

"The drama of sensibility implied that human nature, when not, as in some cases, already perfect, was perfectible by an appeal to the emotions. It wished to show that beings who were good at heart were found in the ordinary walks of life. It so represented their conduct as to arouse admiration for their virtues and pity for their sufferings."

[2] J. W. Krutch, *Comedy and Conscience after the Restoration*, p. 202.

[3] See page 54.

received his reward, he had repented and this repentance was the result of an appeal to his better feelings by the wife he had deserted. The repentance was rather sudden to be sure, and we can well understand Vanbrugh foreseeing a relapse, but there is abundant proof that the public welcomed the first sentimental comedy, and though the tears they shed over the unexpected reconciliation were the first symptoms of that, which was to earn for sentimental comedy the derogatory appellation of *comédie larmoyante,* there is no need to doubt that they came to the spectators themselves as a pleasant surprise.

Cibber, indeed, was not a reformer, calling upon his contemporaries to repent; he was either a very close observer of the signs of the time or, maybe, merely a clever, though unconscious product and exponent of the tendency of his period; this much is certain that he gave the theatre-going public what they wanted, at the psychological moment.

It is of the highest importance, too, that he did so before Collier had published his *Short View.* It is usual in discussions of the drama of this period to attribute any change for the better to Collier, in many cases totally ignoring that, for several years before 1698, influences had been at work that rendered a change of some sort inevitable. Fortunately for himself, in this connection at least, Collier was a Non-Juror. Had he been a Puritan, he would probably have been cried down from the very beginning. [1] We observed before that Collier was a brave man and, even if the times had been less propitious, he would probably have sounded his trumpet-note. All the same, the sentimental

[1] As an extreme instance of this overrating of Collier's influence, we quote from "Quellen Studien zu C. Cibbers Lustspiel *The Careless Husband,*" by Dr. Ernst Michels, p. 6:

"Man hüte sich indessen, mit den Dichtern dieser Epoche allzuscharf ins Gericht zu gehen und ihnen die Hauptschuld zuzuschreiben; den meisten war offenbar jedes Gefühl dafür geschwunden, dass bei dem moralischen Tiefstand der innere Gehalt ihrer Schöpfungen verloren gehen musste; anstatt die Menschen zu sich hinaufzuziehen, waren sie die Sklaven des entarteten Geschmacks.

Erst Colliers Schrift *A short View* öffnete der Welt die Augen und beleuchtete den Abgrund, in den sie geraten war. Einer der ersten, die seinem Rufe Folge leisteten, war C. Cibber."

drama was bound to come, for just as every country gets the government it deserves, every period produces the dramatic art of which it is pregnant,[1] and the idea of a wicked generation being saved from total perdition by the intervention of Collier, who like the prophets of old, bids them mend their ways and repent, is simply absurd.[2]

Cibber's next play, *Woman's Wit* or *The Lady in Fashion* was acted at Drury Lane in 1697, but proved a failure, as the author admits in his *Apology,* where he adds that in order that "it might be peaceably forgotten", he did not give it a place in the two volumes of plays, he published in 1721.

After this he wrote, or adapted, some twenty-five plays, of which may be mentioned: *Love Makes a Man,*[3] *She Wou'd and She Wou'd Not* or *The Kind Impostor, The Careless Husband,*

[1] In his *History of Restoration Drama,* p. 5, professor Nicoll expresses the same idea a little too emphatically by saying: "All dramatic art depends ultimately for its form and content on the audience.... The spectators of 1590 gave birth to *As You Like it;* the spectators of 1600 to *Hamlet*".

It is just possible the same spectators would not have been quite so successful, if they had not happened to have a Shakespeare living amongst them.

[2] At an early date Cibber's importance in this respect, was recognised: "As a writer of comedies, Cibber must be placed in a very superior rank; before Jeremy Collier attacked the profaneness of dramatic writers, he first taught the stage to talk decently and morally. He was properly the inventor of the higher comedy, a species of the drama in which persons of high birth and eminent rank are introduced; for the faint efforts, in that style, of Etheredge and Steele, in *Sir Fopling Flutter* and *The Funeral* are scarceley worthy our notice." (*Dram. Misc.,* III, p. 504).

[3] In her introduction to an undated edition of this play, printed in London, Mrs. Inchbald remarks: "A third author of no mean repute, exerted his skill in uniting and adorning the ancient foundation of this work, (the dramas of *The Elder Brother* and *The Custom of the Country)* according to the modern taste of 1700 and introduced the whole composition to the public under the present title, with the additional name affixed of Colley Cibber.

Whilst many a judicious critic boasted of knowing what kind of drama the public ought to like, Cibber was the lucky dramatist generally to know what they would like, whether they ought or not. If he secured their interest, he defied their understanding; and here, in the following scenes, so far he engages the heart in every event, that the head does not once reflect upon the improbabilities, or even impossibilities, with which the senses are delighted."

The Comical Lovers,[1] *The Lady's Last Stake* or *The Wife's Resentment, The Non-Juror,*[2] *The Double Gallant* or *The Sick Lady's Cure,*[3] *Caesar in Egypt,*[4] *The Refusal* or *The Ladies' Philosophy,*[5] *The Provoked Husband* or *The Journey to London,*[6] *Ximena* or *The Heroic Daughter,*[7] and stage-adaptations of some of Shakespeare's plays, for example, *Papal Tyranny in the Reign of King John* and *Richard III.*

Cibber's adaptations of Shakespeare have been repeatedly and, to a certain extent, justly condemned, but it is only fair to remember that *Richard III* kept the stage in the form given to it by Cibber for over a century, and if it did nothing else, kept the memory of Shakespeare's play alive at a time, when England's and the world's greatest dramatist was but too apt to be forgotten.

Of the plays mentioned above *The Non-Juror* had a great influence on Cibber's life, for on the one hand it was the immediate cause of his appointment as Poet Laureate, on the other it was the publication and performance of this piece that fanned Pope's hatred of Cibber into such a blaze, that through it he was blinded into committing the worst blunder of his poetical career, the substitution of Cibber for Theobald as the hero of the *Dunciad.*[8]

There cannot be any doubt that this play was a great financial success, much greater than it really deserved. In an interesting paper called: *Some cursory Remarks on the Play call'd* The Non-Juror, *written by Mr. Cibber,* published in London in 1718, H. S. (Henry Steele) writes that he has been "a constant spectator for these fourteen nights successively, and with some Pain, in being oblig'd to attend early to be conveniently seated: I find no lessening of the Audience for its being often repeated, but a great Improvement" (p. 6). And again on page 19: "I could write an Encomium upon every line of this excellent Comedy; but I don't care to antedate all the pleasure you'll receive by reading; and I can't help saying once more, that no one has

1 Based on Dryden's *Marriage à la Mode.*
2 Based on Molière's *Tartuffe.*
3 Based on Mrs. Centlivre's *Love at a Venture* and Burnaby's *Visiting Day.*
4 Based on Fletcher's *The False One.*
5 Based on Molière's *Femmes Savantes.*
6 A completion of Vanbrugh's *The Journey to London.*
7 Based on Corneille's *Le Cid.*
8 See Appendix III.

larger capacity for writing a good Comedy, nor ever was a Company fitter to act one." Finally, we are informed in the postcript that on the Thursday before the publication of the article, the King came to see the play and seemed to be mightily pleased with it, so much so, that Cibber got leave to dedicate the play to His Majesty. H. S. would advise all families to procure the play and he hopes to see it "as common in every house as a Prayer-Book or the *Duty of Man.*"

Ximena is *The Cid,* into which a great many alterations were introduced, the principal of these being the happy ending, with which Cibber provided it. Prefixed to the play is a detailed examination of *The Cid* while at the same time Cibber gives his reasons for changing it in several ways. The arguments may not seem convincing, but they are certainly worth reading and prove that Cibber did not set about his adaptations in a haphazard way.

The Provoked Husband is particularly interesting in being an adaptation and continuation of Vanbrugh's unfinished *Journey to London.* The play, however, underwent considerable changes in connection with Cibber's preconceived theories as to the requirements of comedy. In the introduction to the play Cibber says that all he had been able to gather from Vanbrugh as to the intended catastrophe, was, "that the Conduct of his imaginary fine Lady had so provok'd him, that he design'd actually to have made her Husband turn her out of his Doors. But when this Performance came, after his Decease, to my hands, I thought such violent Measures, however just they might be in real Life, were too severe for Comedy, and would want the proper Surprise, which is due to the end of a Play." In the prologue Cibber gave Vanbrugh his due: [1] but when the play was per-

[1] This play took birth from Principles of Truth,
To make amends for Errors past, of youth.
A Bard, that's now no more, in riper Days,
Conscious review'd the Licence of his Plays.
And though Applause his wanton Muse had fir'd,
Himself condemn'd what sensual Minds admir'd.
At length, he own'd, that Plays should let you see
Not only, what you are, but ought to be;
Though Vice was natural, 't was never meant
The Stage should shew it, but for Punishment.

ormed for the first time on Jan. 10, 1728, Cibber's enemies tried to have it damned, in which they were not successful, for it had a run of 28 nights. On January 31st. it was published, after which people found they had been trying to hiss down not Cibber, but Vanbrugh.[1] One year after this (Jan. 7th, 1729) Cibber's pastoral *Love in a Riddle* was performed and damned. Cibber withdrew the piece and changed it into a ballad-opera, *Damon and Phillida,* which was acted successfully.[2]

Before proceeding to a discussion of *The Careless Husband,* we wish once more to emphasize the importance of Cibber's work in the history of the development of the Sentimental drama. As Mr. Bernbaum has pointed out,[3] of the four sentimental comedies published between 1696 and 1703 only the first won a lasting success, while the other three may almost be called failures. *The fair Example* ran about 7 or 8 nights; *The Twin Rivals* and *The Lying Lover* ran six, and both Farquhar and Steele acknowledged that they were not successful. The new genre was threatened with extinction when it was saved by Cibber's *The Careless Husband.*

In conclusion to this chapter we print the *Hymn to the Laureat*[4] by Mrs. Mary Chapman, the evident sincerity of which makes it worth being reproduced.

I

Cibber, accept these feeble Lays
From an unskilful Muse,
Who tries with artless Notes, to praise,
What Envious Men abuse.

The Living proudly would exclude his Lays,
And to the buried Bard resigns the Praise.

1 *Apology* II, p. 125. Also in *Biographia Dramatica:*

"Cibber's enemies bestowed the highest applause on the Part which related to Lord Townly's Provocations from his Wife, which was mostly Cibber's, at the same time that they condemned and opposed the *Journey to London* Part, which was almost entirely Vanbrugh's."

2 Jeanette Marks, *English Pastoral Drama,* p. 90.

3 *The Drama of Sensibility,* p. 91 & p. 139.

4 From *The London Medley,* London, Jan. 1730.

II

Nature and Art in Thee combine;
Thy Comedies excel:
With Wit and sense replete; they shine:
And read politely well.

III

Who sees th' inconstant *Loveless* range,
But mourns *Amanda*'s Fate?
Each Female Heart approves his Change,
And pants for such a State.

IV

When Lady *Betty* treads the Stage,
All Modish Prudes submit:
What *Foppington* adorns our Age,
With the same Grace and Wit?

V

In *Townley* see the Modern Wife!
How full of Vice! How blam'd!
How ruin'd by the Modern Life!
How valu'd when reclaim'd!

VI

May empty Journals [1] weekly rail;
May all dull Bards repine:
If wit unequal'd shou'd prevail,
The Laurel's justly Thine.

[1] A reference to *Mist's Journal.*

COLLEY CIBBER AS LORD FOPPINGTON

From a painting by Grisoni, in the possession of the Garrick Club, London.

VI

THE CARELESS HUSBAND

§ 1 – *Its Stage History Evidence of its Early Popularity*

After describing how surprised he was, when, in 1704, he saw Mrs. Oldfield act Leonora in *Sir Courtly Nice,* Cibber writes in his *Apology*: [1]

"Upon this unexpected sally, then, of the power and disposition of so unforeseen an actress, it was that I again took up the first two acts of the *Careless Husband,* which I had written the summer before and had thrown aside in despair of having justice done to the character of Lady Betty Modish by any one woman then among us;...,but, as I have said, Mrs. Oldfield having thrown out such new proffers of a genius, I was no longer at a loss for support; my doubts were dispelled, and I had now a new call to finish it: accordingly, the *Careless Husband* took its fate upon the Stage the winter following, in 1704." It was acted at Drury Lane Theatre, on December 7th and was published in 1705.

In his *Hand-list of Plays,* Professor Nicoll records 198 performances of the play, ranging from Thursday, Dec. 12th, 1704 to Friday, April 4th, 1749. Though it is clear the list was composed with the greatest care, there is no reason to suppose it to be exhaustive, and even if it were, the evidence it provides is sufficient to prove that the comedy was very popular indeed.

The original cast of the play was as follows:

Sir Charles Easy — Wilks
Lord Foppington — Cibber
Lord Morelove — Powell
Lady Betty Modish — Mrs. Oldfield

[1] Apology II, p. 5.

Lady Easy — Mrs. Knight
Lady Graveairs — Mrs. Moore
Edging — Mrs. Lucas

The play had a fairly long initial run and was restored on January 9th. 1705, with the notice: "At the Desire of Several Persons of Quality". That it continued popular may be inferred from the circumstance that it was considered good enough to be played "for the benefit of Mr. Wilks" as appeared from the notice for the performance of Feb. 27th. 1705. The two veterans, Cibber and Wilks, both acted their original parts in the performance of March 5th. 1733. [1] There cannot be any doubt that *The Careless Husband* marks the summit of Cibber's achievement in comedy and, perhaps for that very reason, it was from the first attributed to anybody but himself, amongst others to no less a person than the Duke of Argyle. [2]

John Dennis, who indiscriminately attacked a great many of his contemporaries, and whose arguments, except in one particular instance, [3] do little nowadays besides give amusement, if the reader is not too much repelled by their coarseness, said of Steele and Cibber: [4] "You have both of you, for several years together, been the celebrated Authors of other people's works", and again: "You (i.e. Steele) and your Viceroy (i.e. Cibber) bravely and boldly seize upon other men's Plays; cause new title pages to be printed; and see: to the amazement of some few Readers, they pass with the rest for your own." Cibber certainly was a most inveterate borrower and the pedigree of some of his plays is appalling. [5] So far, however, all

[1] Harry Glicksman, The Stage History of Colley Cibber's *The Careless Husband.* Publ. Mod. Language Ass. of America, vol. 36.

[2] *Dram. Misc.*, III, p. 438.

[3] *The Stage defended, from Scripture, Reason, Experience, and the Common Sense of Mankind for two thousand years,* London 1726.

[4] *The Character of Sir John Edgar,* Jan. 19, 1719.

[5] Cf. F. W. Bateson, *The Double Gallant of Colley Cibber.* The Review of Eng. Studies, Vol. I, No. 3, July 1925. Mr. Bateson comes to the conclusion that Cibber certainly had before him Mrs. Centlivre's *Love at a Venture* (in its turn taken from *Le Galand Doublé,* by T. Corneille) as far as the mainplot was concerned. The underplot was borrowed from *The Reform'd Wife* and *The Ladies' Visiting Day,* both attributed to Charles Burnaby.

attempts to trace *The Careless Husband,* or parts of it, to other writers of plays of that or a preceding period have failed. There are certainly a great many literary reminiscences, partly from his own plays, partly from *Sir Courtly Nice* and *The Relapse,* and mostly concerning the one character of Lord Foppington, but these were almost inevitable in the case of Cibber and of them we shall have to say more later on. [1] Samuel Johnson, no friend of Cibber's and therefore quite prepared to believe the worst of him, could not but allow considerable merit to some of his comedies and said there was no reason to believe that *The Careless Husband* was not written by him. [2] In his *General View of the Stage,* Wilkes [3] says that were the play *The Careless Husband* curtailed of one scene he would not fail to pronounce it not only the best comedy in English, but in any other language.

Even Pope admitted the general excellence of *The Careless Husband* in the well-known passage: [4]

> "All this may be; the People's Voice is odd,
> "It is, and it is not, the voice of God.
> "To *Gammer Gurton* if it give the bays,
> "And yet deny *The Careless Husband* praise,
> "Or say our Fathers never broke a rule;
> "Why then, I say, the Public is a fool.

Charles Dibdin said of *The Careless Husband* that it was a school for elegant manners, and an example for honourable actions. [5]

In a letter written Oct. 17th. 1769, Walpole mentions Garrick's *Pindarics* and adds: "Cibber wrote as bad odes, but then Cibber wrote *The Careless Husband* and his own life, which both deserve immortality."

In the *Spectator* No. 106, for June 8, 1710, Steele writes: "I have

[1] This point was investigated by Ernst Michels: Quellenstudien zu C. Cibber's Lustspiel *The Careless Husband.* Diss. Marburg 1908.

[2] G. Birkbeck Hill, *Life of Johnson,* II, p. 340.

[3] Quoted by De Witt C. Croissant.

[4] *Imitations of Horace II,* 1, l. 89 ff.

[5] Quoted by De Witt C. Croissant.

at present under my tutelage a young poet, who, I design, shall entertain the town the ensuing winter. And as he does me the honour to let me see his comedy as he writes it, I shall endeavour to make the parts fit the geniuses of the several actors, as exactly as their habits can their bodies. And because the two I have mentioned *(Cibber* and *Wilks)* are to perform the principal parts, I have prevailed with the house to let the *Careless Husband* be acted on Tuesday next, that my young author may have a view of the play, which is acted to perfection, both by them and all concerned in it; as being born within the walls of the theatre, and written with an exact knowledge of the abilities of the performers.

Mr. Wilks will do his best in this play, because it is for his own benefit; [1] and Mr. Cibber, because he writ it. Besides which, all the great beauties we have left in town, or within call of it, will be present, because it is the last play of the season."

Cibber in many places insisted that *The Careless Husband* was entirely his own play and as he proved on several occasions that he was by no means ashamed of owning that he owed a great deal to other authors, his testimony ought to count for something as well. More than once [2] does he inform us that, whenever he undertook to make some dormant play of an old author fitter for the stage, according to his judgment, it was the desire not to be idle that set him to work, just as a good housewife will mend old linen when she has no better employment. When however he was "more warmly engaged by a subject entirely new" he aimed at writing something worthy of a better pen than his, and however unqualified he might be to instruct others, he who so ill governed himself, proudly maintained that there were some plays entirely his own in which he clearly tried to *"prodesse* as well as *delectare".*

Among these plays he counts *The Careless Husband,* of the popularity of which he was justly proud in his own semi-ironical way. Strange to say, it was not immediately appreciated by the spectators, which failure Cibber attributed to the fact that it was

[1] Evidently Wilks thought the play good enough to choose it for his benefit. Cf. also p. 64.

[2] Apology I, p. 144.

written by himself. He remarks [1] that most of his plays, with the emphatic exception of the first, had a better reception from the public when his own personal interest in them was not so great as it had been at first. In support of this statement he tells us that his adaptation of *Richard the Third,* [2] did not raise him five pounds on the third day, though for several years afterwards it always drew a crowded audience. *The Fop's Fortune* lagged on the fourth day, "and only held up its Head by the Heels of the French Tumblers, who it seems had so much Wit in their Limbs, that they forced the Town to see it, till it laugh'd itself into their good Graces." *The Kind Impostor* did not pay the charges on the sixth day, but later the profit it brought Cibber, the manager, to some degree compensated him for the disappointment its poor reception at first caused him as an author. And finally he records that it was at first a moot point whether *The Careless Husband* should live or die, "but the Houses it has since filled have reproach'd the former Coldness of its Auditors."

§ 2 – *The Story of the Play*

The Scene is laid at Windsor. Sir *Charles Easy* cannot find any charms in his own wife, who as he admits, is very much admired by other people. He carries on an intrigue with Lady *Graveairs* and in addition to that has an affair with his wife's maid. All this is known to Lady *Easy,* who, however pretends she does not see anything, because she feels sure that her husband has some regards for her and might become quite estranged from her, if she made a scene or let him feel he was constantly being watched.

In this she is quite right, for, partly owing to her seeming indifference Sir *Charles's* zest for the intrigue with Lady *Graveairs* has become considerably less, so that when the play opens he is trying to find a way to get rid of her.

[1] In the *Address to the Reader,* prefixed to *Ximena.*

[2] We ought to bear in mind, however, that in the first few years, they had to play it minus Act I, the zealous Master of the Revels having expunged it without sparing a line, because the distress of King Henry VI, described in it, might remind people of King James II, then living in France!

Husband and wife have a conversation in which Sir *Charles* tries to find out whether his wife knows anything about his intrigues and, if so, how much. He even goes so far as to ask her what she would do if she were ever to discover that he was unfaithful to her, to which she replies that she would cry her eyes out in some dark place and forget her tears when he spoke kindly to her.

At this juncture Lord *Morelove,* a friend of Sir *Charles,* is announced. This nobleman is madly in love with Lady *Betty Modish,* to whom he has been paying his court for a considerable time, and who has been drawing him on and then making fun of him. She takes all sorts of liberties with him, makes him cut a ridiculous figure in public, and tries her very best to shock his ideas of decency without actually exposing herself. When she feels she has gone too far, she makes her peace with him.

Sir *Charles Easy* now tries to convince Lord *Morelove* that the only way to make sure of Lady *Betty* is to pretend that he has given her up. In order to give him an opportunity to do so, they invite her to dinner, together with Lord *Foppington,* an inveterate fop, who feels sure he is able to win the love of any woman, whose heart he condescends to lay siege to.

On this particular occasion he has decided to conquer Lady *Betty,* who humours him and flirts with him in order to pique Lord *Morelove.* The latter is trying to act upon Sir *Charles's* advice, but finds this is beyond him and he even forgets himself so far as to expostulate with Lady *Betty* on the immodesty and danger of her conduct. The end of it is that she exasperates him so much that he closes with the proposal made to him by Sir *Charles* to start a flirtation with Lady *Graveairs,* who happens to be quite ready for this, as she feels herself neglected by Sir *Charles.* This stratagem at last leads to the expected result: Lady *Betty,* who likes to play with her faithful suitor and display her power over him, begins to realise, with the assistance of Lady *Easy,* that she really loves him and could not bear to lose him.

When he finds that she has been made thoroughly uneasy and that her dormant love has been roused, Sir *Charles* leaves her alone with Lord *Morelove,* and retires to his rooms.

Here he sees the maid and when some time after, Lady *Easy* comes home, she discovers her husband and her maid, asleep in two easy chairs in Sir *Charles's* room. Instead of upbraiding him with this, she takes her Steinkirk [1] from her neck and puts it upon Sir *Charles's* head, for fear he shall catch cold. Sir *Charles* discovers this when he wakes and is so struck with the goodness and considerateness of his wife, that he realises the wickedness of his former course of life and decides to turn over a new leaf.

There is a scene of reconciliation between husband and wife; Lady *Graveairs,* the lady's maid and Lord *Foppington* are all duly punished and Lady *Betty* promises to marry Lord *Morelove.*

§ 3 — *The Characters of the Play*

Sir Charles Easy is a very distinct advance upon the ordinary hero of the Restoration drama, although he is far from impeccable from the point of view of morality. His relations with Lady Graveairs, as far as we can see, are marked by a certain reserve and also in his affair with Edging we notice that, although he finds himself unable to love his wife, he is quite ready to acknowledge her many good qualities and will not allow her maid to take any liberties with her name, because of her relations with himself: "When you speak of my Wife you are to say your lady; and you are never to speak of your lady to me in regard of her being my Wife—for look you, Child, you are not her strumpet but Mine; therefore I only give you leave to be saucy with me". [2]

Then again, he philosophizes about life: "How like Children do we judge of Happiness", and wonders why he is the only one, who does not appreciate his wife's beauty and goodness. He does not yet worry about it, but we realise that he understands there is something wrong in it all and that there may be some hope for him yet, if at any time he should be made to feel the wrong he has been doing in his recklessness.

[1] In H. D. Traill, *Social England,* IV, p. 606, we find: "After the battle of Steinkirk" (where William III was defeated in 1692) "the Steinkirk, or black cravat, came into fashion, in place of the white lace tie."

[2] Act I.

That he may be a staunch friend upon occasion, is proved by his attitude to Lord Morelove and the advice he gives him is ample evidence that he possesses a good deal of psychological insight, for it shows the only way to the affections of Lady Betty. He recognises Foppington's worthlessness, but all the same he warns Morelove not to underestimate him as a rival, and altogether manages things so nicely that, while promoting the end his friend has in view, he succeeds in reversing their relative positions in the affair with Lady Graveairs, for he is effectually supported in his desire to find a decent excuse for breaking off his relations with her, by Morelove's readiness to flirt with her in order to try and rouse Lady Betty's jealousy.

That he should not be able to resist temptation, when on coming home he finds it thrown in his way in the person of Edging, hardly surprises us, after what we have seen of his character and its latent qualities; neither is there any occasion for excessive astonishment, when we witness his conversion, brought about by a sudden disgust of his old ways and the deep impression which the final proof of his wife's long-suffering love has made upon him.

Lord Foppington. About this character there is the following note in the Globe Edition of Pope's works: "The character of Lord Foppington is taken from Vanbrugh".[1] The statement is short and decided, but, as is usual in the case of remarks, bearing on Cibber's work, it is hardly correct and certainly does the creator of the character a great injustice. Vanbrugh's Lord Foppington was based om Cibber's *Sir Novelty Fashion,*[2] who in his turn bears a likeness to Etheredge's *Sir Fopling Flutter* and it is far from improbable that the latter owes several traits to Mascarille in Molière's *Les Précieuses Ridicules.*[3]

A careful comparison of the two pieces *(The Relapse* and *The*

[1] *Imitations of Horace* II, ep. I, l. 92.

[2] Admitted by Saintsbury in *A short History of English Literature,* p. 494, in the following words: "It is a little odd that *The Relapse* is an avowed continuation of a play by another dramatist, Colley Cibber, produced the year before, and entitled *Love's Last Shift*.... Lord Foppington (the Sir Novelty Fashion of the earlier play) is the last and by far the best of the line begun by Sir Fopling Flutter."

[3] Vide Michels, p. 41.

Careless Husband) will show that the only things in *The Careless Husband* directly owing to Vanbrugh are Lord Foppington's name and title. By the time that *The Careless Husband* was published, the fashionable fool was an established figure on the stage and Cibber was recognised as the best actor to take that particular part. The references to Cibber as the fool *par excellence* are numerous in the literature of the time and nowhere are they so frequent as in Cibber's own writings, [1] in which he frankly admits that, if he could play the character of the coxcomb to people's satisfaction, it was merely because there was so much of the coxcomb in his own composition.

If therefore we maintain that Cibber drew Lord Foppington from the life, we mean that for several of the characteristics of this remarkable figure, he drew upon his own person, for example Lord Foppington's recklessness and habits of loose-living, [2] his humour and smartness at repartee and, last but not least, his readiness to join in the laugh when it turned against himself.

The character is everything a stage-libertine could be expected to be: a lover of women and a lover of horses, a husband not only unfaithful, but absolutely indifferent to his wife's reputation as well as to her charms, but fortunately he has some redeeming qualities, to which reference was made above.

In his relations with women he is not only devoid of all decent feelings, but also so absolutely confident of success in everything he undertakes that it simply does not occur to him that Lady Betty might be trifling with him, instead of being prepared to have her name added to the long roll of his conquests. Indeed his conceit in this respect carries him to such extremes that he

[1] E. g. Apology I, p. 17: "It often makes me smile to think how contentedly I have set myself down to write my own life;.... This you will easily account for, when you consider that nothing gives a coxcomb more delight than when you suffer him to talk of himself; which sweet liberty I here enjoy for a whole volume together!

[2] *Dram. Misc.*, III, p. 460: "Mrs. Porter, upon reading a part, in which C. had painted virtue in the strongest and most lively colours, asked him how it came to pass, that a man, who could draw such admirable portraits of goodness, should yet live as if he were a stranger to it. "Madam", said Colley, "the one is absolutely necessary, the other is not."

actually thinks Lady Easy is in love with him, or at all events envious of Lady Betty's apparent success.

However, pride will have a fall, and his self-confidence must have received a severe shock on finding that he had been used, in Lady Betty's own terms, merely as an "Instrument of our Reconciliation", but the only comment her apology elicits from him is that he is never disappointed but when he finds a lady of the same mind for two hours together. Shortly after he hears that he is not the only one that has been duped, and that Lady Betty herself has been the victim of Sir Charles's stratagem, which amuses him so much that, as he says, if he were to expire that moment, his last breath would go out in a laugh.

Our last impression of him is not an unfavourable one; we feel inclined to forget his faults and remember only his humour, while we cannot help being once more reminded of Cibber himself, who looked upon his follies as the best part of his fortune, and was more concerned to be a good husband of them than of that.[1]

Lord Morelove. This is the least satisfactory character in the play, one of diffidence and indecision, so that we can hardly imagine Sir Charles, who himself is of quite a different stamp, feeling any real friendship for such a man. It is by no means strange that it took Lady Betty some time to marry a poor creature like that and, though we understand from the very beginning that her doom is sealed, it is impossible not to pity her.

Lady Betty. About her Cibber informs us that "there are many sentiments in the character of Lady Betty Modish that I may almost say were originally her (i.e. Mrs. Oldfield's) own, or only dressed with a little more care than when they negligently fell from her lively humour: had her birth placed her in a higher rank of life, she had certainly appeared, in reality, what in this play she only excellently acted, an agreeably gay woman of quality, a little too conscious of her natural attractions."[2]

She is the most lifelike of all the persons in the play and her contributions to the dialogue are amusing as well as witty. She is too fond of a flirtation, but on the other hand she feels

[1] Apology I, p. 12. [2] Apology I, p. 5.

absolutely sure of herself and when Lady Easy expresses her surprise at the fact that her friend can stand Lord Foppington's insolent admiration of her beauty, she says: "My dear, fine Fruit will have Flies about it: but, poor things, they do it no Harm: For, if you observe, People are always most apt to chuse that, that the flies have been busie with."

Lord Foppington realises that it would be a great success to get the better of a creature, as smart as she is; he may express it in his own peculiar way, but be feels a real admiration for her and thoroughly enjoys the duel between her and Lady Graveairs, with Lord Morelove, in which she is more than a match for each in turn.[1] She is lively and capable, well able to look after herself, but she has not much heart, as we may infer not only from the way in which she treats the man she intends to marry, but also from other touches.[2] As a witty character, however, she is very attractive and we can well imagine that the part might, even in our own day, be a great success, if entrusted to a clever actress.

Lady Easy. It seems that this character, too, owes something to a lady, Cibber knew in real life, namely to Mrs. Brett, the wife of Colonel Brett.[3] This lady, "after having forfeited the title of Lady Macclesfield by divorce, was married to Colonel Brett, and, it is said, was well-known in all polite circles. Colley Cibber, I am informed, had so high an opinion of her taste and judgment as to genteel life, and manner, that he submitted every scene of his *Careless Husband* to Mrs. Brett's revisal and correction. Colonel Brett was reported to be too free in his gallantry with her Lady's maid. Mrs. Brett came into a room one day in her own house, and found the Colonel and

[1] Act IV, p. 55: "Not but if your Ladiship pleases I' ll endeavour to keep your Back hand a little: Tho', upon my Soul, you may safely set me up at the Line, for, Knock me down, if ever I saw a Rest of Wit better play'd, than that last in my Life."

[2] Act II, p. 17: After being told by Lady Easy to consider Lady Foppington, she says: "I know she hates me in her heart; and I can't endure malicious People so I us'd to dine there once a Week, purely to give her Disorder. If you had but seen her when my Lord and I fool'd a little, the creature look'd so ugly."

[3] Vide p. 6.

her maid both fast asleep in two chairs. She tied a white handkerchief round her husband's neck, which was a sufficient proof that she had discovered his intrigue; but she never at any time took notice of it to him. This incident, as I am told, gave occasion to the well-wrought scene of Sir Charles and Lady Easy and Edging." [1]

If that is true, the transformation of the notorious Mrs. Brett into the exemplary Lady Easy strikingly illustrates that the sentimental dramatist aimed not at a truthful but a flattering picture of life. [2] Lady Easy is indeed a striking portrait of an excellent and capable wife, who, though by no means blind to her husband's many faults, is discerning enough to see below the surface and to do justice to his good qualities at the same time. In the play she is the exponent of Cibber's sentimental ideal at its best and the impression one gets of her personality is such, that it does not seem at all unlikely that the conversion of the husband in the final scene may be lasting.

Vanbrugh had a different opinion and based the title of his own play *The Relapse* on that conception, but there is no need to agree with him; on the contrary we think the reconciliation scene was carefully led up to and realistic, notwithstanding the bombastic and almost sickening expressions the two indulge in after the reconciliation has taken place.

Lady Graveairs and *Edging* are characters of minor importance: of the former we are told that she is young, beautiful and rich, which statement we must accept, though, from the way in which she is treated by everybody in the play, we should hardly have thought so. Edging on the other hand, while of even less importance than her aristocratic rival, gives an impression almost of realism; her different moods are well drawn.

§ 4 – *The Morality of the Play*

It is usual for critics to sneer at the attempts at "moral" plays, as far as Cibber is concerned, but even if it is true, as one of

[1] Birkbeck Hill I, p. 174, Note 2.

[2] E. Bernbaum, *The Drama of Sensibility*, p. 94.

them says [1] that Cibber conscientiously located all his indecencies in the sub-plot, which consequently became sufficiently attractive to support the central story, that only helps to prove that the main-plot itself was not only moral, but even decent.

There cannot be any doubt that Cibber meant *The Careless Husband* to be a moral play, and he certainly succeeded in giving his contemporaries that impression. According to Davies the scene of reconciliation was wrought up with incidents so natural and interesting and in a style so truly affecting that it afforded a perpetual scource of pleasure to the audience. "So well", he says, [2] "did Cibber, though a professed libertine through life, understand the dignity of virtue, that no comic author has drawn more delightful and striking pictures of it". As, however, this is by no means generally recognised, [3] it may be well to consider the plot and see how far Cibber succeeded in working out the theory that guided him in the composition of the play.

To begin with, it should be understood that, if a play is to be considered a moral one, it is by no means necessary that every character of the play should come up to any strict standard of morality, for the exposition of vice and its ultimate defeat by real goodness is one of the aims of sentimental or moral comedy. In many recent plays, we are confronted with nothing but vice, the sole object being that the spectator should be repelled by it; even Jeremy Collier himself knew that his best argument was that in the drama of his day, vice was not merely represented on the stage, but rewarded.

In *The Careless Husband,* p. 65, Lady Betty remarks: "Plays now indeed, one need not so much be afraid of; for since the late short-sighted View of 'em, Vice may go on and prosper: the Stage dares hardly show a Vicious Person speaking like himself, for fear of being call'd Prophane for Exposing him."

[1] J. Marks, *English Pastoral Drama,* p. 132.

[2] *Dram. Misc.,* III. 460.

[3] It is interesting to compare the following statement: "But the purpose of this play is genuinely moral, to exhibit the triumph of pure long-suffering affection, when its object is a man not spoilt at heart", (Ward, *A History of English Dramatic Literature* II, p. 597) with: "The general atmosphere of *The Careless Husband* is immoral." (Allardyce Nicoll, *Early 18th Century Drama,* p. 161).

The remarks of Lord Foppington ought then to be considered in this light, for in the play, in addition to some very few expressions on the part of Sir Charles, he is the only character, whose conversation bears the stamp of immorality or indecency. Now it is a fact that the audience liked the part of Foppington and so would any modern audience, for the sake of his wit, his sparkling contributions to the dialogue and perhaps also for the daring sentiments uttered by him, but in the play itself there is no sign of approbation; on the contrary Lord Foppington sees poetical justice meted out to him to its fullest extent: he loses his money, is used as a tool by the woman he had considered an easy prey, is laughed at by all his friends and, worst of all, is ousted by so contemptible a rival as Lord Morelove.

Sir Charles himself is far from irreproachable, but from the beginning we see his peace of mind disturbed as a result of his intrigue with Lady Graveairs, while at the same time Edging gives him cause for uneasiness, by her behaviour towards Lady Easy; the final scene with Edging is treated in such a way that we feel the author's disapprobation all the time. It was necessary to introduce something of the kind, because only thus could the force of Lady Easy's self-sacrificing love be fully revealed, be crowned with success and rewarded immediately after. It is true that Sir Charles is not punished, but then he repents and for that reason his sins are forgiven. The two partners of his wickedness are duly punished, Lady Graveairs being even reduced to the necessity of accepting an invitation from her magnanimous rival, while Edging is sure of being ignominiously dismissed at some time in the near future, an event that is put off merely because Lady Easy is afraid people will guess its reason.

Lady Betty occupies a kind of intermediate position between the four characters just mentioned on the one hand, and Lord Morelove and Lady Easy on the other. Her reward or punishment, it is very much a matter of taste in what light one considers it, her definite engagement to Lord Morelove, is just what it ought to be.

The only character that possesses real goodness and moral courage at the same time is Lady Easy and she is successful throughout the play; at the moment that she decides to ignore

Lady Graveairs' letter to her husband, which was to her the final proof that he was not faithful to her, the intrigue has become distasteful to Sir Charles. The last adventure that might have been the occasion for an irreparable breach between her and her husband, is by her loving wisdom and reserve, turned into a final victory over her rivals.

That Cibber himself considered her his greatest success, may be seen from the prologue to *The Lady's Last Stake,* where he says:

> Therefore our author drew you once the Life
> Of Careless Husband and Enduring Wife,
> Who by her Patience (tho' much out of Fashion)
> Retriev'd, at last, the Wanderer's Inclination.
> Yet some there are, who still arraign the Play,
> At her tame Temper shock'd, as who shou'd say,
> The Price for a dull Husband, was too much to pay.
> Had he been strangled sleeping, who shou'd hurt ye?
> When so provok'd—Revenge had been a Virtue.

To conclude, we can say that in *The Careless Husband,* Cibber produced a genuinely moral play, in which vice was punished and goodness rewarded and in which, moreover, oaths and obscene language were avoided as far as was consistent with the characters of the people represented in it.

§ 5 – *The Construction of the Plot*

In this respect, too, *The Careless Husband* attains to a very high standard of excellence and while the drama of the time was indeed "very far from realising the modern ideal, by which the dramatist seizes upon a crisis in the lives of his characters, states its conditions and follows its evolutions to an end, regarding everything else as a surplusage, yet, in Cibber, as earlier in Congreve, we recognise an ideal above the practice of the time". [1]

In his prologue to *She Wou'd, and She Wou'd not,* his ideal is described in the following terms:

[1] F. E. Schelling, *English Drama,* p. 275.

His Action's in the Time of Acting done,
No more than from the Curtain, up and down.
While the first Music plays, he removes his Scene
A little Space, but never shifts again.
From his Design no Person can be spar'd
Or Speeches lopt, unless the whole be marr'd:
No scenes of Talk for talking's sake are shewn,
Where most abruptly, when their Chat is done,
Actors go off, because the Poet — can't go on.
His first Act offers something to be done,
And all the rest but lead that Action on;
Which when pursuing Scenes i'th'end discover,
The Game's run down, of course the Play is over."

The main plot and the by-plot are intimately interwoven and the byplot helps to promote the development of the main action.

Sir Charles, one of the principal characters in the main plot, takes a very active part in the secondary action; to a less degree this is also the case with Lady Graveairs and Lady Easy, while conversely, Lady Betty through her flirtation, induces Lord Morelove to pretend a liking for Lady Graveairs, in this way helping Sir Charles to free himself from her. In addition to this the by-plot serves to throw a more favourable light upon the character of the hero.

Taking all this into consideration, we can fully endorse the statement that *The Careless Husband* is a really brilliant comedy of intrigue. [1]

[1] F. E. Schelling, *English Drama,* p. 282.

THE TEXT

The text of *The Careless Husband* reproduces faithfully the quarto copy of the editio princeps in the Bodleian Library, also as far as capitalisation, punctuation, and abbreviations are concerned. Evident errors in punctuation, due to carelessness have been corrected, but any change of that nature is invariably indicated at the foot of the page. In the footnotes are also registered the initial word or words of each page of the original edition. The text has has been collated with that of the following editions:

A. The quarto of 1705 (London).
B. The duodecimo of 1710 (London).
C. The quarto of 1721 (London).
D. The duodecimo of 1723 (Dublin).
E. The duodecimo of 1731 (London).
F. The duodecimo of 1733 (London).

For A, C, D, E, F, the copies in the British Museum Library were used, for B, a copy in the Amsterdam University Library. In the process of collation it was found that A, B, D, were evidently based on the editio princeps (in the notes referred to as P), whereas E and F were based on C, which forms part of the complete edition of Cibber's works, edited by himself.

The variants of these editions are pointed out in the footnotes, with the exception of the numerous differences in the use of capitals and punctuation, in which no consistent system is recognisable.

Mrs. ANNE OLDFIELD

From a painting after Jonathan Richardson, in the possession of the National Portrait Gallery, London.

The Careless Husband

A

COMEDY

as it is ACTED at the

THEATRE ROYAL

BY

Her MAJESTY's Servants

Written by C. CIBBER

Yet none Sir Fopling *Him, or Him can call,*
He's Knight o' th' Shire, and Represents you all.
Qui Capit, Ille Facit.

LONDON,
Printed for William Davis, *at the* Black Bull, *over-against the Royal Exchange in* Cornhill, 1705.

To the Most Illustrious,

JOHN

Duke and Earl of Argile, Marquis of Lorne, Lord Kintyre, Campbel and Lorne, Heretable Master of the Houshold, Colonel and Captain of her Majesty's Troop of Horse-Guards in Scotland, and Knight of the most Ancient and Noble Order of St. Andrew.

This Play at last through many Difficulties, has made way to throw itself at your Grace's Feet: And, considering what well-meant Attempts were made to intercept it in its Course to so great an Honour, I have had reason not to think it intirely successful, till (where my Ambition always design'd it) I found it safe in your Protection: Which, when several means had fail'd of making it less Worthy of the Spleen, ended with the Old Good Nature that was offer'd to my First Play, *viz.* That it was none of my own: But that's a Praise I have indeed some reason to be proud of, since your Grace from Evincing Circumstances is Able to divide the Malice from the Compliment.

The Best Criticks have long, and justly complain'd that the Coursness of most Characters in our late Comedies have been unfit Entertainments for People of Quality, especially the Ladies:

3 A, C, D, E, F, Argyle. C, D, E, F, omit the titles after Argyle.

A, Argyle, Her Majesty's Lord High Commissioner for the Kingdom of Scotland, Marquis of Kintyre and Lorne, Earl of Campbel & c. Heretable Justice General for the Shire of Argyle, Isles, and others; Heretable Sheriff of the said shire; Heretable Great Master of the Household in Scotland, one of the extraordinary Lords of the Sessions; Brigadier General and Captain of Her Majesty's Life Guard of Horse; Brigadier General and Colonel of a Regiment of Fusiliers, in the Service of their High and Mightinesses the States General, one of her Majesty's most Honourable Privy Council, and Knight of the most Ancient and Most Noble Order of the Thistle.

10 B, successfull. 13 C, D, E, F, Good-nature.

18 The Best Criticks. P, 2nd leaf, verso.

19 A, Courseness. C, Coarsness. D, E, F, Coarseness.

And therefore I was long in Hopes, that some able Pen (whose Expectation did not Hang upon the Profits of success) wou'd generously attempt to reform the Town into a better Tast, than the World generally allows 'em: But nothing of that kind having lately appear'd, that wou'd give me an Opportunity of being Wise at anothers Expence, I found it Impossible any longer to Resist the secret Temptation of my Vanity, and so ev'n struck the first Blow my self: and the Event has now convinc'd me, that whoever sticks closely to Nature can't easily write above the Understanding of the Galleries, tho' at the same Time he may Possibly deserve Applause of the Boxes.

This Play before its Tryal on the Stage was Examin'd by several People of Quality, that came into your Graces Opinion of its being a Just, a Proper, and Diverting Attempt in Comedy; but few of 'em carry'd the Compliment beyond their private Approbation: For when I was wishing for a little farther Hope, they stopt short of your Grace's Penetration, and only kindly wisht me what they seem'd to fear, and you assur'd me of, a General Success.

But your Grace has been pleas'd, not only to encourage me with your Judgment; but have likewise by your Favourable Influence in the Bounties that were rais'd me for the Third and Sixth Day, defended me against any Hazards of an entire Disappointment from so bold an Undertaking: And therefore, whatever the World may think of me, as one they call a *Poet;* yet I am confident, as your Grace understands me, I shall not want your Belief, when I assure you that this *Dedication* is the Result of a profound Acknowledgment, an Artless Inclination proudly Glad, and Grateful.

And if the Dialogue of the following Scenes flows with more easie Turn of Thought and Spirit, than what I have usually produc't; I shall not yet blame some People for saying 'tis not my own, unless they knew at the same time I owe most of it

[23] A, C, D, E, F, Taste. [25] C, D, E, F, would . . . at another's. [27] C, e'en. F, even. [33] A, C, D, E, F, Grace's. [34] Attempt. P. Third leaf, recto. [38] D, wish'd. [42] C, E, F, for me the Third. C, raised. [52] A, C, D, E, F, produc'd. [52] for saying. P, Third leaf, verso.

to the many stolen Observations I have made from your Grace's manner of Conversing.

And if ever the Influence of your Grace's more shining Qualities should perswade me to attempt a *Tragedy,* I shall then with the same Freedom, borrow all the Ornamental Virtues of my Hero, where now I only am indebted for part of the Fine Gentleman. Greatness of Birth and Mind, Sweetness of Temper, flowing from the Fixt and Native Principles of Courage and of Honour, are Beauties that I reserve for a further Opportunity of expressing the Zeal and Gratitude of,

My Lord,

Decem. 15. 1704.

Your Grace's Most Obedient,
Most oblig'd and Humble Servant,

COLLEY CIBBER.

57 C, E, F, persuade.
67 C omits, Decem. 15. 1704. D, E, F, Dec. 1704.

THE
PROLOGUE.

Of all the Various Vices of the Age
And Shoals of Fools Expos'd upon the Stage,
How Few are lasht, that call for Satyrs Rage.
What can you think to see our Plays so full
Of Madmen, Coxcombs and the Driveling Fool;
Of Citts, of Sharpers, Rakes, and Roaring Bullies,
Of Cheats, of Cuckolds, Aldermen, and Cullies?
Wou'd not one swear 'twere taken for a Rule,
That Satyrs Rod in the Dramatick School
Was only meant for the Incorrigible Fool?
As if too Vice and Folly were confin'd
To the Vile Scum alone of Humane Kind.
Creatures a Muse should scorn, such abject Trash
Deserve not Satyrs but the Hangman's Lash.
Wretches so far shut out from sense of Shame,
Newgate, or Bedlam only shou'd Reclaim
For Satyr ne'er was meant to make Wild Monsters Tame.
No Sirs —
We rather think the Persons fit For Plays
Are they whose Birth, and Education says
They've every Help, that shou'd Improve Mankind
Yet still live Slaves to a vile Tainted Mind;
Such as in Wit are often seen t'Abound,
And yet have some weak Part, where Folly's found:
For Follies sprout like Weeds, Highest in Fruitful Ground.
And 'tis Observd the Garden of the Mind
To no Infestive Weed's so much Inclin'd
As the Rank Pride, that some from Affectation find.

[1] P, leaf 4 recto. [3] C, D, E, F, Satyr's. [6] E, F, Cits. [9] C, D, E, F, Satyr's. [12] C, D, E, F, human. [13] E, F, shou'd. [14] C, D, E, F, Satyr's. [17] A, ne're. [22] P, still like Slaves. [26] A, C, D, E, F, observ'd.

A Folly too well known to make its Court
With most success among the Better sort.
Such are the Persons we to Day provide,
And Natures Fools for once are laid aside.
This is the Ground on which our Play we Build;
But in the structure must to Judgment yield:
And where the Poet Fails in Art, or Care,
We Beg your Wonted Mercy to the Player.

29 P, make its Cours. 32 C, D, E, F, Nature's.

PROLOGUE.

Upon the last Campaign, Written by a Person of Quality; design'd for the Sixth Day, but not spoken.

A paying Nation hates the Fighting Trade,
And Lingring War in usual Methods made:
When Armies walk about from Wood to River,
And Threescore Thousand only get together
To Eat, and Drink, consult, and find the way
How without fighting they may earn their Pay,
When prudent Generals get by safeguard giving,
An honest, quiet comfortable living;
But never fight it up to a Thanksgiving.
These manage War with the Physicians Skill,
And use such means, as neither Cure, nor Kill:
Like the wise Doctors, safe by their Degrees,
They give weak Doses, but take swinging Fees.
The Trade continuing, which can never end
While the sick state has any thing to spend.
Thanks then to him, who strikes at the Disease,
And Bravely tries to set the World at ease:
For if such fighting last but one Year more,
Two Danube *Victories will quit the score,*
And soon recruit our almost Lavisht Store.
A Happy Peace regains our Treasure lost,
Our own the Glory, and our Foes the Cost.
No Favour let the Homebred Sparks expect;
But scorn from Men, and from the Fair neglect.
Beaux, that spend all their time in soft love-making;
Those tender Souls, whose Hearts are always aking,
Shun 'em Ye Fair, prevent their Am'rous Boasting;

[1] P, Leaf 4 verso. [11] P omits stop after Thanksgiving. [12] E, F, Physician's. [22] C, D, E, F, lavish'd. [25] A, Homebread. [29] C, Shun em.

Nor Poorly yield to Idle Talk, and Toasting.
If you have Favours, which you must bestow,
Give 'em the Soldiers, they deserve 'em now.
Who make proud Tyrants stoop, shou'd only kneel to you.
Minerva *guides our General to Fame*
No Cruelties in War affect his Name,
Mild in the Camp, by no success made Vain.
A Gentle Goddess Animates his Mind;
Bold for his Friends, to Conquer'd Foes as Kind.
Design'd by Heav'n for Anna's *Happy Reign.*
Whose generous Soul seeks only to Restrain
Unbounded Tyranny, and lawless Might,
Revenge Oppression, and restore the Right:
War not her choice, but necessary Fence,
Truth to Promote, and Humble insolence.
Where'er her Influence flys, it Joy creates,
And Peace, and Safety brings to Distant States:
With such success her Chief begins his Race,
That his first Battle Brightly does Efface
The Tedious Labours of our Modern Wars;
Out-does at once Old Soldiers, and the Tarrs.
In him no sauntring in the Feild we find,
No Doubt Remains where Victory Inclin'd.
His Sword Decides — no Double Praise is given;
Where neither side is pleas'd, yet Both thank Heaven.
From War he quickly Kingdoms will release;
Rapine, and Rage soon Turn to Joy, and Peace,
And by Destruction make Destruction cease.

[33] A, E, F, should. [37] A Gentle P, leaf 5 recto. [45] E, F, flies. [48] C, Battel. [50] A, D, Out does. F, Outdoes. [50] A, C, D, E, F, Tars. [51] C, D, E, F, Field [54] C, D, E, F, Heav'n.

THE

EPILOGUE.

Conquest and Freedom are at length our own;
Fals Fears of slavery now no more are shewn;
Nor Dread of Paying Tribute to a Forreign Throne.
All Stations now the Fruits of Conquest share,
Except (if small with Great things may Compare)
Th'opprest Condition of the lab'ring Player.
We're still in Fears (as you of late from France)
Of the Despotick Power of Song, and Dance:
For while Subscription, like a Tyrant Reigns.
Nature's Neglected and the Stage in Chains,
And English *Actors Slaves to swell the* Frenchman's *Gains.*
Like Esop's *Crow, the poor out-witted Stage,*
That liv'd on wholsome Plays i'th' latter Age,
Deluded once to sing, ev'n justly serv'd,
Let fall her Cheese to th'Fox's Mouth, and starv'd.
O that your judgment (as your Courage has
Your Fame extended) wou'd assert our Cause;
That nothing English *might submit to Foreign Laws.*
If we but live to see that joyful Day,
Then of the English *Stage reviv'd we may,*
As of your Honour now, with proper Application, say.
So when the Gallick *Fox by Fraud of Peace*
Had lull'd the British *Lion into Ease,*
And saw that Sleep compos'd his couchant Head,
He bids him wake, and see himself betray'd
In Toils of Treach'rous Politicks around him laid:

1 The Epilogue on leaf 5 recto. 9 C, Despotic. 11 C, Natture's. 19 C, would. 21 If we. P, leaf 5 verso.

Shews him how one close Hour of Gallick *thought*
Retook those Towns for which he Years had fought.
At this th' indignant Savage rowls his fiery Eyes,
Dauntless, tho' blushing at the base Surprize,
Pauses a while—But finds Delays are vain:
Compell'd to fight, he shakes his shaggy Main;
He grinds his dreadful Fangs, and stalks to Blenheim's *Plain.*
There with erected Crest, and Horrid Roar
He Furious, Plunges on through Streams of Gore,
And Dyes with False Bavarian *Blood the Purple* Danube's *shore.*
In one pusht Battle frees the Destin'd Slaves;
Revives Old English *Honour, and an Empire saves.*

The Perſons.

Lord Morelove,	Mr. *Powel.*
Lord Foppington,	Mr. *Cibber.*
Sir *Charles Eaſy,*	Mr. *Wilks.*
Lady *Betty Modiſh,*	Mrs. *Oldfield.*
Lady Eaſy,	Mrs. *Knight.*
Lady Grave-airs,	Mrs. *Moore.*
Mrs. *Edging,* Woman to Lady Eaſy,	Mrs. *Lucas.*

The SCENE Windſor.

32 C, F, rolls. 42 C, E, Battel. 50 C, E, F, Mrs. More.

Note. D prints the following names: Mr. Ralph Elrington, Mr. Griffith, Mr. Gifford, Miss Lyddell, Mrs. Lyddell, Mrs. Vanderbank, Mrs. Martin.

THE CARELESS HUSBAND

ACT I.

Scene, *Sir* CHARLES EASY'S *Lodgings.*

Enter Lady Easy *alone.*

Lady *Easy.* Was ever Woman's Spirit, by an injurious Husband, broke like mine? A vile, licentious Man! must he bring Home his Follies too? Wrong me with my very Servant! O! how tedious a Relief is Patience! And yet in my Condition 'tis the only Remedy: for to reproach him with my Wrongs is taking on my self the Means of a Redress, bidding Defiance to his Falshood, and naturally but provokes him to undo me. Th' uneasie Thought of my continual Jealousie may teize him to a fixt Aversion; and hitherto, tho' he neglects, I cannot think he Hates me—It must be so; since I want Power to please him, he never shall upbraid me with an Attempt of making him uneasie. —My Eyes and Tongue shall yet be blind and silent to my Wrongs; nor would I have him think my Virtue cou'd suspect him, 'till by some Gross, Apparent Proof of his Misdoing he forces me to see,—and to forgive it.

Enter Edging *hastily.*

Edg. — O Madam!

La. *Ea.* — What's the Matter?

Edg. — I have the strangest thing to shew your Ladyship —such a Discovery—

La. *Ea.* You are resolv'd to make it without much Ceremony, I find; what's the Business, pray?

Edg. The Business, Madam! I have not Patience to tell you, I am out of Breath at the very Thoughts on't, I shall not be able to speak this half Hour.

[7] C & D, uneasy. F, The uneasy; Jealousy. [8] C, teaze. [11] C. D. F, uneasy. [18] C, D, E, F, L. Ea., throughout the play. [21] La. Ea. P, p. 2.

La. *Ea.* Not to the Purpose, I believe, but methinks you talk impertinently with a great deal of Ease.

Edg. Nay, Madam, perhaps not so impertinent as your Ladyship thinks; there's that will speak to the purpose, I am sure —A Base Man— *(Gives a Letter.*

La. *Ea.* What's this, an open Letter? Whence comes it?

Edg. Nay read it, Madam, you'll soon guess—if these are the Tricks of Husbands, keep me a Maid still, say I.

La. *Ea. [Looking on the Superscription]* To Sir Charles Easy! Ha! Too well I know this hateful Hand—O my Heart! But I must veil my Jealousie, which 'tis not fit this Creature should suppose I am acquainted with. *(Aside)* This Direction is to your Master, how came you by it?

Edg. Why, Madam, as my Master was lying down, after he came in from Hunting, he sent me into his Dressing-Room to fetch his Snuff-Box out of his Wastcoat-Pocket, and so, as I was searching for the Box, Madam, there I found this wicked Letter from a Mistress; which I had no sooner read, but, I declare it, my very Blood rose at him again, methought I cou'd have tore him and her to pieces.

La. *Ea.* Intolerable! This odious Thing's jealous of him her self, and wants me to join with her in a Revenge upon him—Sure I am fallen indeed! But 'twere to make me lower yet, to let her think I understand her. *(Aside.*

Edg. Nay pray, Madam, read it, you'll be out of Patience at it.

La. *Ea.* You are bold, Mistress; has my Indulgence, or your Master's good Humour, flatter'd you into the Assurance of reading his Letters? A Liberty I never gave my self—Here—lay it where you had it immediately—shou'd he know of your Sauciness, 'twou'd not be my Favour cou'd protect you.

(Ex. L. Easy.

Edg. Your Favour! Marry come up! Sure I don't depend upon your Favour!—'tis not come to that, I hope—Poor Creature—don't you think I am my Master's Mistress for nothing—you shall find, Madam, I won't be snapt up as I have been—Not but it vexes me to think she shou'd not be as uneasie as I; I am

30 F, Letter! 36 C, F, Jealousy. 45 C, F, torn. 51 C, of your. 59 A, Masters. 61 C, F, uneasy.

sure he's a base Man to me, and I could cry my Eyes out that she shou'd not think him as Bad to her every Jot. If I am wrong'd sure she may very well expect it, that is but his Wife—A conceited Thing—she need not be so Easie neither—I am as handsom as she, I hope—Here's my Master,—I'll try whether I am to be huff'd by her, or no. *(Walks behind.*

Enter Sir Charles Easy.

Sir *Cha.* So! The Day is come again—Life but rises to another Stage, and the same dull Journey is before us—How like Children do we judge of Happiness! When I was stinted in my Fortune almost every thing was a Pleasure to me, because most things then being out of my Reach, I had always the Pleasure of hoping for 'em; now Fortune's in my Hand she's as insipid as an old Acquaintance—It's mighty silly, Faith—Just the same thing by my Wife too; I am told she's extreamly Handsom—nay, and have heard a great many People say she is certainly the Best Woman in the World—why I don't know but she may, yet I could never find that her Person, or good Qualities, gave me any Concern—In my Eye the Woman has no more Charms than my Mother.

Edg. Hum!—He takes no Notice of me yet—I'll let him see, I can take as little Notice of him.

(She walks by him gravely, he turns her about and holds her, she struggles.

Pray Sir.

Sir *Cha.* A pretty pert Air that—I'll humour it—What's the Matter, Child? Are not you well? Kiss me, Hussy.

Edg. No, the Duce fetch me, if I do.

Sir *Cha.* Has any thing put thee out of Humour, Love?

Edg. No, Sir, 'tis not worth my being out of Humour at—tho' if ever you have any thing to do with me again I'll be Burn'd.

Sir *Cha.* Some Body has bely'd me to thee.

Edg. No, Sir, 'tis you have bely'ed your self to me—did not I ask you, when you first made a Fool of me, if you would be

[65] C, F, easy; A, D, E, F, handsome. [68] Enter. P, p. 3. [76] A, D, E, F, handsome; F, extremely. [92] C, D, F, anything to say to me.

always constant to me, and did not you say I might be sure you wou'd? And here, instead of that, you are going on in your old Intrigue with my Lady *Graveairs.*—

Sir *Cha.* So.—

Edg. Beside, don't you suffer my Lady to huff me every Day, as if I were her Dog, or had no more Concern with you—I declare I won't bear it, and she shan't think to huff me—for ought I know I am as Agreeable as she, and tho' she dares not take any Notice of your Baseness to Her, you shan't think to use Me so,—and so pray take your nasty Letter—I know the Hand well enough,—for my part I won't stay in the Family to be abus'd at this rate; I that have refus'd Lords and Dukes for your sake: I'd have you to know, Sir, I have had as many Blue and Green Ribbons after me, for ought I know, as would have made me a Falbala Apron.

Sir *Cha.* My Lady *Graveairs!* My nasty Letter! and, I won't stay in the Family!—Death! I'm in a pretty Condition—What an unlimited Privilege has this Jade got from being a Whore.

Edg. I suppose, Sir, you think to use every body as you do your Wife.

Sir *Cha.* My Wife, hah! Come hither, Mrs. *Edging,* hark you, Drab.

Edg. Oh! *(Seizing her by the Shoulder.*

Sir *Cha.* When you speak of my Wife you are to say your Lady, and you are never to speak of your Lady to me in any regard of her being my Wife—for look you, Child, you are not Her Strumpet but Mine, therefore I only give you leave to be saucy with Me;—in the next place you are never to suppose there is any such Person as my Lady *Graveairs;* and lastly, my pretty one, how came you by this Letter?

Edg. It's no Matter, perhaps.

Sir *Cha.* Ay, but if you shou'd not tell me quickly, how are you sure I won't take a great Piece of Flesh out of your Shoulder?—My Dear. *(Shakes her.*

Edg. O Lud! O lud! I will tell you, Sir.

Sir *Cha.* Quickly then.— *(Again.*

[98] F, Intriegue. [109] A, Ribbonds. [111] won't. P, p. 4. [116] D, Mistress Edging. [127] D, should.

Edg. Oh! I took it out of your Pocket, Sir.

Sir *Cha.* When?

Edg. Oh! This Morning, when you sent me for your Snuff-box.

Sir *Cha.* And your Ladyship's pretty Curiosity has look'd it over, I presume—ha— *(Again.*

Edg. O lud! dear Sir, don't be angry—indeed I'll never touch one again.

Sir *Cha.* I don't believe you will, and I'll tell you how you shall be sure you never will.

Edg. Yes, Sir.

Sir *Cha.* By stedfastly believing, that the next time you offer it, you will have your pretty white Neck twisted behind you.

Edg. Yes, Sir. *(Curtesing.*

Sir *Cha.* And you will be sure to remember every thing I have said to you?

Edg. Yes, Sir.

Sir *Cha.* And now, Child, I was not angry with your Person, but your Follies; which since I find you are a little sensible of—don't be wholly discourag'd—for I believe I—I shall have Occasion for you again—

Edg. Yes, Sir.

Sir *Cha.* In the mean time let me hear no more of your Lady, Child.

Edg. No, Sir.

Sir *Cha.* Here she comes; begone.

Edg. Yes, Sir—Oh! I was never so frighten'd in my Life. *(Ex.* Edg.

Sir *Cha.* So! Good Discipline makes good Soldiers. It often puzzles me to think, from my own Carelessness, and my Wife's continual good Humour, whether she really knows any thing of the strength of my Forces—I'll sift her a little.

Enter Lady Easy.

My Dear how do you do? You are dress'd very early to Day; are you going out?

La. *Ea.* Only to Church, my Dear.

142 D, steadfastly. 152 A, Yes, Sir. *(Curtesing).* 156 P, comes, begone. A, E, F, be gone. 157 Edg. P, p. 5.

Sir *Cha.* Is it so late then?

La. *Ea.* The Bell has just Rung.

Sir *Cha.* Well, Child, how does Windsor Air agree with you? Do you find your self any Better yet? Or have you a Mind to go to London again?

La. *Ea.* No indeed, my Dear; the Air's so very pleasant, that if it were a Place of less Company, I could be content to end my Days here.

Sir *Cha.* Prithee, my Dear, what sort of Company would most please you?

La. *Ea.* When Business wou'd permit it Yours, and in your Absence a sincere Friend, that were truly happy in an honest Husband, to sit a chearful Hour, and talk in mutual Praise of our Condition.

Sir *Cha.* Are you then really very happy, my Dear?

La. *Ea.* Why shou'd you question it? *(Smiling on him.*

Sir *Cha.* Because I fancy I am not so good to you as I should be.

La. *Ea.* Pshah!

Sir *Cha.* Nay, the Duce take me if I don't really confess my self so bad, that I have often wonder'd how any Woman of your Sense, Rank and Person, could think it worth her while to have so many useless good Qualities.

La. *Ea.* Fie, my Dear.

Sir *Cha.* By my Soul I'm serious.

La. *Ea.* I can't boast of my good Qualities; nor if I could, do I believe you think 'em useless.

Sir *Cha.* Nay, I submit to you—Don't you find 'em so? Do you perceive that I am one Tittle the better Husband for your being so good a Wife?

La. *Ea.* Pshah! You Jest with me.

Sir *Cha.* I don't really—Tell me truly, was you never jealous of me?

La. *Ea.* Did I ever give you any sign of it?

Sir *Cha.* Um—that's true—but do you really think I never gave you Occasion?

[173] E, cou'd. [175] E, Pry'thee. [177] D, would. [182] F, should. [184] F, Pshaw! [189] F, Fy. [191] P, Qualities, nor if I could do I. [196] F, pshaw. [197] F, Sir *Cha.* Upon my Life I don't—Tell me truly. [200] Sir *Cha.* P, p. 6.

La. *Ea.* That's an odd Question—but suppose you had?

Sir *Cha.* Why then, what good has your Virtue done you, since all the good Qualities of it could not keep me to your self?

La. *Ea.* What occasion have you given me to suppose I have Not kept you to my self?

Sir *Cha.* I given you Occasion— Fie! My Dear—you may be sure—I—I—look you, that is not the thing, but still a—(Death! What a Blunder have I made!)—a still, I say, Madam, you shan't make me believe you have never been Jealous of me, not that you ever had any real Cause, but I know Women of your Principles have more Pride than those that have no Principles at all; and where there is Pride there must be some Jealousie —so that if you are Jealous, my Dear, you know you wrong me, and—

La. *Ea.* Why then upon my Word, my Dear, I don't know that ever I wrong'd you that way in my Life.

Sir *Cha.* But suppose I had given you a real Cause to be Jealous, how would you do then?

La. *Ea.* It must be a very substantial one that makes me Jealous.

Sir *Cha.* Say it were a substantial one; suppose now I were well with a Woman of your own Acquaintance, that under pretence of frequent Visits to you, should only come to carry on an Affair with me—Suppose now my Lady *Graveairs* and I were great?—

La. *Ea.* Wou'd I could not Suppose it. *(Aside.*

Sir *Cha.* If I come off here I believe I am pretty safe—*(Aside).* Suppose, I say, my Lady and I were so very familiar, that not only your self, but half the Town should see it.

La. *Ea.* Then I should cry my self sick in some dark Closet, and forget my Tears when you spoke kindly to me.

Sir *Cha.* The most convenient piece of Virtue sure, that ever Wife was Mistress of. *(Aside.*

La. *Ea.* But pray, my Dear, did you ever think that I had any ill Thoughts of my Lady *Graveairs?*

Sir *Cha.* O Fie! Child, only you know she and I us'd to be a little free sometimes, so I had a Mind to see if you thought there was any harm in it: But since I find you very easie, I

207 F, Fy! 214 F, Jealousy. 218 F omits, you. 226 D, cou'd. 236 F, Fy! 238 C, F, easy.

think my self oblig'd to tell you, that upon my Soul, my Dear, I have so little regard to her Person, that the Duce take me, if I would not as soon have an Affair with thy own Woman.

La. *Ea.* Indeed, my Dear, I should as soon suspect you with one as t'other.

Sir *Cha.* Poor Dear—shou'dst thou—give me a Kiss.

La. *Ea.* Pshah! You don't care to Kiss me.

Sir *Cha.* By my Soul I do—I wish I may die if I don't think you a very fine Woman.

La. *Ea.* I only wish you wou'd think me a good Wife. *(Kisses her.)* But pray, my Dear, what has made you so strangely Inquisitive?

Sir *Cha.* Inquisitive—Why—a—nay I don't know, one's always saying one foolish thing or another—Toll le roll *(sings and talks.)* My Dear, what! are we never to have any Ball here? Toll le roll. I fancy I could recover my Dancing again, if I would but Practise, Toll loll loll!

La. *Ea.* This Excess of Carelessness to me excuses half his Vices, if I can make him once think seriously—Time yet may be my Friend.

Enter a Servant.

Ser. Sir, my Lord *Morelove* gives his Service—

Sir *Cha.* Lord *Morelove!* Where is he?

Ser. At the Chocolate-House; he call'd me to him as I went by, and bid me tell your Honour he'll wait upon you presently.

La. *Ea.* I thought you had not expected him here again this Season, my Dear.

Sir *Cha.* I thought so too, but you see there's no depending upon the Resolution of a Man that's in Love.

La. *Ea.* Is there a Chair?

Ser. Yes, Madam. *(Ex. Servant.*

La. *Ea.* I suppose Lady *Betty Modish* has drawn him hither.

Sir. *Cha.* Ay, poor Soul, for all his Bravery, I am afraid so.

La. *E*a. Well, my Dear, I han't time to ask my Lord how

[244] Sir Cha. P, p. 7. [245] D, Psha. F, Pshaw. [251] D omits, nay. [253] A, B, C, E, F, omit, what.

he does now; you'll excuse me to him, but I hope you'll make him Dine with us.

Sir *Cha.* I'll ask him; if you see Lady *Betty* at Prayers make her Dine too, but don't take any notice of my Lord's being in Town.

La. *Ea.* Very well! If I should not meet her there I'll call at her Lodgings.

Sir *Cha.* Do so. *(Re-enter the Servant.*

La. *Ea.* My Dear, your Servant. *(Ex. La.* Easy.

Sir *Cha.* My Dear, I'm yours. Well! One way or other this Woman will certainly bring about her Business with me at last: For tho' she can't make me happy in her own Person, she lets me be so intollerably easie with the Women that can, that she has at least brought me into a fair way of being as weary of them too.

Enter Servant and Lord Morelove.

Ser. Sir, my Lord's come.

L. *Mo.* Dear *Charles!*

Sir *Cha.* My dear Lord! This is an Happiness undreamt of; I little thought to have seen you at Windsor again this Season; I concluded of Course that Books and Solitude had secur'd you 'till Winter.

L. *Mo.* Nay, I did not think of coming my self, but I found my self not very well in *London,* so I thought—a—little Hunting, and this Air—

Sir *Cha.* Ha! ha! ha!

L. *Mo.* What do you laugh at?

Sir *Cha.* Only because you should not go on with your Story: If you did but see how sillily a Man fumbles for an Excuse, when he's a little asham'd of being in Love, you would not wonder what I laugh at; ha! ha!

L. *Mo.* Thou art a very happy Fellow—nothing touches thee—always Easie—Then you conclude I follow Lady *Betty* again?

Sir *Cha.* Yes, Faith do I, and to make you easie, my Lord, I cannot see why a Man that can ride Fifty Miles after a poor

[280] C, D, E, omit, Re-enter the Servant. [285] C. intolerably. F, easy. [288] Enter. P, p. 8. [300] E, F, silly. [304], [305] C. F, easy.

Stag, should be asham'd of running Twenty in Chace of a fine Woman, that, in all probability, will make him so much the better Sport too. *(Embracing.*

L. *Mo.* Dear *Charles* don't flatter my Distemper; I own I still follow her: Do you think her Charms have Power to excuse me to the World?

Sir *Cha.* Ay! ay! A fine Woman's an Excuse for any thing.

L. *Mo.* You take a great deal of Pains to give me Hope, but I can't believe she has the least degree of Inclination for me.

Sir *Cha.* I don't know that—I am sure her Pride likes you, and that's generally your fine Lady's Darling Passion.

L. *Mo.* Do you suppose if I cou'd grow indifferent it wou'd touch her?

Sir *Cha.* Sting her to the Heart—Will you take my Advice?

L. *Mo.* I have no Relief but that. Had I not thee now and then to talk an Hour, my Life were insupportable.

Sir *Cha.* I am sorry for that, my Lord—but mind what I say to you—But hold, first let me know the Particulars of your Quarrel with her.

L. *Mo.* Why—about Three Weeks ago, when I was last here at *Windsor,* she had for some Days treated me with a little more Reserve, and another with more Freedom than I found my self easie at.

Sir *Cha.* Who was that other?

L. *Mo.* One of my Lord *Foppington*'s Gang, the Pert Coxcomb that's just come to a small Estate, and a great Perriwig—he that Sings himself among the Women—What d'ye call him?—He won't speak to a Gentleman when a Lord's in Company—You always see him with a cane dangling at his Button, his Breast open, no Gloves, one Eye tuck'd under his Hat and a Toothpick—*Startup!* That's his Name.

Sir *Cha.* O! I have met him in a Visit—but pray go on.

[307] C, D, E, F, chase. [310] P, comma after Distemper. [312] P, World. [313] and [314] C, D, E, F, . . . for any thing; and the Scandal of being her Jest, is a Jest itself; we are all forc'd to be their Fools, before we can be their Favourites. L. Mo. You are willing to give me Hope, but.

[318] D, F, could. [321] P, but that, had I not. [322] P, Life we. [325] C, F, your late Quarrel. [329] C, F, easy. [330] Sir Cha. P, p. 9. [332] D, and a great Perruke. [334] C, D, F, speak to a Commoner when.

L. *Mo.* So, disputing with her about the Conduct of Women, I took the Liberty to tell her how far I thought she err'd in hers; she told me I was rude, and that she would never believe any Man could love a Woman, that thought her in the wrong in any thing she had a Mind to, at least if he dar'd to tell her so— This provok'd me into her whole Character, with as much Spite, and civil Malice, as I have seen her bestow upon a Woman of true Beauty, when the Men first Toasted her; so in the middle of my Wisdom she told me she desir'd to be Alone, that I would take my odious proud Heart along with me, and trouble her no more—I—bow'd very low, and, as I left the Room, vow'd I never wou'd, and that my proud Heart Should never be humbl'd by the Outside of a fine Woman— About an Hour after I whip'd into my Chaise for *London,* and have never seen her since.

Sir *Cha.* Very well, and how did you find your proud Heart by that time you got to *Hounslow?*

L. *Mo.* I am almost asham'd to tell you—I found her so much in the right, that I curs'd my Pride for contradicting her at all, and began to think that no Woman could be in the wrong to a Man that she had in her Power.

Sir *Cha.* Ha! Ha! well I'll tell you what you shall do. You can see her without trembling, I hope.

L. *Mo.* Not if she receives me well.

Sir *Cha.* If she receives you well you will have no occasion, for what I am going to say to you—First you shall Dine with her.

L. *Mo.* How! where! when!

Sir *Cha.* Here! here! At Two a Clock.

L. *Mo.* Dear *Charles!*

Sir *Cha.* My Wife's gone to invite her; when you see her first be neither too Humble, nor too Stubborn; let her see, by the ease in your Behaviour, you are still pleas'd in being near her, while she is upon reasonable Terms with You. This will either open the Door of a Ecclarcisement, or quite shut it against you—if she is still resolv'd to keep you out—

344 D, Caracter. 352 C, whipp'd. 258 C, D, F, to think according to her Maxim, that. 369 P, prints comma after stubborn. 372 B, a Eclaircissement. E, an Eclarcisement. 373 C, D, and if she is still.

L. *Mo.* Nay, if she insults me Then, perhaps I may recover Pride enough to rally her by an over-acted Submission.

Sir *Cha.* Why you improve, my Lord; this is the very thing I was going to propose to you.

L. *Mo.* Was it, Faith! Hark you, dare you stand by me.

Sir *Cha.* Dare I! Ay, to my last drop of Assurance, against all the insolent Airs of the proudest Beauty in Christendom.

L. *Mo.* Nay, then Defiance to her—We Two—Thou hast inspir'd me, I find my self as Valiant as a flatter'd Coward.

Sir *Cha.* Courage, my Lord—I'll warrant we beat her.

L. *Mo.* My Blood stirs at the very thought on't; I long to be engag'd.

Sir *Cha.* She'll certainly give Ground, when she once sees you are thoroughly provok'd.

L. *Mo.* Dear *Charles,* thou art a Friend indeed.

Enter a Servant.

Ser. Sir, my Lord *Foppington* gives his Service, and if your Honour's at leisure he'll wait on you as soon as he's dress'd.

L. *Mo.* Lord *Foppington!* is he in Town?

Sir *Cha.* Yes—I heard last Night he was come. Give my Service to his Lordship, and tell him I shall be glad he'll do me the Honour of his Company here at Dinner. *(Ex. Ser.)* We may have occasion for him in our Design upon Lady *Betty.*

L. *Mo.* What use can we make of him?

Sir *Cha.* We'll see when he comes, at least there's no Danger in him, not but I suppose you know he's your Rival.

L. *Mo.* Pshah! a Coxcomb.

Sir *Cha.* Nay, don't despise him neither—He's able to give you Advice; for tho' he's in Love with the same Woman, yet to him she has not Charms enough to give a Minutes Pain.

L. *Mo.* Prithee! What Sense has he of Love?

Sir *Cha.* Faith very near as much as a man of Sense ought to have; I grant you he knows not how to value a Woman truly deserving, but he has a pretty just Esteem for most Ladies about Town.

[374] L. Mo. P, p. 10. [380] A, Aires. [399] F, Pshaw! [402] A, minuits. C, D, E, F, minute's.

L. *Mo.* That he follows, I grant you—for he seldom visits any of Extraordinary Reputation.

Sir *Cha.* Have a Care, I have seen him at Lady *Betty Modish*'s.

L. *Mo.* To be laugh'd at.

Sir *Cha.* Don't be too confident of that, the Women now begin to laugh With him, not At him: For he really sometimes rallies his own Humour with so much Ease and Pleasantry, that a great many Women begin to think he has no Follies at all, and those he has, have been as much owing to his Youth, and a great Estate, as want of natural Wit: 'Tis true, he's often a Bubble to his Pleasures, but he has always been wisely vain enough to keep himself from being too much the Ladies Humble Servant in Love.

L. *Mo.* There indeed I almost envy him.

Sir *Cha.* The Easiness of his Opinion upon the Sex will go near to pique you—We must have him.

L. *Mo.* As you please—but what shall we do with our selves till Dinner?

Sir *Cha.* What think you of a Party at Picquet?

L. *Mo.* O! You are too hard for me.

Sir *Cha.* Fie! fie! What, when you play with his Grace.

L. *Mo.* Upon my soul, he gives me Three Points.

Sir *Cha.* Does he? Why then you shall give me but Two—Here, Fellow, get Cards. Allons!— *(Exeunt.*

ACT II.

SCENE I.

The Scene *Lady* BETTY MODISH'*s Lodgings.*

Enter Lady BETTY, *and Lady* EASY, *meeting.*

La. *Bet.* Oh! My Dear! I am overjoy'd to see you! I am strangely Happy to Day; I have just receiv'd my New Scarf from *London,* and you are most Critically come to give me your Opinion of it.

415 great. P, p. 11. 416 P, omits comma after has. 423 E, picque. 428 F, Fy! Fy! P, omits comma after what. 1 C, D, E, F, L. *Bet.,* troughout.

La. *Ea.* O! Your Servant, Madam; I am a very indifferent Judge, you know: what, is it with Sleeves?

La *Bet.* O 'tis impossible to tell you what it is!—'Tis all Extravagance both in Mode and Fancy, my Dear I believe there's Six Thousand Yards of Edging in it—Then such an Enchanting Slope from the Elbow—something so New, so Lively, so Noble, so Coquet and Charming—but you shall see it, my Dear—

La. *Ea.* Indeed I won't, my Dear; I am resolv'd to mortifie you for being so wrongly fond of a Trifle.

La. *Bet.* Nay now, my Dear, you are Ill-natur'd.

La. *Ea.* Why truly, I am half angry to see a Woman of your Sense, so warmly concern'd in the Care of her Outside; for when we have taken our best Pains about it, 'tis the Beauty of the alone that gives us Lasting Value.

La. *Bet.* Ah! My Dear, my Dear! You have been a married Woman to a fine Purpose indeed, that know so little of the Taste of Mankind: Take my Word, a new Fashion upon a fine Woman is often a greater Proof of her Value, than you are aware of.

La *Ea.* That I can't comprehend, for you see among the Men nothing's more ridiculous than a new Fashion, those of the first Sense are always the last that come into 'em.

La. *Bet.* That is, because the only Merit of a Man is his Sense; but doubtless the greatest Value of a Woman is her Beauty; an homely Woman at the Head of a Fashion would not be allow'd in it by the Men, and consequently not follow'd by the Women: So that to be successful in ones Fancy is an evident sign of ones being admir'd, and I always take Admiration for the best Proof of Beauty, and Beauty certainly is the Source of Power, as Power in all Creatures is the Heighth of Happiness.

La. *Ea.* At this rate you wou'd rather be thought Beautiful than Good?

La. *Bet.* As I had rather Command, than Obey: The wisest homely Woman can't make a Man of Sense of a Fool, but the veriest Fool of a Beauty shall make an Ass of a statesman; so that in short I can't see a Woman of Spirit has any Business

[10] F, Sloop from the Elbow. [11] F, Cocquet. [12] C, E, F, mortify. [19] La. Bet. P, p. 12. [31] C, E. F, one's. [32] C, D, E, F, one's. [34] D, E, height.

in this World, but to Dress— and make the Men like her.

La. *Ea.* Do you suppose this is a Principle the Men of Sense will admire you for?

La. *Bet.* I do suppose, that when I suffer any Man to like my Person he sha'nt dare to find Fault with my Principle.

La *Ea.* But Men of Sense are not so easily humbled.

La *Bet.* The easiest of any; one has Ten Thousand times the Trouble with a Coxcomb.

La. *Ea.* Nay, that may be; for I have seen you throw away more good Humour in hopes of a *Tendresse* from my Lord *Foppington,* who loves all Women alike, than wou'd have made my Lord *Morelove* perfectly happy, who loves only you.

La. *Bet.* The Men of Sense, my Dear, make the best Fools in the World, their Sincerity and good Breeding throws 'em so intirely into ones Power, and give one such an agreeable Thirst of using 'em ill, to Shew that Power—'tis impossible not to quench it.

La. *Ea.* But methinks My Lord *Morelove*'s Manner to You might move any Woman to a kinder sense of his merit.

La. *Bet.* Ay! But wou'd it not be hard, my Dear, for a poor weak Woman to have a Man of his Quality and Reputation in her Power, and not to let the World see him there? Wou'd any Creature sit New Dress'd all Day in her Closet? Cou'd you bear to have a sweet-fancy'd Suit, and never shew it at the Play or the Drawing-Room?

La. *Ea.* But one wou'd not ride in 't methinks, or harass it out, when there's no occasion.

La. *Bet.* Pooh! My Lord *Morelove*'s a meer *Indian* Damask, one can't wear him out; O'my Conscience I must give him to my Woman at last, I begin to be known by him: Had not I best leave him off, my Dear? For (poor Soul) I believe I have a little Fretted him of late.

La. *Ea.* Now 'tis to me Amazing, how a Man of his Spirit can bear to be us'd like a Dog for Four or Five Years together —but Nothing's a Wonder in Love; yet pray, when you found you cou'd not like him at first why did you ever encourage him?

[55] C, D, E, F, entirely. C, E, F, one's. D, F, gives. [59] A, sence. [62] C, D, and not let. [63] ture sit. P, p. 13. [64] F, fansy'd. [73] D, Now this to me.

La. *Bet.* Why, what wou'd you have one do? For my part I cou'd no more chuse a Man by my Eye than a Shoe, one must draw 'em on a little to see if they are right to ones Foot.

La. *Ea.* But I'd no more fool on with I Man I cou'd not like, than I'd wear a Shoe that pinch'd me.

La. *Bet.* Ay but then a poor Wretch tells one he'll widen 'em, or do any thing, and is so civil and silly, that one does not know how to turn such a Trifle, as a Pair or Shoes, or an Heart, upon a Fellow's Hands again.

La. *Ea.* Well! I confess you are very happily distinguish'd among most Women of Fortune, to have a Man of My Lord *Morelove*'s Sense and Quality so long and Honourably in love with you: For now a Days one hardly ever hears of such a Thing as a Man of Quality in love with the Woman he wou'd marry: To be in Love now is only having a Design upon a Woman, a modish way of declaring War against her Virtue, which they generally attack first, by Toasting up her Vanity.

La. *Bet.* Ay, but the World knows that is not the Case between my Lord and me.

La. *Ea.* Therefore I think you happy.

La. *Bet.* Now I don't see it; I'll swear I'm better pleas'd to know there are a great many foolish Fellows of Quality that take occasion to toast me frequently.

La. *Ea.* I vow I shou'd not thank any Gentleman for toasting me, and I have often wonder'd how a Woman of your Spirit cou'd bear a great many other Freedoms I have seen some Men take with you.

La. *Bet.* As how, my Dear—come, prithee be Free with me, for you must know I love dearly to hear my Faults—Who is 't you have observ'd to be too free with me?

La. *Ea.* Why, there's my Lord *Foppington:* Cou'd any Woman but You bear to see him with a respectful Fleer stare full in her Face, draw up his Breath, and cry—Gad, you're handsom.

La. *Bet.* My Dear—fine Fruit will have Flies about it; but, poor things, they do it no Harm: For, if you observe, People are

[78] E, F, choose. [79] C, D. F, one's. [89] D, E, F, now-a days. [97] P, See it, I'll swear. [104] P, La. Mo. [107] La. Ea. P, p. 14. [109] C, D, E, F, handsome. [111] C, are generally most apt.

always most apt to chuse that, that the Flies have been busie with, ha! ha!

La. *Ea.* Thou art a strange giddy Creature.

La. *Bet.* That may be, from so much Circulation of Thought, my Dear.

La. *Ea.* But my Lord *Foppington*'s married, and one wou'd not fool with him for his Lady's sake; it may make her uneasie, and—

La *Bet.* Poor Creature, her Pride indeed makes her carry it off without taking any Notice of it to me, tho' I know she hates me in her Heart, and I can't endure malicious People, so I us'd to dine there once a Week purely to give her Disorder. If you had but seen her when my Lord and I fool'd a little, the Creature look'd so Ugly.

La. *Ea.* But I shou'd not think my Reputation safe, my Lord *Foppington*'s a Man that talks often of his Amours, but seldom speaks of Favours that are refus'd him.

La. *Bet.* Pshah! will any thing a Man says make a Woman less agreeable? Will his Talking spoil ones Complexion, or put ones Hair out of order? And for Reputation—look you, my Dear, take it for a Rule, that as amongst the lower Rank of People no Woman wants Beauty that has Fortune, so amongst People of Fortune no Woman wants Virtue that has Beauty: But an Estate and Beauty join'd is of an unlimited—nay a Power Pontifical, makes one not only Absolute, but Infallible—A fine Woman's never in the Wrong, or if we were, 'tis not the Strength of a poor Creature's Reason that can unfetter him— O! how I love to hear a Wretch curse himself lor loving on, or now and then coming out with a—

"Yet, for the Plague of Human Race,
"This Devil has an Angel's Face.

La. *Ea.* At this rate, I don't see you allow Reputation to be at all Essential to a Fine Woman.

La *Bet.* Just as much as Honour to a Great Man: Power always is above Scandal: Don't you hear People say, the King of *France* owes most of his Conquests to Breaking his Word?

112 E, F, choose. C, F, busy. 118 C, F, uneasy. 129 F, Pshaw! 130 & 131 C, D, F, one's. 135 F, are of an unlimited... make. 138 A, Creatures.

and wou'd not the Confederates have a fine time on 't, if they were only to go to War with Reproaches? Indeed, my Dear, that Jewel Reputation is but a very fanciful business; One shall not see an Homely Creature in Town but wears it in her Mouth, as monstrously as the *Indians* do Bobs at their Lips, and it really becomes 'em just alike.

La. *Ea.* Have a care, my Dear, of being too eagerly Fond of Power: for nothing is more ridiculous than the Fall of Pride, and Woman's Pride at best may be suspected to be more a Distrust, than a real Contempt of Mankind: for when we have said all we can, a Deserving Husband is certainly our best Happiness; and I don't question but my Lord *Morelove's* Merit in a little time will make you think so too; for whatever Airs you give your self to the World, I am sure your Heart don't want good Nature.

La. *Bet.* You are mistaken, I am very ill-natur'd, tho' your good Humour won't let you see it.

La. *Ea.* Then, to give me a Proof on't, let me see you refuse to go immediately and dine with me, after I have promis'd Sir *Charles* to brlng you.

La *Bet.* Pray don't ask me.

La. *Ea.* Why?

La. *Bet.* Because, to let you see I hate good Nature, I'll go without Asking, that you mayn't have the Malice to say I did you a Favour.

La. *Ea.* Thou art a mad Creature. *(Exeunt.*

The SCENE *changes to Sir* Charles*'s Lodgings.*
Lord Morelove *and Sir* Charles *at Picquet.*

Sir *Cha.* Come, my Lord, one single Game for the Tout, and so have done.

Sir *Cha.* L. *Mo.* No, hang 'em, I have enough of 'em: Ill Cards are the dullest Company in the World—How much is it?

Sir *Cha.* Three Parties.

L, *Mo.* Fifteen Pound—very well.

(While L. Mo. *counts out his Mony a Servant gives Sir* Cha. *a Letter, which he reads to himself.*

150 F, fansyful. 150 Jewel. P, p. 15. 152 D, omits the. 154 C, D, F, my Dear, of trusting too far to Power alone. 171 D, F, *Exeunt arm in arm.* 178 C, E, F, money.

Sir *Cha. (To the Servant)* Give my Service; say I have Company dines with me; if I have time I'll call there in the Afternoen—ha! ha! ha!

L. *Mo.* What's the Matter?

Sir *Cha.* The Old Affair— My Lady *Graveairs.*

L. *Mo.* O! prithee how does that go forward?—here—

Sir *Cha.* As agreeably as a Chancery Suit: For now it's come to the intollerable Plague of my not being able to get rid on't; as you may see— *(Giving the Letter.)*

L. *Mo. (Reads.)* "Your Behaviour since I came to *Windsor*
"has convinc'd me of your Villany, without my being
"surpriz'd, or angry at it: I desire you would let me see
"you at my Lodgings immediately, where I shall have
"a better Opportunity to satisfie you, that I never can, or
"Positively will be, as I have been, Yours.

A very Whimsical Letter! Faith, I think she has hard luck with you; if a Man were oblig'd to have a Mistress, her Person and Condition seem to be cut out for the Ease of a Lover: For she's a Young, Handsome, Wild, Well-jointed Widow—But what's your Quarrel?

Sir *Cha* Nothing—she sees the Coolness happens to be first of my side, and her Business with me now, I suppose, is to convince me, how Heartily she's vex'd, that she was not before Hand with me.

L. *Mo.* Her Pride, and your Indifference must occasion a Pleasant Scene sure; what do you intend to do?

Sir *Cha.* Treat her with a Cool Familiar Air, till I pique her to forbid me her sight, and then take her at her Word.

L. *Mo.* Very Gallant and Provoking.

Enter a Servant.

Ser. Sir, my Lord *Foppington*'s come— *(Exit.*

Sir *Cha* O—now, my Lord, if you have a Mind to be let into the Mystery of making Love without Pain, here's one that's a Master of the Art, and shall declaim to you—My Dear

178 P, comma after Service. 179 P, with with, and comma after me. 183 C, D, F, go on? F, pr'ythee. 185 C, E, F, intolerable. 187 L. Mo. P, p. 16. 188 C, D, Villainy. 191 C, D, E, F, Opportunity to convince you. 196 C, E, F, well-jointured. 198 D, F, on my Side. 207 E. F, omit 's come. 209 C, E, F, My dear Lord Foppington.

Enter Lord FOPPINGTON.

Lord *Foppington!*

L. *Fop*. My Dear Agreeable! *Que Je t'embrasse! Pardi! Il y a cent anns, que Je ne T'ai veu*—my Lord, I am your Lordship's most obedient Humble Servant.

L. *Mo*. My Lord, I kiss your Hands—I hope we shall have you here some time; you seem to have laid in Stock of Health to be in at the Diversions of the Place—You look extreamly well.

L. *Fop*. To see ones Friends look so, my Lord, may easily give a *Vermeile* to ones Complexion.

Sir *Cha*. Lovers in Hope, my Lord, always have a visible *Brillant* in their Eyes and Air.

L. *Fop*. What dost thou mean, *Charles?*

Sir *Cha*. Come, come, my Lord, confess what really brought you to *Windsor,* now you have no Business here.

L. *Fop*. Why two Hours, and Six of the Best Nags in Christendom, or the Devil Drive me.

L. *Mo*. You make haste, my Lord.

L. *Fop*. My Lord, I always Fly when I pursue—But they are well Kept indeed—I love to have Creatures go as I bid 'em: You have seen 'em, *Charles,* but so has all the World—*Foppington*'s Long-Tails are known in every Road in *England*.

Sir *Cha*. Well, my Lord, but how came they to bring you this Road? You don't use to take these Irregular Jaunts without some Design in your Head of having more than Nothing to do.

L. *Fop*. Pshah! prithee Pax! *Charles,* thou know'st I am a Fellow *sans Consequence,* be where I will.

Sir *Cha*. Nay, nay, we must nave it—come, come, your Real Business here?

L. *Fop*. Why then, *Entre Nous,* there is a certain *Fille de Joye* about the Court here that loves Winning at Cards better than all the Fine Things I have been able to say to her, so I have brought an Odd Thousand Pound Bill in my Pocket, that I design

215 C, D, F, in a Stock. 216 C, D, F, extremely. 218 C, D, F, one's. 217 C omits, my Lord. 218 B. Vermeille. 222 C, D, F, omit, my Lord. 223 D, F, omit, here. 228 well Kept. P, p. 17. 234 C, D, Pshah! Pox! prithee. F, Pshaw! Pox! pr'ythee. 236 C, D, F, Nay, nay, this is too much among Friends, my Lord; come, come—we must have it, your real.

Tete à Tete to play off with her at Picquet, and now the Business is out.

Sir *Cha.* Ai! and a very Good Business too, my Lord.

L. *Fop.* If it be well done, *Charles.*

Sir *Cha.* That's as you Manage your Cards, my Lord.

L. *Mo.* This must be a Woman of some Consequence, by the Value you set upon her Favours.

Sir *Cha.* Pshah! Nothing's above the Price of a Fine Woman.

L. *Fop.* Nay look you, Gentlemen, the Price may not happen to be altogether so high neither: For, all this while, I fancy I know enough of the Game to make it but an even Bet, that I get her for Nothing.

L. *Mo.* How so, my Lord?

L. *Fop.* Because, if she Happens to lose a Good Sum to Me, I shall Buy her with her own Mony.

L. *Mo.* That's New, I confess.

L. *Fop.* You know, *Charles,* 'tis not Impossible but I may be Five Hundred Pound Deep with her, then Bills may fall short, and the Devil's in 't if I want Assurance to ask her to Pay me some Way, or other.

Sir *Cha.* And a Man must be a Churl indeed that won't take a Lady's Personal Security; hah! hah! ha!

S. *Fop.* Heh! heh! heh! Thou art a Devil, *Charles.*

L. *Mo.* Death! How happy is this Coxcomb! *(Aside.*

L. *Fop.* But to tell you the Truth, Gentlemen, I had another pressing Temptation, that brought me hither, which was—my Wife.

L. *Mo.* That's kind indeed: my Lady has been here this Fortnight, she'll be Glad to see you.

L. *Fop.* That I don't know; for I design this Afternoon to send her to *London.*

L. *Mo.* What! the same Day you Come, my Lord? That wou'd be Cruel.

L. *Fop.* Ay, but it will be mighty Convenient, for she is positively of no manner of Use in my Amours.

242 D, Piquet. 247 C, D, F, omit, some. 249 C, D, F, Sir Cha. O! Nothing's. 251 C omits, all this while. E, fansie. F, fansy. 252 C omits that. E, F, Bett, I get. 255 C, happen. 256 D, Money. 265 P, Coxcomb? 268 C, D, F, this Month. 272 L. Mo. P, p. 18. D, F, would.

L. *Mo.* That's your Fault, the Town thinks her a very Deserving Woman.

L. *Fop.* If she were a Woman of the Town, perhaps I shou'd think so too: But she happens to be my Wife, and when a Wife is once given to deserve more than her Husband can Pay, in my Mind she has no Merit at all.

L. *Mo.* She's extreamly well bred, and of a very Prudent Conduct.

L. *Fop.* Um—Ay the Woman's Proud enough.

L. *Mo.* And to This, all the World allows her Handsom.

L. *Fop.* The World's very Civil, my Lord; and I should take it as a Favour done to me, if they cou'd find an Expedient to unmarry the Poor Woman from the only Man in the World that can't think her Handsom.

L. *Mo.* I believe there are a Great many in the World that are sorry 'tis not in their Power to Unmarry her.

L. *Fop.* I am a Great many in the World's very Humble Servant, and whenever they find 'tis in their Power, their High and Mighty Wisdoms may command me at a Quarter of an hour's Warning.

L. *Mo.* Pray, my Lord, what did you marry for?

L. *Fop.* To pay my Debts at Play, and disinherit my Younger Brother.

L. *Mo.* But there are some Things due to a Wife.

L. *Fop.* And there are some Debts I don't care to pay—to both which I plead Husband, and my Lord.

L. *Mo.* If I shou'd do so, I shou'd expect to have my own Coach stopt in the Street, and to meet my Wife with the Windows up in a Hackny.

L. *Fop.* Then wou'd I put in Bail, and order a separate Maintenance.

L. *Mo.* So pay Double the Sum of the Debt, and be Married for Nothing.

L. *Fop.* Now I think Deferring a Dun, and getting Rid of

[280] C, D, F, Husband's Inclinations can. [282] C, F, extremely. C, of very. [284] P, comma after enough. [285] D, E, F, Add to This. D, E, handsome. [286] C, F, extremely Civil; D, E, extreamly. [289] D, E, handsome. [302] D, I'd expect. E, F, should expect. [307] F, marry'd.

ones Wife, are Two the most Agreeable Sweets in the Liberties of an *English* Subject.

L. *Mo.* If I were married I wou'd as soon part from my Estate, as my Wife.

L. *Fop.* Now I wou'd not, Sun-burn me if I wou'd.

L. *Mo.* Death! my Lord, but since you are thus indifferent, why wou'd you needs marry a Woman of so much Merit? Cou'd not you have laid out your Spleen upon some Ill-natur'd Shrew, that wanted the Plague of an Ill-Husband, and have let Her alone to some Plain, Honest Man of Quality that wou'd have deserv'd her?

L. *Fop.* Why faith, my Lord, that might have been consider'd, but I really grew so Passionately Fond of her Fortune, that, Curse catch me, I was quite Blind to the rest of her Good Qualities: For to tell you the Truth, if it were possible the Old Putt of a Peer cou'd have toss'd her into t'other Five Thousand Pound, for 'em, by my Consent, she shou'd have relinquisht her Merit and Virtues to any of her Younger Sisters.

Sir *Cha.* Ay, ay, my Lord, Virtues in a Wife are Good for nothing but to make her Proud, and put the World in Mind of her Husband's Faults.

L. *Fop.* Right, Charles: And strike me Blind, but the Women of Virtue are now grown such Ideots in Love, They expect of a Man, just as they do of a Coach-horse, that One's Appetite, like t'other's Flesh, shou'd increase by Feeding.

Sir *Cha.* Right, my Lord, and don't consider that *toutjours Chapons bouillés* will never do with an *English* Stomach.

L. *Fop.* Ha! ha! ha! To tell you the Truth, *Charles,* I have known so much of that sort of Eating, that I now think, for an Hearty Meal, no Wild-Fowl in *Europe* is Comparable to a Joint of *Banstead* Mutton.

L. *Mo.* How do you mean?

L. *Fop.* Why, that for my Part, I had rather have a Plain Slice of my Wife's Woman, than my Guts full of e'er an Ortolan Dutchess in Christendom.

[310] C, F, one's. [312] F, marry'd. [315] C, D, F, Death! but. D, F, indifferent, my Lord. F, would. [319] Plain. P, p. 19. [321] P omits, 50. [323] C, D, F, if it had been. [324] E, tossed me in t'other. P, omits comma. C, omits, Pound. [325] E, F, relinquish'd. [342] A, Ortollan. C, Duchess.

L. *Mo.* But I thought, my Lord, your Business now at *Windsor* had been your Design upon a Woman of Quality.

L. *Fop.* That's true, my Lord, tho' I don't think your Fine Lady the Best Dish my self, yet a Man of Quality can't be without such Things at his Table.

L. *Mo.* O! then you only desire the Reputation of Having an Affair with her?

L. *Fop.* I think the Reputation is the most Inviting Part of an Amour with most Women of Quality.

L. *Mo.* Why so, my Lord?

L. *Fop.* Why who the Devil wou'd run thro' all the Degrees of Form and Ceremony, that lead one up to the last Favour, if it were not for the Reputation of Understanding the Nearest Way to get over the Difficulty?

L. *Mo.* But, my Lord, since the World sees you make so little of the Difficulty, does not the Reputation of your being too General an Undertaker frighten the Women from Engaging with you? for they say no Man can love but One at a time.

L. *Fop.* That's just One more than ever I came up to: For, stap my Breath, if ever I lov'd One in my life.

L. *Mo.* How do you get 'em then?

L. *Fop.* Why sometimes as they get other People, I dress, and let them get me: Or, if that won't do, as I got my Title, I buy 'em.

L. *Mo.* But how can you, that Profess Indifference, think it worth your while to come so often up to the Price of a Woman of Quality?

L. *Fop.* Because you must know, my Lord, that most of 'em begin Now to come down to Reason, I mean, those that are to be had, for some die Fools: But with the Wiser sort, 'tis not of late so very Expensive; now and then a *Partie Quarrée,* a Jaunt or two in an Hack to an *Indian* House, a little *China,* an Odd Thing for a Gown, or so, and in Three Days after you meet her at the Conveniency of Trying in on *Chez Mademoiselle d'Epingle.*

[344] C, your chief Business. [350] C, F, of an Affair. [358. 359] C, F, omit since the World sees you make so little of the Difficulty. [359] C, F, being so General. [362] L. Fop. P, p. 20. C, F, Stop my. [374] A, C, D, E, F, Partie Quarrie. [376] C, so, in Three. [377] C, D, F, Trying it Chez. A, madmoiselle. E, F, madamoiselle.

Sir *Cha.* Ay, ay, my Lord, and when you are there, you know, what between a little Chat, a Dish of Tea, Madmoiselle's Good Humour, and a *Petit Chanson,* or two; the Devil's in 't if a Man can't fool away the Time, 'till he sees how it looks upon her by Candle-light, ha! ha!

L. *Fop.* Heh! Heh! Well said, *Charles,* I'gad I fancy thee and I have unlac'd many a Reputation there—Your Great Lady is as soon undrest as her Woman, ha! ha!

L. *Mo.* I cou'd never find it so; the Shame, or Scandal of a Repulse, always made me afraid of Attempting a Woman of Condition.

Sir *Cha.* Ha! Ha! I gad, my Lord, you deserve to be ill us'd, your Modesty's enough to Spoil any Woman in the World; but my Lord and I understand the Sex a little better, we see plainly that Women are only Cold, as some Men are Brave, from the Modesty or Fear of those that attack 'em.

L. *Fop.* Right, *Charles,* a Man shou'd no more give up his Heart to a Woman, than his Sword to a Bully, they are Both as Insolent as the Devil after it.

Sir *Cha.* How do you like that, my Lord?

(Aside to L.Mo.

L. *Mo.* Faith, I envy him.—But, my Lord, suppose your Inclination shou'd Stumble upon a Woman truly Virtuous, wou'd not a Formal Repulse from such an One put you strangely out of Countenance?

L. *Fop.* Not at all, my Lord, for if a Man don't mind a Box on the Ear in a fair Struggle with a Fresh Country Girl, why the Devil shou'd he be concern'd at an Impertinent Frown for an Attack upon a Woman of Quality?

L. *Mo.* Then you have no Notion of a Lady's Cruelty?

L. *Fop.* Ha! ha! let me Blood, if I think there's a greater Jest in Nature. I am ready to Crack my Guts with laughing to see a senseless Flirt, because the Creature happens to have a little Pride that she calls Virtue about her, give her self all the

379 E, F madamoiselle. A, mademoiselle; Canson. 382 C, D, F omit, ha! ha! 383 E, fansy. 385 D, undress'd. 385 C omits ha! ha! 389 F, I'gad. 399 F, Should. D, would. 400 C, D, a Severe Repulse. 403 D, F, o'the Ear. F, Why the Duce. 407 L. Fop. P, p. 21.

Insolent Airs of Resentment and Disdain to an Honest Fellow, that all the while does not care three Pinches of Snuff, if she and her Virtue were to run with their last Favours through the First Regiment of Guards—Ha! ha! it puts me in Mind of an Affair of mine, so Impertinent—

L. *Mo.* O! that's impossible, my Lord, pray let's hear it.

L. *Fop.* Why I happen'd once to be well in a certain Man of Quality's Family, and his Wife lik'd me.

L. *Mo.* How do you know she lik'd you?

L. *Fop.* Why, from the very Moment I told her I lik'd her, she never durst trust her self at the End of the Room with me.

L. *Mo.* That might be her not liking you.

L. *Fop.* My Lord—Women of Quality don't use to speak the thing plain—but to satisfie you, that I did not want Encouragement, I never came there in my Life, that she did not immediately Smile, and Borrow my Snuff-Box.

L. *Mo.* She lik'd your Snuff, at least—Well, but how did she use you?

L. *Fop.* By all that's Infamous she Jilted me.

L. *Mo.* How? Jilt you?

L. *Fop.* Ay, Death's Curse, she Jilted me.

L. *Mo.* Pray let's hear.

L. *Fop.* For when I was pretty well convinc'd she had a Mind to me, I one Day made her a Hint of an Appointment; upon which, with an Insolent Frown in her Face (that made her look as Ugly as the Devil) she told me, that if ever I came thither again, her Lord should know that she had forbidden me the House before; ha! ha! Did you ever hear of such a Slut?

Sir *Cha.* Intolerable!

L. *Mo.* But how did her Answer agree with you?

L. *Fop.* Passionately well—For I star'd full in her Face, and Busted out a laughing; at which she turn'd upon her Heel, gave a Crack with her Fan like a Coach-whip, and Bridled out of the Room with the Air and Complexion of an Incens'd Turkey-Cock.

L. *Mo.* What did you then? *(A Servant whispers Sir Charles.*

[417] F, to be very well. [424] E, F, Satisfy. [425] C, D, F, Life, but she did immediately. [438] D omits, ha! ha! [439] D, intollerable. [441] F, L. Fop. O Passionately B, bursted. F, burst.

L. *Fop.* I—Look'd after her, Gap'd, threw up the Sash, and fell a Singing out of the Window, so that you see, my Lord, while a Man is not in Love, there's no great Affliction in Missing ones way to a Woman.

Sir *Cha.* Ay, ay, you talk this very well, my Lord; but now let's see how you dare behave your self upon Action—Dinner's serv'd, and the Ladies stay for us—There's one within, that has been too Hard for as Brisk a Man as your self.

L. Mo. I know whom you mean—Have a Care, my Lord, she'll prove your Courage for you.

L. Fop. Will she! then she's an Undone Creature: For let me tell you, Gentlemen, Courage is the whole Mystery of Love, and of more Use than Conduct is in War; for the Bravest Fellow in *Europe* may beat his Brains out against the stubborn Walls of a Town—But

"Women, born to be Controll'd
"Stoop to the Forward, and the Bold. *(Exeunt.*

Act III

The Scene Continues.

Enter Lord Morelove *and Sir* Charles.

Lord *Morelove.*

So! Did not I bear up bravely?

Sir *Cha.* Admirably! With the Best bred Insolence in Nature, you insulted like a Woman of Quality, when her Country-bred Husband's Jealous of her in the wrong Place.

L. *Mo.* Ha! ha! Did you Observe, when I first came into the Room, how carelesly she Brush'd her Eyes over me, and when the Company saluted me, stood all the while with her Face to the Window? ha! ha!

Sir *Cha.* What Astonish'd Airs she gave her self, when you ask'd her what made her so grave upon her Old Friends?

L. *Mo.* And when ever I offer'd any thing in talk, what Affected

449 C, E, F, one's. 450 Sir Cha. P, p. 22. 452 F, omits that. 454 D, F, I guess who you mean. 457 F, of making Love. 6 B, C, D, E, F, carelessly. 10 F, whenever.

Care she took to Direct her Observations of it to a third Person?

Sir *Cha.* I observ'd she did not Eat above the Rump of a Pidgeon all Dinner Time.

L. *Mo.* And how she Colour'd when I told her her Ladyship had lost her Stomach.

Sir *Cha.* If you keep your Temper she's Undone.

L. *Mo.* Provided she sticks to her Pride, I believe I may.

Sir *Cha.* Ah! Never fear her, I warrant in the Humour she is in, she would as soon part with her Sense of Feeling.

L. *Mo.* Well! What's to be done next?

Sir *Cha.* Only observe her Motions; for by her Behaviour at Dinner, I am sure she designs to Gall you with my Lord *Foppington,* if so you must even stand her Fire, and then Play my Lady *Graveairs* upon her, whom I'll immediately Pique, and prepare for your Purpose.

L. *Mo.* I understand you—the Properest Woman in the World too; for she'll certainly Encourage the least Offer from me, in hopes of Revenging her late Slights upon you.

Sir *Cha.* Right, and the very Encouragement she gives you, at the same time will give me a Pretence to Widen the Breach of my Quarrel to her.

L. *Mo.* Besides, *Charles,* I own I am fond of any Attempt that will forward a Misunderstanding there, for your Lady's sake; A Woman so truly Good in her Nature, ought to have something more from a Man, than bare Occasions to Prove her Goodness.

Sir *Cha.* Why then upon Honour, my Lord, to give you a Proof that I am Positively the Best Husband in the World, my Wife—never yet found me out.

L. *Mo.* That may be her being the Best Wife in the World: She, may be, won't find you out.

Sir *Cha.* Nay, if she won't tell a Man of his Faults, when she sees 'em, how the Duce should he mend 'em? But however you see I am going to leave 'em off as fast as I can.

L. *Mo.* Being tir'd of a Woman is indeed a pretty tolerable Assurance of a Man's not designing to Fool on with her—Here

[14] F, Pigeon. [23] Sir Cha. P, p. 23. [30] B, D, E, F, omit, late. [39] C, you Proof.

she comes, and, if I don't mistake, Brim full of Reproaches—You can't take her in a better Time—I'll leave you.

Enter Lady Graveairs.

L. *Mo.* Your Ladyship's most Humble Servant; is the Company Broke up, pray?

La. *Gra.* No, my Lord, they were just talking of Basset; my Lord *Foppington* has a Mind to Tally, if your Lordship would encourage the Table.

L. *Mo.* O Madam, with all my Heart! But Sir *Charles,* I know, is hard to be got to it; I'll leave your Ladyship to prevail with him.

(Exit Lord Morelove.

(Sir Charles *and Lady* Graveairs *salute Coldly, and Trifle some time before they speak.*

La. *Gra.* Sir *Charles,* I sent you a Note this Morning—

Sir *Cha.* Yes, Madam, but there were some Passages I did not expect from your Ladyship; you seem'd to Tax me with things that—

La. *Gra.* Look you, Sir, 'tis not at all Material whether I tax'd you with any thing or no: I don't in the least desire to hear you clear your self, upon my Word you may be very easie as to that Matter; for my Part I am mighty well satisfy'd, that things are as they are; all that I have to say to you is—that you need not give your self the Trouble to call at my Lodgings this Afternoon, if you should have Time, as you were pleas'd to send me Word—and so your Servant, Sir, that's all. *(Going.*

Sir *Cha.* Hold, Madam.

La. *Gra.* Look you, Sir *Charles,* 'tis not your calling me back that will signifie any thing, I can assure you.

Sir *Cha.* Why this Extraordinary Haste, Madam?

La. *Gra.* In short, Sir *Charles,* I have taken a great many things from you of late, that you know I have often told you I wou'd Positively bear no longer: But I see things are in vain, and the more People strive to Oblige People, the less they are thank'd for't: And since there must be an End of ones Ridiculous-

49 E, F, Brim-full. 53 E, they are just. 62 you with, P, p. 24. 65 C. F, satisfy'd, Things are as they are; all I have. 67 P, need give. 72 C, signify. 78 C, D, E, F, one's.

ness one time or other, I don't see any time so proper as the Present, and therefore, Sir, I desire you would dispose things accordingly—your Servant—

Sir *Cha.* Nay, Madam, let's start Fair however; you ought at least to stay 'till I have got it in my Head too, and then, if we must part—

Affectedly

Adieu you silent Grots, and shady Groves,
Ye soft Amusements of our Growing Loves;
Adieu the whisper'd Sighs, that Fann'd the Fire,
And all the Thrilling Joys of young Desire.

La. *Gra.* O mighty well, Sir: I am very glad we are at last come to a Right Understanding, the only way I have long wish'd for; not but I'd have you to know I see your Design through all this Painted Ease of Resignation: I know you'd give your Eyes to make me Uneasie now—

Sir *Cha.* O Fie, Madam, upon my Word I would not make you Uneasie if it were in my Power.

La. *Gra.* O dear Sir, you need not take such Care, upon my Word you'll find I can part with you without the least Disorder—I'll try at least, and so once more, and for ever, Sir, your Servant. Not but you must give me leave to tell you, as my last Thought of you too, that I do think—you are a Villain—

(Exit hastily.

Sir *Cha.* O your very Humble Servant, Madam—*(Bowing low.)* What a Charming Quality is a Woman's Pride, that's strong enough to refuse a Man her Favours—when he's weary of 'em—Ah! *(Lady* Graveairs *returns.*

La. *Gra.* Look you, Sir *Charles*—don't presume upon the Easiness of my Temper: For to Convince you that I am Positively in Earnest in this Matter, I desire you would let me have what Letters you have had of mine since you came to *Windsor,* and I expect you'll return the rest, as I will yours, as soon as we come to *London.*

Sir *Cha.* Upon my Faith, Madam, I never keep any, I always put Snuff in 'em, and so they wear out.

[80] P, would things. A, you'd dispose. C, E, you'd think of things. D, F, Servant *(Going, he holds her).* [83] C, F, till I am as ready as your Ladyship, and then. [85] C, D, F, ye silent. [92] D, all your Painted. [93] C, F, Uneasy. [94] F, fy. [95] F, Uneasy. [103] enough. P, p. 25.

La *Gra.* Sir *Charles,* I must have 'em; for Positively I won't stir without 'em.

Sir *Cha.* Ha! Then I must be Civil, I see. Perhaps, Madam, I have no Mind to part with them or you.

La *Gra.* Look you, Sir, all those sort of things are in vain, now there's an End of every thing between us—If you say you won't give 'em, I must even get 'em as well as I can—

Sir *Cha.* Ha! That won't do then, I find.

La *Gra.* Who's there? Mrs. *Edging.*—Your keeping a Letter, Sir, won't keep me I'll assure you.

Enter Edging.

Edg. Did your Ladyship call me, Madam?

La. *Gra.* Ay, Child, pray do me the Favour to fetch my Hood and Scarf out of the Dining-Room.

Edg. Yes, Madam –

Sir *Cha.* O! Then there's Hope again.

Edg. Ha! She looks as if my Master had Quarrell'd with her; I hope she's going away in a Huff—she sha'nt stay for her Scarf, I warrant her— This is Pure. *(Aside.* *Exit.*

(After some Pause Lady Graveairs *speaks.*

La. *Gra.* Pray, Sir *Charles,* before I go give me leave now, after all, to ask you why have us'd me thus?

Sir *Cha.* What is it you call Usage, Madam?

La. *Gra.* Why then, since you will have it, how comes it you have been so grossly Careless and Neglectful of me of late: Only tell me seriously wherein I have deserv'd it?

Sir *Cha.* Why then seriously, Madam—

Re-enter Edging.

We are Interrupted—

Edg. Here's your Ladyship's Scarf, Madam.

La *Gra.* Thank you, Mrs. *Edging*—O law! Pray will you let some Body get me a Chair to the Door.

114 C, D, E, I see. *(Aside)* Perhaps. 118 D, E, F, e'en. 119 D, I find. *(aside).* 120 P prints, Keeping Letter, but there is a space for a. A, Keeping Letter. B, Keeping Letters. P, comma after there. 125 C. E, fetch my Scarf. 127 C, E, F, again. *(Aside).* 128 E, quarrel'd. 129 A, E, shan't. 130 C, E, F, Exit Smiling. 136 A, D, grosly. 137 C, D, deserv'd this? 141 L. Gra. P, p. 26.

Edg. Humh! She might have told me that at first, if she had been in such Haste to go— *(Exit.*

La. *Gra.* Now, Sir.

Sir *Cha.* Why then seriously, I say, I am of late grown so very Lazy in my Pleasures, that I had rather lose a Woman, than go through the Plague and Trouble of having or keeping her; and to be free, I have found so much even in my Acquaintance with you, whom I confess to be a Mistress in the Art of Pleasing, that I am from henceforth resolv'd to follow no Diversion that Rises above the Degree of an Amusement—and that Woman that Expects I should make her my Business; why—like my Business, is then in a fair way of being forgot: When once she comes to Reproach me with Vows, and Usage, and Stuff, I had as lieve hear her talk of Bills, Bonds, and Ejectments, her Passion becomes as troublesome as a Law suit, and I would as soon Converse with my Sollicitor—In short, I shall never care Six Pence for any Woman that won't be Obedient.

La. *Gra.* I'll swear, Sir, you have a very free way of treating People; I am Glad I am so well acquainted with your Principles however; and you'd have me Obedient?

Sir *Cha.* Why not? My Wife's so, and I think she has as much Pretence to be Proud, as your Ladyship.

La. *Gra.* Lard! is there no Chair to be had, I wonder?

Enter Edging.

Edg. Here's a Chair, Madam.

La. *Gra.* 'Tis very well, Mrs *Edging:* Pray will you let some Body get me a Glass of Fair Water.

Edg. Hah! Her Huff's almost over, I suppose. I see he's a Villain still. *(Exit.*

La. *Gra.* Well, that was the prettiest Fancy about Obedience sure that ever was—Certainly a Woman of Condition must be infinitely Happy under the Dominion of so Generous a Lover! But how came you to forget Kicking and Whipping all this while;

143 C, E, that before, if. 146 C omits, why. 156 C, F, no Pleasure that. 157 C, D, F, of Amusement. 161 A, live. C, E, F, lief. 163 D, E. F, Solicitor. 167 D, have me be Obedient? 173 P, Mr. *Edging*. 175 C, he is.

methinks you shou'd not have left so fashionable an Article out of your Scheme of Government.

Sir *Cha.* Um! no, there's too much trouble in that, tho' I have known 'em of Admirable Use in the Reformation of some Humoursome Gentlewomen.

La. *Gra.* But one thing more, and I have done—Pray what Degree of Spirit must the Lady have, that is to make her self Happy under so much Freedom, Order and Tranquility?

Sir *Cha.* O! she must at least have as much Spirit as your Ladyship, or she'd give me no Pleasure in breaking it.

La. *Gra.* O! that would be troublesome—No, you had better take one that's broken to your Hand; there are such Souls to be hir'd, I believe; things that will Rub your Temples in an Evening 'till you fall fast a-sleep in their Laps, Creatures too that think their Wages their Reward; I fancy, at last, that will be the Best Method for the Lazy Passion of a Marry'd Man, that has out-liv'd his any other Sense of Gratification.

Sir *Cha.* Look you, Madam, I have told you that Reproaches will never do your Business with me: I have lov'd you very well a great while; now you would have me love you better, and longer, which is not in my Power to do, and I don't think there's any Plague upon Earth like a Dun, that comes for more Mony than one's ever likely to be Able to pay.

La *Gra.* A Dun! Do you take me for a Dun, Sir? Do I come a Dunning to you? *(Walks in an Heat.*

Sir *Cha.* S't! Don't expose yourself—Here's Company.

La *Gra.* I care not—A Dun!—You shall see, Sir, I can Revenge an Affront, tho' I despise the Wretch that offers it—A Dun; O! I could die with laughing at the Fancy. *(Exit.*

Sir *Cha.* So! She's in Admirable Order—Here comes my Lord, and I'm afraid in the very Nick of his Occasion for her.

Enter Lord Morelove.

L. *Mo.* O *Charles!* Undone again! All's Lost and Ruin'd.

Sir *Cha.* What's the matter, now?

[185] B, Humoursom. [186] La. Gra. P, p. 27. [191] C, D, E, F, No! that would be troublesome—you had. [198] C, E, F, omit, I have . . . with me. [203] C, E, money. [206] C, D, E, F, H'st.

L. *Mo.* I have been Playing the Fool yonder even to Contempt, my senseless Jealousie has confess'd a Weakness I never shall forgive my self—She has Insulted on it to that Degree too, I can't bear the Thought—O *Charles!* this Devil still is Mistress of my Heart, and I could dash my Brains to think how grossly too I've let her know it.

Sir *Cha.* Ah! How it would Tickle her if she saw you in this Condition: Ha! ha! ha!

L. *Mo.* Prithee don't Torture me: Think of some Remedy for present Ease, or I shall Burst—

Sir *Cha.* Well, well, let's hear pray what has she done to you?

L. *Mo.* Why ever since I left you she treated me with so much Coolness and ill Humour, and that Thing of a Lord with so much laughing Ease, such an acquainted, such a spiteful Familiarity, that she at last saw and triumph'd in my Uneasiness.

Sir *Cha.* Well! and so you left the Room in a Pet?

L. *Mo.* O worse, worse still! for at last, with half Shame and Anger in my Looks, I thrust my self before my Lord, press'd her by the Hand, and in a Whisper Trembling begg'd her, in Pity of her self and me, to shew her good Humour only where she knew it was truly Valued, at which she broke from me with a Cold Smile, sate her down by the Peer, whisper'd him, and Burst into a loud Laughter in my Face.

Sir *Cha.* Ha! ha! then would I have given Fifty Pound to have seen your Face: Why what, in the Name of Common Sense, had you to do with Humility? Will you never have enough on 't? Death! 'twas setting a lighted Match to Gun-powder to blow your self up.

L. *Mo.* I see my Folly now, *Charles;* but what shall I do with the Remains of Life that she has left me?

Sir *Cha.* O throw it at her Feet by all means, put on your Tragedy Face, catch fast hold of her Petticoat, whip out your Handkercher, and in point Blank Verse desire her, one way or other, to make an End of the Business.

216 C, F. Jealousy. 219 F, I have. D, grosly. 223 E, F, Pr'ythee. C, of some present. 225 D, E, F, you? ha! ha! 227 E, F, and ill Nature. 229 liarity. P, p. 28. 229 C, E, F, that at the last she saw. 230 E, F, Pet? ha! 232 C, D, F, between my Lord and her. 236 A, C, E, F, sat. 239 F, why, what. 246 C, E, F, handkerchief.

L. *Mo*. What a Fool dost thou make me? *(Smiling.*

Sir *Cha*. I only shew you, as you come out of her Hands, my Lord.

L. *Mo*. How Contemptibly have I behav'd my self?

Sir *Cha*. That's according as you Bear her Behaviour.

L. *Mo*. Bear it, no—I thank thee, Charles, thou hast wak'd me now—and if I bear it—What have you done with my Lady *Graveairs?*

Sir *Cha*. Your Business I believe—She's ready for you, she's just gone down Stairs, and if you don't make haste after her, I expect her back again, with a Knife or a Pistol, presently.

L. *Mo*. I'll go this Minute.

Sir *Cha*. No, stay a little, here comes my Lord; we'll see what we can get out of him first.

L. *Mo*. Methinks I now could laugh at her.

Enter Lord Foppington.

L. *Fop*. Nay, prithee, Sir *Charles,* let's have a little of thee—We have been so *Chagrin* without thee, that, stap my Breath, the Ladies are gone half a-sleep to Church for want of thy Company.

Sir *Cha*. That's hard indeed, while your Lordship was among 'em: Is Lady *Betty* gone too?

L. *Fop*. She was just upon the Wing: But I caught her by the Snuff-Box, and she pretends to stay to see if I'll give it again, or no.

L. *Mo*. Death! 'tis that I gave her, and the only Present she ever would receive from me—Ask him how he came by it? *(Aside to S.* Cha.

Sir *Cha*. Prithee don't be Uneasie—Dit she give it you, my Lord?

L. *Fop*. Fait, *Charles,* I can't say she did, or she did Not; but we were Playing the Fool, and I took it—*a la*—Pshah! I can't tell thee in *French* neither, but *Horace* touches it to a Nicety, 'twas—*Pignus Direptum Male Pertinaci.*

L. *Mo*. So! but I must bear it—If your Lordship has a Mind to the Box, I'll stand by you in the Keeping of it.

[248] C, D, E, F, *In a whining tone* instead of *Smiling*. [257] P, hast. [262] D. Methinks now I could. [264] F, prythee. [265] F, stop. [270] C, F, give it her. [274] F, Prythee. [274] C, F, Uneasy. [275] L. Fop. P, p. 29.

L. *Fop.* My Lord, I am Passionately Oblig'd to you, but I am afraid I can't Answer your Hazarding so much of the Lady's Favour.

L. *Mo.* Not at all, my Lord: 'Tis Possible I may not have the same Regard to her Frown that your Lordship has.

L. *Fop.* *(Aside.)* That's Bite, I'm sure, I know he'd give a Joint of his little Finger to be as well with her as I am—But here she comes! *Charles,* stand by me—Must not a Man be a Vain Coxcomb now, to think this Creature follow'd one?

Sfr *Cha.* O! Nothing so Plain, my Lord.

L. *Fop.* Flattering Devil!—

Enter Lady Betty.

La. *Bet.* Pshah! my Lord *Foppington*! Prithee don't play the Fool now, but give me my Snuff-Box: Sir *Charles,* help me to take it from him. *(Goes to L.* Fop.

Sir *Cha.* You know, I hate Trouble, Madam.

La. *Bet.* Pooh! you'll make me stay 'till Prayers are half over now.

L. *Fop.* If you'll promise me not to go Church I'll give it you.

La *Bet.* I'll promise Nothing at all, for Positively I will have it. *(Struggles with him.*

L. *Fop.* Then Comparatively I won't Part with it. *(Struggling with her.*

La. *Bet.* O you Divil! you have Kill'd my Arm! Oh! Well seriously, if you'll let me have it I'll give you a Better.

L. *Mo.* O *Charles!* that has a View of Distant Kindness in it. *(Aside to Sir* Cha.

L. *Fop.* Nay now I keep it Superlatively, I find there's a secret Value in it.

La *Bet.* O Dismal! upon my Word, I am only asham'd to give it you, do you think I would offer such an Odious-Fancy'd Thing to any Body I had the least Value for?

Sir *Cha.* Now it Comes a little Nearer, methinks it does not seem to be any Kindness at all. *(Aside to L.* Mo.

282 F, I cannot. 286 F, That's a Bite. C, F, omit I know. D, Joynt. 287 C, D, F, after I am *(aside).* 290 D, F, O! omitted. 293 E, F, Pr'ythee, 295 C, Stage-direction omitted. 303 C, D, F, seriously, omitted. 308 E, F, fansy'd.

L. *Fop.* Why really, Madam, upon second View it has not extreamly the Mode of a Lady's Utensil; are you sure it never held any thing but Snuff!

La. *Bet.* O! you Monster!

L. *Fop.* Nay, I only ask, because it seems to me to have very much the Air and Fancy of Monsieur *Smoakantsot*'s Tobacco-box.

L. *Mo.* I can Bear no more.

Sir *Cha.* Why don't then; I'll step in to the Company, and return to your Relief, when there's Occasion. *(Exit Sir* Cha.

L. *Mo.* (*To L.* Bet.) Come, Madam, will your Ladyship give me leave to End the Difference?—Since the Slightness of the Thing may let you bestow it without any Mark of Favour, shall I beg it of your Ladyship?

La. *Bet.* O my Lord! no Body sooner—I beg you give it my Lord.

(Looking very earnestly upon L. Fop. *who smiling gives it to L.* Mo. *and then Bows gravely to her.*

L. *Mo.* Only to have the Honour of Restoring it to your Lordship, and if there be any other Trifle of mine your Lordship has a Fancy to, tho' it were a Mistress, I don't know any Person in the World, that has so Good a Claim to my Resignation.

L. *Fop.* O my Lord, this Generosity will distract me.

L. *Mo.* My Lord, I do you but common Justice; But from your Conversation, I had never known the true Value of the Sex: You positively Understand 'em the Best of any Man Breathing, and therefore I think every One of Common Prudence ought to resign to you.

L. *Fop.* Then positively your Lordship's the most Obliging Person in the World, for I'm sure your Judgment can never like any Woman that is not the Finest Creature in the Universe. *(Bowing to L.* Bet.

L. *Mo.* O! Your Lordship does me too much Honour: I have the Worst Judgment in the World, no Man has been more deceiv'd in it.

L. *Fop.* Then your Lordship, I presume, has been apt to chuse in a Mask, or by Candle-light.

313 F, extremely. 319 Sir Cha. P, p. 30. P, comma after then. 320 C, D, F, Relief, immediately. 327 C, F, *earnestly on.* 337 C, omits and. 345 E, choose.

L. *Mo.* In a Mask indeed, my Lord, and of all Masks the most Dangerous.

L. *Fop.* Pray what's that, my Lord?

L. *Mo.* A. Bare Face.

L. *Fop.* Your Lordship will pardon me, if I don't so readily Comprehend How a Woman's Bare Face can hide her Face.

L. *Mo.* It often hides her Heart, my Lord, and therefore I think it a more Dangerous Mask than a Peice of Velvet: That's rather a Mark, than a Disguise of an Ill Woman: But the Mischiefs skulking behind a Beauteous Form give no Warning, they are always Sure, Fatal, and Innumerable.

La. *Bet.* O Barbarous Aspersion! My Lord *Foppington,* have you Nothing to say for the poor Women?

L. *Fop.* I must confess, Madam, nothing of this Nature ever Happen'd in my Course of Amours: I always Judge the Beauteous Form of a Woman to be the most Agreeable Part of her Composition, and when a Lady once does me the Honour to Toss That into my Arms, I think my self Oblig'd in Honour not to Quarrel about the rest of her Equipage.

La. *Bet.* Why ay, my Lord, there's some Good Humour in that now.

L. *Mo.* He's Happy in a Plain English Stomach, Madam,—I could Recommend a Dish that's perfectly to your Lordship's Goust, where Beauty is the only Sauce to it.

La. *Bet.* So! *(Aside.*

L. *Fop.* My Lord, when my Wine's Right I never care it shou'd be Zested; a Fine Woman, like a Fine Oyster, needs no Sawce but her own.

L. *Mo.* I know some Ladies wou'd thank you for that Opinion.

La. *Bet.* My Lord *Morelove*'s really grown such a Churl to the Women, I don't only think he is Not, but can't Conceive how he ever cou'd be in Love.

L. *Mo.* Upon my Word, Madam, I once thought I was. *(Smiling.*

354 C, I think it Sometimes. 356 D. sculking. 363 -position; P, p. 31. 363 C, F, and when once a Lady does. 364 C, D, E, Oblig'd in good Nature. F, Obliged in good Nature. 370 E, F, Gust. 372 C omits *Aside.* 373 D, should. 373 D, F, and a Fine Woman &c., omitted. 378 D, F, could.

La *Bet.* Fie! fie! how cou'd you think so? I fancy now you had only a mind to Domineer over some poor Creature, and so you thought you were in love, ha! ha!

L. *Mo.* The lady I lov'd Madam, grew so Unfortunate in her Conduct, that she at last brought me to Treat her with the same Indifference and Civility as I now pay your Ladyship.

La. *Bet.* And Ten to One, Just at that time she never thought you such tolerable Company; ha! ha!

L. *Mo.* That I can't say, Madam, for at that time she grew so Affected, there was no Judging of her Thoughts at all.

(Mimicking her Manner.

La. *Bet.* What, and so you left the Poor Lady? O you Inconstant Creature!

L. *Mo.* No, Madam, to have Lov'd her on had been Inconstancy; for she was never Two Hours together the same Woman.

(La. Bet. *and L.* Mo. *seem to talk.*

L. *Fop. (Aside.)* Ha! ha! ha! he has a Mind to Abuse her, I find; so I'll ev'n give him an Opportunity of doing his Business with her at once for ever—My Lord, I perceive your Lordship's going to be Good Company to the Lady, and for her sake, I don't think it Good Manners in me to Disturb it.

Enter Sir Charles.

Sir *Cha.* My Lord *Foppington.*

L. *Fop.* O *Charles!* I was just Wanting thee—Hark thee—I have Three Thousand Secrets for thee—I have made such Discoveries—to tell thee all in One Word—*Morelove*'s as Jealous of me as the Devil; heh! heh! heh!

Sir *Cha.* Is 't possible? has she given him any Occasion?

L. *Fop.* Only Rally'd him to Death upon my Account; she told me within Just now she'd use him like a Dog, and begg'd me to Draw off for an Opportunity.

Sir *Cha.* O! Keep in while the Scent lyes, and she's your own, my Lord.

[380] F, fy! fy! F, fansy. [387] C, ha! ha! is omitted. [389] C, D, F, omit Manner. [394] D, E, F, I see he has a Mind. [394] C, omits I see. [395] A. Oppertunity. C, e'en. [398] D, F, to Disturb you. [405] Slr Cha. P, p. 32. [406] P, comma after Account. [409] C, E, F, lies.

L. *Fop.* I cant tell that, *Charles,* but I'm sure she's fairly Unharbour'd; and when once I throw off my Inclinations, I usually follow em 'till the Game has enough on't, and between thee and I she's pretty well Blown too, she can't Stand long, I believe; for Curse catch me, if I have not rid down half a Thousand Pound after her already.

Sir *Cha.* What do you mean?

L. *Fop.* I have lost Five Hundred to her at Picquet since Dinner.

Sir *Cha.* You are a Fortunate Man faith—you are resolv'd not to be thrown out, I see.

L. *Fop.* Hang it! What shou'd a Man come out for, if he does not keep up to the Sport?

Sir *Cha.* Well Pusht, my Lord.

L. *Fop.* *Tayo!* Have at her.—

Sir *Cha.* Down! down, my Lord—ah—'ware Hanches.

L. *Fop.* Ah! *Charles. (Embracing him.)* Prithee let's Observe a little, there's a Foolish Cur, now I have run her to a Stand, has a Mind to be at her by himself and thou shalt see she won't stir out of her Way for him. *(They stand aside.*

L. *Mo.* Ha! ha! Your Ladyship's very Grave of a sudden, you look as if your Lover had insolently recover'd his Common Senses.

La. *Bet.* And your Lordship is so very Gay, and Unlike your self, one wou'd swear you were Just Come from the Pleasure of making your Mistress afraid of You.

L. *Mo.* No faith, quite Contrary: For do you know, Madam, I have Just found out, that upon your Account I have made my self One of the Most Ridiculous Puppies upon the Face of the Earth, I have upon my Faith!—nay and so Extravagantly such—ha! ha! ha! that it's at last become a Jest ev'n to my self, and I can't help laughing at it for the Soul of me.

La. *Bet.* I want to Cure him of that Laugh now-—*(disdainfully, and aside.)* My Lord, since you are so Generous I'll tell you another Secret; do you know too, that I still find (spite of all your Great Wisdom and my Contemptible Qualities, as you are pleas'd now and then to call 'em), Do you know, I say, that

411 A, F, can't. 421 F, should. 423 C, D, F, push'd. 426 F, Pr'ythee. 439 C, omits ha! ha! ha! 441 C, E, F, omit *disdainfully and.* 445 F, call them. P, omits comma before Do.

I see under all this, you still love me with the same Helpless Passion, and can your vast Foresight Imagine, that I won't use you Accordingly for these Extraordinary Airs you are Pleas'd to give your self?

Ld. *Mo.* O by all means, Madam, 'tis fit you shou'd, and I expect it, whenever it is in your power—Confusion! *(Aside.*

L. *Bet.* My Lord, you have talk'd to me this half Hour, without confessing Pain, *(Pauses and affects to Gape.)* only remember it.

Ld. *Mo.* Hell and Tortures!—

L. *Bet.* What did you say, my Lord?

Ld. *Mo.* Fire, and Furies!

L. *Bett.* Ha! ha! he's Disorder'd—Now I am Easie—My Lord *Foppington*, have you a mind to your Revenge at *Picquet?*

L. *Fop.* I have always a mind to an opportunity of entertaining your Ladyship, Madam.

Ld. *Mo.* *Charles*—The Insolence of this Woman might furnish out a thousand Devils.

Sir *Cha.* And your Temper is enough to furnish out a thousand such Women. Come away—I have Business for you upon the Terrace.

Ld. *Mo.* Let me but speak one word to her—

Sir *Cha.* Not a Syllable—the Tongue's a Weapon you'll always have the worst at: For I see you have no Guard, and she carries a Devilish Edge—

L. *Bett.* My Lord, don't let any thing I've said frighten you away; for if you have the least Inclination to stay, and Rail, you know the old Conditions; 'tis but your asking me Pardon next Day, and you may give your Passion any liberty you think fit.

Ld. *Mo.* Daggers and Death!

Sir *Cha.* Are you Mad?

Ld. *Mo.* Let me speak to her now or I shall burst—

Sir *Cha.* Upon Condition you'll speak no more of her to me, my Lord, do as you please.

Ld. *Mo.* Prithee Pardon me—I know not what to do.

[450] L. Mo. P, p. 33. [457] C, F, Easy. [460] F, inserts *(L. Bet coquets with L. Fop.)* [461] F, O! Charles. [470] C, I have said. [471] C, to stay and Rail. [480] E, Pr'ythee.

Sir *Cha*. Come along—I'll set you to work I warrant you—Nay, nay, none of your parting Ogles.—Will you go?

Ld. *Mo*. Yes,—and I hope—for ever.

(Exit Sir Cha. pulling away Ld. Mo.

Ld. *Fop*. Ha! ha! ha! Did ever Mortal Monster set up for a Lover with such unfortunate Qualifications.

L. *Bett*. Indeed, my Lord *Morelove* has something strangely singular in his Manner.

Ld. *Fop*. I thought I should have burst to see the Creature pretend to Railery, and give himself the Airs of one of Us. But, run me through Madam, your Ladyship push'd like a Fencing-Master; that last thrust was a *Coup de Grace* I believe—I'm afraid his Honour will hardly meet your Ladyship in hast again.

L. *Bett*. Not unless his Second Sir *Charles* keeps him better in Practice, perhaps. Well, the Humour of this Creature has done me signal Service to day, I must keep it up for fear of a second Engagement.

Ld. *Fop*. Never was poor Wit so foil'd at his own Weapon sure.

L. *Bett*. Wit! Had he ever any Pretence to it?

Ld. *Fop*. Ha! ha! he has not much in Love, I think, tho' he wears the Reputation of a very pretty young Fellow, among some sort of People; but Strike me stupid, if ever I could discover Common Sense in all the Progress of his Amours: He expects a Woman shou'd like him for endeavouring to convince her, that she has not one good Quality belonging to the whole Composition of her Soul and Body.

L. *Bett*. That, I suppose, is only in a modest Hope, that she'll mend her Faults to qualifie her self for his vast Merit, ha! ha!

Ld. *Fop*. Poor *Morelove!* I see she can't endure him. *(Aside.*

L. *Bett*. Or if one really had all those Faults, he does not consider, that Sincerity in Love is as much out of Fashion as sweet Snuff; No Body takes it now.

Ld. *Fop*. O! no Mortal, Madam, unless it be here and there a Squire, that's making his lawful Court to the Cherry-cheek Charms of my Lord Bishop's great fat Daughter in the Country.

489 C, Rally. 492 Honour. P, p. 34. 497 D, E, F, *(aside)*. 504 F, should. 508 C, F, qualify.

L. *Bett.* O what a surfeiting Couple has he put together— *(Throwing her hand carelessly upon his.*

Ld. *Fop.* Fond of me, by all that's tender—Poor Fool, I'll give thee Ease immediately. *(Aside.)*—But, Madam, you were pleas'd just now to offer me my Revenge at *Picquet*—Now here's no Body within, and I think we can't make use of a better Opportunity.

L. *Bett.* O! no: Not now, my Lord! I have a Favour I wou'd fain beg of you first.

Ld. *Fop.* But time, Madam, is very precious at this Place, and I shall not easily forgive my self, if I don't take him by the Forelock—

L. *Bett.* But I have a great mind to have a little more Sport with my Lord *Morelove* first, and wou'd fain beg your Assistance.

Ld. *Fop.* O! Withal my Heart; and, upon second thoughts, I don't know but piquing a Rival in Publick may be as good Sport, as being well with a Mistress in private: For after all, the Pleasure of a fine Woman is like that of her own Virtue, not so much in the thing, as the Reputation of having it. *(Aside)*—But how, Madam, can I serve you in this Affair?

L. *Bett.* Why methought, as my Lord *Morelove* went out, he shew'd a stern Resentment in his look, that seem'd to threaten me with Rebellion, and downright Defiance: Now I have a great Fancy, that you and I shou'd follow him to the *Terrace,* and laugh at his Resolution before he has time to put it in Practice.

Ld. *Fop.* And so punish his Fault before he commits it! ha! ha! ha!

L. *Bett.* Nay, we won't give him time, if his Courage shou'd fail, to repent it.

Ld. *Fop.* Ha! ha! let me Blood, if I don't long to be at it! ha! ha!

L. *Bett.* O! 'twill be such Diversion to see him bite his Lips, and broil within, only with seeing us ready to split our sides in laughing at nothing, ha! ha!

Ld. *Fop.* Ha! ha! I see the Creature does really like me.

528 F, would. 532 A, Vertue. 534 C, F, Well, Madam, but how can I. 544 P, fail to. 545 C, Ha! ha! ha!

(Aside) And then, Madam, to hear him hum a broken Piece of a Tune in Affectation of his not minding us—'twill be so foolish when we know he loves us to Death all the while, ha, ha!

L. *Bett.* And if at last his sage Mouth shou'd open in surly Contradiction of our Humour, then will we, in pure opposition to his, immediately fall foul upon every thing that is not Gallant, and Fashionable; Constancy shall be the Mark of Age and Ugliness, Vertue a Jest, we'll rally Discretion out of Doors, lay Gravity at our Feet, and only Love, Free Love, Disorder, Liberty and Pleasure be our standing Principles.

Ld. *Fop.* Madam, you transport me: For if ever I was obliged to Nature for any one tolerable Qualification, 'twas positively the Talent of being Exuberantly pleasant upon this Subject—I am impatient—my Fancy's upon the Wing already —let's fly to him.

L. *Bett.* No, stay till I am just got out, our going together won't be so proper.

Ld. *Fop.* As your Ladyship pleases, Madam—But when this Affair is over, you won't forget that I have a certain Revenge due.

L. *Bett.* Ay! ay! after Supper I am for you—Nay, you shan't stir a step, my Lord— *(Seeing her to the Door.*

Ld. *Fop.* Only to tell you, you have fix'd me yours to the last Existence of my Soul's eternal Entity—

L. *Bett.* O, your Servant— *(Exit L.* Betty.

Ld *Fop.* Ha! ha! stark mad for me, by all that's Handsome! Poor *Morelove:* That a Fellow who has ever been abroad, shou'd think a Woman of her Spirit is to be taken as the Confederates do Towns, by a Regular Siege, when so many of the *French* Successes might have shewn him the surest way is to whisper the Governor: How can a Coxcomb give himself the Fatigue of Bombarding a Woman's Understanding, when he may with so much ease make a Friend of her Constitution—I'll see, if I can shew him a little *French* Play with Lady *Betty*—let me see—Ay—I'll make an end of it the old way, get her into Picquet at her own Lodgings—not mind one Tittle of my Play, give her

[567] C, F, No, no; stay. [581] him. P, p. 36.

every Game before she's half up, that she may judge the strength of my Inclination by my hast of losing up to her Price; then of a sudden, with a familiar Leer, cry—Rat *Picquet*—sweep Counters, Cards, and Money upon the Floor, *et donc—l'Affaire est Faite.* *(Exit.*

The End of the Third Act.

ACT IV.

The SCENE *the* TERRACE

Enter Lady Easy *and Lady* Betty.

L. *Easy.*

My Dear, you really talk to me as if I were your Lover, and not your Friend; or else I am so dull, that by all you've said I can't make the least Guess at your real Thoughts—Can you be serious for a Moment?

L. *Bett.* Not easily: But I would do more to oblige you.

L. *Ea.* Then pray deal ingenuously, and tell me without Reserve, are you sure you don't love my Lord *Morelove?*

L. *Bett.* Then seriously—I think not—but because I won't be positive, you shall judge by the worst of my Symptoms—First, I own I like his Conversation, his Person has neither Fault, nor Beauty .... well enough, I don't remember I ever secretly wisht my self married to him, or that I ever seriously resolv'd against it.

L *Ea.* Well! so far you are tolerably safe: But come, as to his manner of addressing to you, what Effect has that had?

L. *Bett.* Humh *(Smiling)* I am not a little pleas'd to observe few Men follow a Woman with the same Fatigue and Spirit, that he does me; am more pleas'd when he lets me use him ill; and if ever I have a favourable Thought of him, 't is when I see he can't bear that Usage.

L. *Ea.* Have a Care, that last is a dangerous Symptom: He pleases your Pride, I find.

589 B, C, D, E, F, haste. C, D, Scene, the Castle Terrace. F, the Castle Terrass. 6 P, ingeniously. 12 D, F, wish'd. 16 C, omits *(Smiling)*. 21 L. Ea P, p. 37.

L. *Bett.* Oh! perfectly, in that I own no Mortal ever can come up to him.

L. *Ea.* But now, my Dear! now comes the main Point—Jealousie! are you sure you have never been toucht with it? Tell me that with a safe Conscience, and then I pronounce you clear.

L. *Bett.* Nay, then I defie him; for positively I was never jealous in my Life.

L. *Ea.* How, Madam! have you never been stirr'd enough to think a Woman strangely forward for being a little familiar in Talk with him? or are you sure his Gallantry to another never gave you the least Disorder? Was you never, upon no Accident, in an Apprehension of losing him?

L. *Bett.* Hah—Why, Madam—Bless me!—wh, wh— why sure you don't call this Jealousie, my Dear?

L. *Ea.* Nay, nay, that is not the Business; Have you ever felt any thing of this Nature, Madam?

L. *Bett.* Lord! don't be so hasty, my Dear—any thing of this nature—O Lu'd! I swear I don't like it: Dear Creature bring me off here; I am half frighted out of my Wits.

L. *Ea.* Nay, if you can railly upon't, your Wound is not over deep I'm afraid.

L. *Bett.* Well, that's comfortably said however.

L. *Ea.* But come, to the Point! how far have you been jealous?

L. *Bett.* Why—O bless me!—he gave the Musick one night to my Lady *Languish* here upon the *Terrace;* and tho' she and I were very good Friends, I remember I cou'd not speak to her in a week for't—Oh!

L. *Ea.* Nay, now you may laugh if you can; for, take my word, the Marks are upon you—but come—what else!

L. *Bett.* O nothing else upon my word, my Dear.

L. *Ea* Well, one Word more, and then I proceed to Sentence: Suppose you were heartily convinced, that he actually follow'd another Woman?

L. *Bett.* But pray, my Dear, what Occasion is there to suppose any such thing at all?

[26] C, F, Jealousy. [26] C, F, touch'd. [28] C, F, defy. [33] C, D, F, were you. [36] C, F, Jealousy. [39] P, any thiny. [41] C, Lud. F, here; for I am.[42] B, F, rally. [47] F, Terrass. [53] C, D, F, I give Sentence. [54] A, convinc'd.

L. *Ea.* Guilty upon my Honour.

L. *Bett.* Pshah! I defie him to say, that ever I own'd any Inclination for him.

L. *Ea.* But you have given him Terrible leave to guess it.

L. *Bett.* If ever you see us meet again, you'll have but little Reason to think so, I can assure you.

L. *Ea.* That I shall see presently; for here comes Sir *Charles,* and I am sure my Lord can't be far off.

Enter Sir Charles.

Sir *Cha.* Servant Lady *Betty*—My dear, how do you do?

L. *Ea.* At your Service, my Dear—But pray what have you done with my Lord *Morelove?*

L. *Bett.* Ay, Sir *Charles,* pray how does your Pupil do? Have you any hopes of him. Is he Docible?

Sir *Cha.* Well, Madam, to confess your Triumph over me, as well as him, I own my hopes of him are lost. I offer'd what I cou'd to his Instruction, but—he's incorrigibly yours, and undone—and the news, I presume, does not displease your Ladyship.

L. *Bett.* Fy, fy, Sir *Charles,* you disparage your Friend, I am afraid you don't take Pains with him.

Sir *Cha.* Ha! I fancy, Lady *Betty,* your good Nature wont let you sleep a Nights? Don't you love dearly to hurt People?

L. *Bett.* O! your Servant; then without a Jest, the Man is so unfortunate in his want of Patience, that let me die, if I don't often pity him.

Sir *Cha.* Strange Goodness—O that I were your Lover for a Month or two.

L. *Bett.* What then?

Sir *Cha.* I wou'd make that pretty Heart's Blood of yours Ake in a Fortnight.

L. *Bett.* Auh! I shou'd hate you, your Assurance wou'd make your Addres intolerable.

Sir *Cha.* I believe it wou'd, for I 'd never Address to you at all.

L. *Bett.* O! you Clown you! *(Hitting him with her Fan.*

Sir *Cha.* Why, what to do? to feed a diseas'd Pride, that's

59 F, defy. 61 D, F, L. Ea. No, but. 62 L. Bett. P, p. 38. 75 C, E, fie, fie. 79 P, Servant then. 82 D, F, Ha! Strange. 87 C, E, F, Hugh.

Eternally breaking out in the Affectation of an Ill Nature that—in my Conscience I believe is but Affectation.

L. *Bett.* You, nor your Friends have no great reason to complain of my Fondness I believe. Ha! ha! ha!

Sir *Cha.* *(Looking earnestly on her.)* Thou insolent Creature! How can you make a Jest of a Man, whose whole Life's but one continued Torment from your want of common Gratitude?

L. *Bett.* Torment! For my part I really believe him as easie as you are.

Sir *Cha.* Poor Intollerable Affectation! You know the contrary, you know him blindly yours, you know your Power, and the whole pleasure of your Life's the poor and low abuse of it.

L. *Bett.* Pray how do I abuse it?—If I have any Power.

Sir *Cha.* You drive him to Extreams that make him Mad, then punish him for acting against his Reason: You've almost turn'd his Brain, his common Judgment fails him; he's now, at this very Moment, driven by his Despair upon a Project, in hopes to free him from your Power, that I am sensible, and so must any one be, that has his sense, of course must ruine him with you, for ever: I almost blush to think of it, yet your unreasonable Disdain has forced him to it; and shou'd he now suspect I offer'd but a hint of it to you, as in contempt of his Design, I know he'd call my Life to answer it: But I have no regard to Men in Madness, I rather chose for once to trust in your good Nature, in hopes the Man, whom your Unwary Beauty had made Miserable, your Generosity wou'd scorn to make Ridiculous.

L. *Bett.* Sir *Charles,* you charge me very home, I never had it in my Inclination to make any thing ridiculous that did not deserve it. Pray, what is this Business you think so Extravagant in him?

Sir *Cha.* Something so absurdly Rash and Bold, you'll hardly forgive ev'n me that tell it you.

L. *Bett.* O fie! If it be a fault, Sir *Charles,* I shall consider it as His, not Yours. Pray, what is it?

L. *Ea.* I long to know methinks.

98 E, F, continu'd. 99 C, F, easy. 101 C, F, intolerable. 103 pleasure. P, p. 39. 105 C, F, Extremes. 110 C, F, ruin. 113 F, you, and in. 115 C, chuse. F, choose. 124 F, fy!

Sir *Cha.* You may be sure he did not want my Disswasions from it.

L. *Bett.* Let's hear it.

Sir *Cha.* Why this Man, whom I have known to love you with such Excess of Generous Desire, whom I have heard in his Extatick Praises on your Beauty talk, till from the soft Heat of his distilling Thoughts the Tears have fall'n.

L. *Bett.* O! Sir *Charles.* *(Flushing.*

Sir *Cha.* Nay, grudge not, since 'tis past, to hear what was (tho' you contemn'd it) once his Merit: but now I own, that Merit ought to be forgotten.

L. *Bett.* Pray, Sir be plain.

Sir *Cha.* This Man, I say, whose unhappy Passion has so ill succeeded with you, at last has forfeited all his Hopes (into which, pardon me, I confess my Friendship had lately flatter'd him) his Hopes of ev'n now deserving your lowest Pity or Regard.

L. *Bett.* You amaze me—For I can't suppose his utmost Malice dares assault my Reputation—and what—

Sir *Cha.* No, but he Maliciously presumes the World will do it for him; and indeed he has taken no unlikely means to make 'em busie with their Tongues: For he is this Minute upon the open Terrace, in the highest Publick Gallantry with my Lady *Graveairs.* And to convince the World and me, he said, he was not that Tame Lover we fancied him, he'd venture to give her the Musick to Night: Nay, I heard him, before my Face, speak to one of the Hoboys, to Engage the rest, and desir'd they wou'd all take their Directions only from my Lady *Graveairs.*

L. *Bett.* My Lady *Graveairs!* Truly I think my Lord's very much in the Right on't—for my part, Sir Charles, I don't see any thing in this, that's so very ridiculous, nor indeed that ought to make me think either the better or the worse of him for't.

Sir *Cha.* 'Pshah! 'Pshah! Madam, You and I know, 'tis not in his Power to renounce you; this is but the poor Disguise of a resenting Passion vainly ruffled to a Storm, which the least

127 D, dissuations. C, E, F, dissuasions. 132 C, E, F, Ecstatick. 147 busie P, p. 40. 147 C, F, busy. 148 F, Terrass. 152 C, E, F, Hautboys. 153 F, desired. F, would. 159 F, Pshaw! Pshaw!

gentle look from you can reconcile at will, and laugh into a Calm again.

L. *Bett.* Indeed, Sir *Charles,* I shan't give my self that Trouble, I believe.

Sir *Cha.* So I told him, Madam; Are not all your Complaints, said I, already owing to her Pride, and can you suppose this publick Defiance of it (which you know you can't make good too) won't incense her more against you? — That's what I'd have, said he, starting wildly, I care not what becomes of me, so I but live to see her piqued at it.

L. *Bett.* Upon my word, I fancy my Lord will find himself mistaken,—I shan't be piqued, I believe—I must first have a Value for the Thing I lose, before it piques me: Piqued! ha! ha! ha! *(Disorder'd.*

Sir *Cha.* Madam, you've said the very Thing I urg'd to him; I know her Temper so well, said I, that tho' she doated on you, if you once stood out against her, she'd sooner burst, than shew the least distant motion of Uneasiness.

L. *Bett.* I can assure you, Sir *Charles,* my Lord won't find himself Deceiv'd in your Opinion—Piqued!

Sir *Cha.* She has it! *(Aside.*

L. *Ea.* Alas, poor Woman! how little do our Passions make us?

L. *Bett.* Not, but I wou'd advise him to have a little Regard to my Reputation in this Business, I wou'd have him take heed of Publickly Affronting me.

Sir *Cha.* Right, Madam, that's what I strictly warn'd him of; for among Friends, whenever the World sees him follow another Woman, the Malicious Tea-Tables will be very apt to be free with your Ladyship.

L. *Bett.* I'd have him Consider that, methinks.

Sir *Cha.* But alas! Madam, 'tis not in his Power to Think with Reason, his mad Resentment has destroy'd ev'n his Principles of Common Honesty: He considers nothing but a senseless Proud Revenge, which in this Fit of Lunacy, 'tis Impossible that either Threats or Dangers can Disswade him from.

L. *Bett.* What! does he defie me, Threaten me!—then he

172 E, fansie. 179 C, omits distant. 191 L. Bett. P, p. 41. 195 F, in his Fit. 196 C, D, E, F, dissuade. 197 C, E, F, defy.

shall see, that I have Passions too, and know, as well as he, to stir my Heart 'gainst any Pride that Dares Insult me. Does he suppose I fear him! Fear the little Malice of a slighted Passion, that my own Scorn has stung to a despis'd Resentment! Fear him! O! it provokes me to think he Dares have such a Thought!

L. *Ea.* Dear Creature, don't Disorder your self so.

L. *Bett.* Let me but live to see him once more within my Power, and I'll forgive the Rest of Fortune.

(Walking disorder'd.

L. *Ea. (Aside)* Well! certainly I am very Ill-natur'd; for tho' I see this News has disturb'd my Friend, I can't help being pleas'd with any Hopes of my Lady *Graveairs* being otherwise Dispos'd of—My Dear I am afraid you have provokt her a little too far.

Sir *Cha.* Pshah! not at all—You shall see—I'll sweeten her, and she'll cool like a Dish of Tea.

L. *Bett.* I may see him with his complaining Face again—

Sir *Cha.* I am sorry, Madam, you so wrongly judge of what I've told you; I was in Hopes to have stirr'd your Pity, not your Anger; I little thought your Generosity wou'd punish him for Faults, which you your self resolv'd he shou'd commit—Yonder he comes, and all the World with him: Might I advise you, Madam, you shou'd not Resent this Thing at all—I wou'd not so much as stay to see him in his Fault; nay, I'd be the last that Heard of it: Nothing can sting him more, or so Justly Punish his Folly, as your Utter Neglect of it.

La *Ea.* Come, Dear Creature, be Persuaded, and go home with me; indeed it will shew more Indifferent to avoid him.

L. *Bett.* No, Madam, I'll Oblige his Vanity for once, and stay to let him see how strangely he has Piqued me.

Sir *Cha. (Aside)* O not at all to speak of; you had as good part with a little of that Pride of yours, or I shall yet make it a very troublesome Companion to you.

Goes from them, and whispers Lord Morelove.

Enter Lord Foppington; *and a little after, Lord* Morelove, *Lady* Graveairs, *and other Ladies.*

199 F, against. 200 F, I fear him? 201 F, despised. 202 F, he dare have. 208 D, F, Graveair's. 209 C, D, provok'd. E, provoked. 210 C, D, E, F, Oh! not at all. 216 D, F, should. 222 A, perswaded. 223 C, omits indeed. F, Indifference.

Ld. *Fop.* Ladies, your Servant—O! we have wanted you beyond Reparation—such Diversion!

L. *Bett.* Well! my Lord! have you seen my Lord *Morelove?*

Ld. *Fop.* Seen him!—ha! ha! ha!—I have such things to tell you, Madam—you'll Die—

L. *Bett.* O 'Pray' let's have 'em, for I was never in a better Humour to receive them.

Ld. *Fop.* Hark you. *(They Whisper.*

Ld. *Mo.* So, she's engag'd already. *(To Sir* Charles.

Sir *Cha.* So much the better; make but a just Advantage of my Success, and she's Undone.

Ld. *Fop.*
L. *Bett* } Ha! ha! ha!

Sir *Cha.* You see already what ridiculous Pains she's taking to stir your Jealousie and Cover her own.

Ld. *Fop.*
L. *Bett.* } Ha! ha! ha!

Ld. *Mo.* O never fear me; for, upon my word, it now appears Ridiculous ev'n to me.

Sir *Cha.* And Hark you— *(Whispers Ld.* Mo.

L. *Bett.* Ha! ha! and so the Widow was as full of Airs, as his Lordship.

Sir *Cha.* Only observe that, and 'tis impossible you can fail. *(Aside.*

Ld. *Mo.* Dear *Charles,* You have convinc'd me, and I thank you.

L. *Gra.* My Lord *Morelove,* What do you leave us?

Ld. *Mo.* Ten thousand Pardons, Madam, I was but Just—

L. *Gra.* Nay, nay, no Excuses, my Lord, so you will but let us have you again.

Sir *Cha.* *(Aside to L.* Gra.) I see you have Good Humour, Madam, when you like your Company.

L. *Gra.* And You, I see, for all your mighty Thirst of Dominion, cou'd stoop to be Obedient, if one thought it worth one's while to make you so! Ha! Ha!

233 L. Bett. P, p. 42. 236 C, F, let's hear 'em. C, omits for. 244 C, F, Jealousy, and. 247 F, even. 254 F, Morelove! What, do you. 262 D, F, omit Ha! Ha!

Sir *Cha.* Hah! Power would make her an admirable Tyrant. *(Aside.*

L. *Ea. (Observing Sir* Cha. *and L. Graveairs)* So! there's another Couple have Quarrell'd too, I see—Those Airs to my Lord *Morelove* look, as if Design'd to recover Sir *Charles* into Jealousie: I'll Endeavour to Joyn the Company, and, it may be, that will let me into the Secret. *(Aside.*

My Lord *Foppington,* I vow this is very Uncomplaisant to Engross so Agreeable a Part of the Company to your self.

Sir *Cha.* Nay, my Lord, that is not fair indeed to Enter into Secrets among Friends—Ladies! what say you? I think we ought to Declare against it.

Ladies. O! no Secrets, no Secrets.

L. *Bett.* Well, Ladies, I ought only to ask your Pardon: My Lord's excusable, for I wou'd haul him into a Corner.

Ld. *Fop.* I swear it's very hard tho'! I observe two People of Extream Condition can no sooner grow Particular, but the Multitude of both Sexes are Immediately Up, and think their Properties invaded—

L. *Bett.* Odious Multitude—

Ld. *Fop.* Perish that *Canaille.*

L. *Gra.* O, my Lord, we Women have all Reason to be jealous of Lady *Betty Modish*'s Power.

Ld. *Mo. (To L. Betty.)* As the Men, Madam, All have of my Lord *Foppington;* beside Favourites of great Merit Discourage those of an inferiour Class for their Princes Service: He has already lost you one of your Retinue, Madam.

L. *Bett.* Not at all, my Lord, he has only made Room for another: One must sometimes make Vacancies, or there cou'd be no Preferment.

Ld. *Fop.* Ha! ha! Ladies Favours, my Lord, like Places at Court, are not always held for life you know.

L. *Bett.* No, indeed! if they were, the Poor fine Women wou'd be all us'd like their Wives; and no more minded than the Business of the Nation.

[263] G, Ha! [265] C, E, F, quarrel'd too, I find. [266] C, F, Jealousy. E, join. [269] F, Uncomplaisant, to. [274] Ladies P, p. 43. [277] P, A, C, F, hard ho! [281] C, D, F, the Canaille. [286] C, F, inferior. [286] C, E, Prince's. [290] F, could. C, Preferments. [292] C, life, you know.

L. *Ea.* Have a Care, Madam, an Undeserving Favourite has been the Ruine of Many a Prince's Empire.

Ld. *Fop.* Upon my Soul, Lady *Betty*, we must grow more Discreet; for positively if we go on at this Rate, we shall have the World throw you under the Scandal of Constancy, and I shall have all the Swords of Condition at my Throat for a Monopolist.

L. *Mo.* O! there's no such Fear of that, my Lord, tho' the Men of Sense give it over, there will be always some Idle Fellows vain enough to believe their Merit may succeed as well as your Lordships.

L. *Bett.* Or if they shou'd not, my Lord, cast Lovers, you know, need not fear being long out of Employment, while there are so many well dispos'd People in the World—There are generally Neglected Wives, stale Maids, or Charitable Widows, always ready to relieve the Necessities of a Disappointed Passion—and, by the way, Hark you, Sir *Charles.*

Ld. *Mo. (Aside).* So! she is stirr'd, I see; for all her Pains to Hide it—she wou'd hardly have glanc'd an Affront at a Woman, she was not Piqued at.

L. *Gra. (Aside.)* That Wit was thrown at me, I suppose; but I'll return it.

L. *Bett. (Softly to Sir* Cha.) 'Pray' how came you all this While to Trust your Mistress so Easily?

Sir *Cha.* One is not so Apt, Madam, to be allarm'd at the liberties of an Old Acquaintance, as perhaps your Ladiship ought to be at the Resentment of an Hard-us'd, Honourable Lover.

L. *Bett.* Suppose I were allarm'd, how does that make you easie?

Sir *Cha.* Come, come, be wise at last; my trusting them together may easily convince you, that (as I told you before) I know his Addresses to her are only Outward, and 'twill be your Fault Now, if you let him go on till the World thinks him in Earnest; and a thousand Busie Tongues are set upon Malicious Enquirys into your Reputation.

[297] C, E, F, Ruin. [298] F, Ha! ha! Upon my Soul. [302] C, F, no great Fear. [305] C, E, F, Lordship's. [312] F, she's. D, she's stir'd. [317] L. Bett. P, p. 44. [320] E, F, Ladyship. [322] C, E, alarm'd. D, alarmed. [322] C, D, E, F, alarm'd. [325] F, easy. [328] C, F, busy. [329] C, E, F, enquiries.

L. *Bett.* Why, Sir *Charles,* do you suppose while he behaves himself as he does, that I wont Convince him of my Indifference?

Sir *Cha.* But—Hear me, Madam.

La. *Gra.* *(Aside.)* The Air of that Whisper looks as if the Lady had a mind to be making her Peace again; and, 'tis Possible, his Worship's being so Busie in the Matter too, may proceed as Much from his Jealousie of my Lord with me, as Friendship to her, at least I Fancy so; therefore I'm resolv'd to keep her still Piqued and prevent it, tho' it be only to Gall Him—Sir *Charles,* that is not fair to take a Privilege, that you just now declar'd against in my Lord *Foppington.*

Ld. *Mo.* Well observ'd, Madam.

L. *Gra.* Beside it looks so Affected to whisper, when every Body guesses the Secret.

L. *Mo.* Ha! ha! ha!

L. *Bett.* O! Madam, your Pardon in particular: But 'tis possible you may be mistaken: The Secrets of People that have any Regard to their Actions are not so soon Guess'd, as theirs that have made a Confident of the whole Town.

Ld. *Fop.* Ha! ha! ha!

La. *Gra.* A *Coquette* in her affected Airs of Disdain to a Revolted Lover, I'm afraid must exceed your Ladyship in Prudence, not to let the World see at the same time she'd give her Eyes to make her Peace with him: ha! ha!

Ld. *Mo.* Ha! ha! ha!

L. *Bett.* 'Twou'd be a Mortification indeed, if it were in the Power of a Fading Widow's Charms to prevent it; and the Man must be Miserably reduc'd sure, that cou'd bear to live Buried in Woollen, or take up with the Motherly Comforts of a Swan-skin Petticoat. Ha! ha!

Ld. *Fop.* Ha! ha! ha!

L. *Gra.* Widows, it seems, are not so squeamish to their Interest, they know their own Minds, and take the Man they like, tho' it happens to be one, that a Froward vain Girl has disoblig'd, and is Pining to be Friends with.

Ld. *Mo.* Nay, tho' it happens to be one, that confesses he

[331] F, won't. [335] C, F, busy. [336] C, F, Jealousy. [337] F, Fansy. [339] C, F, omit that. [350] A, D, Coquete. [355] F, 'Twould. [358] F, Wollen. [361] L. Gra. P, p. 45.

once was fond of a piece of Folly, and afterwards asham'd on't.

L. *Bett.* Nay, my Lord, there's no standing against two of you.

L. *Fop.* No Faith, that's odds at Tennis my Lord: Not but if your Ladiship pleases I'll endeavour to keep your Back-hand a little: Tho', upon my Soul, you may safely set me up at the Line; for, knock me down, if ever I saw a Rest of Wit better Play'd, than that last, in my Life.—What say you, Madam, shall we engage?

L. *Bett.* As you please, my Lord.

Ld. *Fop.* Ha! ha! ha! *Allons. Tout de bon, joues mi Lor.*

Ld. *Mo.* O Pardon me, Sir, I shall never think my self in any thing a Match for the Lady.

Ld. *Fop.* To you, Madam.

L. *Bett,* That's much, my Lord, when the World knows you have been so many Years teazing me to play the Fool with you.

Ld. *Fop.* Ah! *Bien joué.*

Ld. *Mo.* At that Game I confess your Ladyship has chosen a much properer Person to improve your Hand with.

Ld. *Fop.* To me, Madam,—My Lord, I presume whoever the Lady thinks fit to play the Fool with, will at least be able to give as much Envy as the Wise Person that had not Wit enough to keep well with her when he was so.

L. *Gra.* O! my Lord! Both Parties must needs be greatly happy, for I dare swear, neither will have any Rivals to disturb 'em.

Ld. *Mo.* Ha! ha!

L. *Bett.* None that will disturb 'em, I dare swear.

Ld. *Fop.* Ha! ha! ha!

Ld. *Mo.*
L. *Gra.* } Ha! ha! ha!
L. *Bett.*

Sir *Cha.* I don't know, Gentlefolks—but you are all in extream good Humour methinks, I hope there's none of it Affected.

L. *Ea.* I shou'd be loath to answer for any but my Lord *Foppington.* *(Aside.*

L. *Bett.* Mine is not, I'll swear.

Ld. *Mo.* Nor mine, I'm sure.

369 A, C, E, F, Ladyship. B, jouez. 381 P, jouè. A, C, E, F, joue. 382 C, Game, I confess your. 396 C, F, extreme.

L. *Gra.* Mine's sincere, depend upon't.

Ld. *Fop.* And may the Eternal Frowns of the whole Sex Doubly Demme, if mine is not.

L. *Ea.* Well, good People, I am mighty glad to hear it. You have all perform'd extreamly well: But if you please you shall ev'n give over your Wit now, while it is well.

L. *Bett.* *(To her self.)* Now I see his Humour I'll stand it out, if I were sure to die for't.

Sir *Cha.* You shou'd not have proceeded so far with my Lord *Foppington,* after what I had told you. *(Aside to Lady Betty.*

L. *Bett.* Pray, Sir *Charles,* give me leave to understand my self a little.

Sir *Cha.* Your Pardon, Madam, I thought a right understanding wou'd have been for both your Interests, and Reputation.

L. *Bett.* For His perhaps.

Sir *Cha.* Nay, then, Madam, it's time for me to take care of my Friend.

L. *Bett.* I never in the least doubted your Friendship to him in any thing that was to shew your self my Enemy.

Sir *Cha.* Since I see, Madam, you have so ungrateful a sence of my Lord *Morelove*'s Merit, and my Service, I shall Never be asham'd of using my Power henceforth to keep him intirely out of your Ladyship's. *(Goes from her.*

L. *Bett.* Was ever any thing so Insolent? I cou'd find in my Heart to run the hazard of a downright Compliance, if it were only to convince him, that my Power, perhaps, is not inferior to His. *(To her self.*

L. *Ea.* My Lord *Foppington,* I think you generally lead the Company upon these Occasions. Pray will you think of some Prettier sort of Diversion for us, than Parties and Whispers.

Ld. *Fop.* What say you, Ladies, shall we step and see what's done at the Basset-Table.

L. *Bett.* With all my Heart, Lady *Easy*—

L. *Ea.* I think 'tis the best thing we can do, and because

404 C. F, Dem me. 405 L. Ea. P, p. 46. 406 C, F, extremely. C, please, you. 416 C, His perhaps. 421 B, ungraceful. 423 E, F, entirely. C, F, *(Goes from her)* omitted. 425 P, Insolent I cou'd. C, F, could.

we won't part to Night, you shall all Sup where you Din'd—What say you, my Lord?

Ld. *Mo.* Your Ladyship may be sure of me, Madam.

Ld. *Fop.* Ay! ay! we'll all come.

L. *Ea.* Then pray let's change Parties a little. My Lord Foppington, you shall Squire me.

Ld. *Fop.* O! you do me Honour, Madam.

L. *Bett.* My Lord *Morelove,* pray let me speak with you.

Ld. *Mo.* Me, Madam?

L. *Bett.* If you please, my Lord.

Ld. *Mo.* Ha! that look shot through me! What can this mean? *(Aside.*

L. *Bett.* This is no proper Place to tell you what it is: But there is one thing I'd fain be truly answer'd in: I suppose you'll be at my Lady *Easy*'s by and by, and if you 'll give me leave there—

Ld. *Mo.* If you please to do me that Honour, Madam, I shall certainly be there.

L. *Bett.* That's all, my Lord.

Ld. *Mo.* Is not your Ladyship for Walking?

L. *Bett.* If your Lordship dare venture with me.

L. *Mo.* O! Madam! *(Taking her Hand.)* How my Heart Dances, what Heavenly Musick's in her Voice, when softned into Kindness. *(Aside.*

L. *Bett.* Ha! his Hand trembles—Sir *Charles* may be mistaken.

L. *Fop.* My Lady *Graveairs,* you wont let Sir *Charles* leave us.

L. *Gra.* No, my Lord, we'll follow you—stay a little. *(To Sir* Cha.

Sir *Cha.* I thought your Ladyship design'd to follow 'em.

L. *Gra.* Perhaps I'd speak with you.

Sir *Cha.* But, Madam, consider we shall certainly be observ'd.

L. *Gra.* Lord, Sir! If you think it such a Favour. *(Ex. hastily.*

Sir *Cha.* Is she gone? let her go, etc. *(Exit Singing.*

The End of the Fourth Act.

[447] L. Bett. P, p. 47. [455] C, F, dares.

71

ACT V

The SCENE *Continues*

Enter Sir CHARLES *and Lord* MORELOVE

Sir *Cha.* Come a little this way—my Lady *Graveairs* had an Eye upon me, as I stole off, and I'm apprehensive will make use of any opportunity to talk with me.

L. *Mo.* O! we are pretty safe here—well! you were speaking of Lady *Betty.*

Sir *Cha.* Ay my Lord,—I say, notwithstanding all this sudden change of her Behaviour, I wou'd not have you yet be too secure of her: For, between you and I, since, as I told you, I have profess'd my self an open Enemy to her Power with You, 'tis not impossible but this new Air of good Humour may very much proceed from a little Woman's Pride, of convincing Me you are not yet Out of her Power.

Ld. *Mo.* Not unlikely: But still can we make no advantage of it?

Sir *Cha.* That's what I have been thinking of—look you—Death! my Lady *Graveairs!*

Ld. *Mo.* Hah! She will have Audience I find.

Sir *Cha.* There's no avoiding her—The Truth is, I have ow'd her a little Good Nature a great while,—I see there is but one way of getting rid of her—I must ev'n appoint her a Day of Payment at last. If you'll step into my Lodgings, my Lord, I'll just give her an Answer, and be with you in a Moment.

Ld. *Mo.* Very well, I'll stay there for you.

(Ex. Lord Morelove.

Enter L. Graveairs *on the other side.*

L. *Gra.* Sir *Charles!*

Sir *Cha.* Come, come, no more of these Reproachful Looks; you'll find, Madam, I have deserv'd better of you than your Jealousy imagines—Is it a Fault to be tender of your Reputation?—fie, fie,—This may be a proper time to Talk, and of my Contriving too,—you see I just now shook off my Lord *Morelove* on purpose.

8 F, since, I told you. 16 Ld. Mo. P, p. 48. 16 C, F, Ha! 28 F, fy, fy.

L. *Gra.* May I believe you?

Sir *Cha.* Still doubting my Fidelity, and mistaking my Discretion for want of Good Nature.

L. *Gra.* Don't think me troublesome—For I confess 'tis Death to think of parting with you: Since the World sees, for you I have neglected Friends and Reputation, have stood the little Insults of Disdainful Prudes, that envy'd me perhaps your Friendship; have born the Freezing Looks of Near and General Acquaintance—Since this is so, don't let 'em Ridicule me too, and say my Foolish Vanity undid me; don't let 'em point at me as a Cast Mistress.

Sir *Cha.* You Wrong me to suppose the Thought, you'll have better of me when we meet: When shall you be at leisure?

L. *Gra.* I confess, I wou'd see you once again, if what I have more to say prove Ineffectual, perhaps it may convince me then, 'tis my Interest to part with you—Can you come to Night?

Sir *Cha.* You know we have Company, and I'm afraid they'll stay too late: Can't it be before Supper? What's a Clock now?

L. *Gra.* It's almost Six.

Sir *Cha.* At Seven then be sure of me; till when, I'd have you go back to the Ladies to avoid Suspicion, and about that time—Have the Vapours.

L. *Gra.* May I depend upon you?— *(Exit L.* Gra.

Sir *Cha.* Depend on everything—A very Troublesome Business This—send me once fairly rid on't—if ever I'm caught in an *Honourable* Affair again!—A Debt now, that a little ready Civility, and away, would satisfie, a Man might Bear with; but to have a Rent-Charge upon ones good Nature, with an unconscionable long Scroll of Arrears too, that wou'd eat out the Profits of the best Estate in *Christendom*—ah! Intollerable! Well! I'll ev'n to my Lord, and shake off the Thoughts on't. *(Exit.*

Enter Lady Betty, *and Lady* Easy.

L. *Bett.* I observe, my Dear, you have Usually this great Fortune at Play, it were enough to make one suspect your good luck with an Husband.

[43] F, would. [49] D, 'till [53] C, Depend on. [55] C, A Debt now that. C, F, satisfy. [57] C, one's. D, ones Good-nature. E, one's Good-nature. F, one's. [58] F, would. [59] best Estate P, p. 49. [59] C, A, E, F, Intolerable. [64] C, F, your good luck.

L. *Ea.* Truly—I don't complain of my Fortune either way.

L. *Bett.* Prithee tell me, You are often advising me to it, are there those real Comfortable Advantages in Mariage, that our Old Aunts, and Grand-mothers wou'd persuade us of?

L. *Ea.* Upon my word, if I had the Worst Husband in the World, I shou'd still think so.

L. *Bett.* Ay, but then the Hazard of Having a good one, my Dear.

L. *Ea.* You may have a Good one, I dare say, if you don't give Airs till you spoil him.

L. *Bett.* Can there be the same, Dear, full Delight in giving Ease, as Pain? O! my Dear, the Thought of Parting with ones Power is Insupportable!

L. *Ea.* And the keeping it, till it dwindles into no Power at all, is most Rufully Foolish.

L. *Bett.* But still to marry before One's Heartily in love—

L. *Ea.* Is not half so Formidable a Calamity—but if I have any Eyes, my Dear, you'll run no great Hazard of that, in Venturing upon my Lord *Morelove*—You don't Know, perhaps, that within this half hour, the Tone of your Voice is strangely Softened to him, ha! ha! ha! ha!

L. *Bett.* My Dear, you are positively, one or other, the most Censorious Creature in the World; and so, I see it's in vain to talk with you—'Pray' will you go back to the Company.

L. *Ea.* Ah! Poor Lady *Betty*.

L. *Bett.* 'Pshah! *(Exeunt.*

The SCENE *Changes to Sir* CHARLES'*s Lodgings.*

Enter Sir Charles *and Lord* Morelove.

L. *Mo.* *Charles!* you have transported me; you have made my Part in the Scene so very easie too, 'tis impossible I shou'd fail in it.

Sir *Cha.* That's what I consider'd: For Now the more you throw your self into her Power, the more I shall be able to Force her into yours.

66 E, F, Pr'ythee. 67 E, F, marriage. 70 D, F, should. 71 D, F, of not having. 73 D, 'till. 75 C, E, F, one's. 78 F, ruefully. 79 A, ones. 89 C, F, omit L. Bett. Pshah! C, omits *Exeunt.* 91 P Lady Morelove. 93 C, F, easy.

Ld. *Mo.* After all (begging the Ladies Pardon) Your Fine Women, like Bullies, are only stout where they know their Men: A Man of an Honest Courage may fright 'em into any thing! Well, I am fully Instructed, and will about it Instantly—Won't you go along with me?

Sir *Cha.* That may not be so Proper; beside I have a little Business upon my Hands.

Ld. *Mo.* O your Servant, Sir—Good by to you—you shan't stir.

Sir *Cha.* My Lord, your Servant— *(Exit* Ld. *Morelove.)* So! Now to dispose of my self, till 'tis time to think of my Lady *Graveairs*—Umh!— I have no great Maw to that Business, methinks—I don't find my self in Humour Enough to come up to the Civil things, that are usually expected in the making up of an old Quarrel— (Edging *Crosses the Stage.*) There goes a Warmer Temptation by half! Ha! into my Wives Bedchamber too—I question if the Jade has any great Business there; I have a great Fancy she has only a mind to be taking the Opportunity of no Body's being at Home, to make her Peace with me—let me see—ay, I shall have time enough to go to her Ladyship afterwards—Beside I want a little Sleep, I find—Your Young Fops may talk of their Women of Quality—but, to me now, there's a strange Agreeable Convenience in a Creature one is not Oblig'd to say much to upon these Occasions. *(Going.*

Enter Edging.

Edg. Did you call me, Sir.

Sir *Cha.* Hah! all's Right—*(Aside.)*—Yes, Madam, I did call you.

Edg. What wou'd you please to have, Sir? *(He sits down.*

Sir *Cha.* Have!—why, I wou'd have you grow a Good Girl, and know when you are well Us'd, Hussy.

Edg. Sir, I don't Complain of any thing, not I.

Sir *Cha.* Well, don't be Uneasy—I am not Angry with you Now—Come, and Kiss me.

Edg. Lard, Sir—

Sir *Cha.* Don't be a Fool now—come hither.

Edg. 'Pshah— *(Goes to him.*

[103] A, C, D, E, F, besides. [108] E, F, umph! [112] C, E, F, Wife's. [123] C, F, Ha! [131] Sir Cha. P, p. 51. [132] F, Pshaw!

Sir *Cha.* No Wry Faces—so—sit down. I won't have you look Grave neither—let me see you smile, you Jade you.

Edg. Hah! hah! *(Laughs and Blushes.*

Sir *Cha.* Ah, you melting Rogue!

Edg. Come, don't you be at your Tricks Now—Lard! can't you sit still and talk with one; I am sure there's ten times more Love in that, and fifty times the Satisfaction, People may say what they will.

Sir *Cha.* Well! now you're Good, you shall have your own way,—I am going to lye down in the next Room; and, since you love a little Chat, come and throw my Night-Gown over me, and you shall talk me to sleep. *(Exit Sir Cha.*

Edg. Yes, Sir—for all his Way, I see he likes me still.

(Exit after him.

The SCENE *Changes to the* TERRACE.

Enter Lady Betty, *Lady* Easy, *and Lord* Morelove.

L. *Mo.* Nay, Madam, there you are too severe upon him; for Bating now and then a little Vanity, my Lord *Foppington* does not want Wit sometimes to make him a very Tolerable Woman's Man.

L. *Bett.* But such Eternal Vanity grows Tiresome.

L. *Ea.* Come, if he were not so loose in his Morals, Vanity methinks might easily be Excus'd considering how much 'tis in Fashion: For 'pray' Observe what's half the Conversation of most of the Fine Young People about Town, but a perpetual Affectation of appearing foremost in the Knowledge of Manners, New Modes, and Scandal; and in that I don't see any body comes up to him.

Ld. *Mo.* Nor I indeed—and Here he comes—'Pray', Madam, let's have a little more of him; no Body shews him to more Advantage than your Ladyship.

L. *Bett.* Nay, with all my Heart, you'll second me, my Lord?

Ld. *Mo.* Upon Occasion, Madam—

L. *Ea.* Engaging upon Parties, my Lord?

(Aside, and smiling to Ld. *Mo.*

[133] E, F, Face. [134] P, omits comma. [135] F, ha! ha! [142] C, E, F, lie. [146] F, Terras. [159] B, C, D, E, omit Madam. [162] P, withal.

Enter Lord Foppington.

Ld. *Fop.* So, Ladies! What's the Affair Now?

L. *Bett.* Why you were, my Lord; I was allowing you a Great many Good Qualities; but Lady *Easy* says, you are a perfect Hypocrite; and that whatever Airs you give your self to the Women, she's Confident you value no Woman in the World Equal to your own Lady.

Ld. *Fop.* You see, Madam, how I am scandaliz'd upon your Account: But it's so Natural for a Prude to be Malicious, when a Man endeavours to be well with any Body but her self; did you never Observe she was Piqu'd at that before? ha! ha!

L. *Bett.* I'll swear you are a Provoking Creature.

Ld. *Fop.* Let's be more Familiar upon't, and give her Disorder: Ha! Ha!

L. *Bett.* Ha! ha! ha!

Ld. *Fop.* Stap my Breath, but Lady *Easy* is an Admirable Discoverer—Marriage is indeed a Prodigious Security of ones Inclination: A Man's likely to take a World of Pains in an Employment, where he can't be turn'd out for his Idleness.

L. *Bett.* I vow, my Lord, that's vastly Generous to all the Fine Women; you are for giving 'em a Despotick Power in Love, I see, to Reward and Punish as they Think fit.

Ld. *Fop.* Ha! ha! Right, Madam, what signifies Beauty without Power? And a Fine Woman when she's Married makes as Ridiculous a Figure, as a Beaten General marching out of a Garrison.

L. *Ea.* I'm afraid, Lady *Betty,* the greatest Danger in your Use of Power, wou'd be from a too Heedless Liberality; you wou'd more mind the Man than his Merit.

Ld. *Fop.* Piqued again, by all that's Fretful—Well, Certainly to give Envy, is a Pleasure inexpressible. *(To* L. Betty.

L. *Bett.* Ha! ha! ha!

L. *Ea.* Does not she shew him well, my Lord?

(Aside to Ld. Mo.

Ld. *Mo.* Perfectly, and me too to my self—For now I almost Blush to Think I ever was uneasie at him. *(To* L. *Easy.*

165 *Enter Lord* Foppington. P, p. 52. 166 P, my Lord, I was. 181 C, E, F, one's. 189 B, out a. 192 F, would. 197 F, me to myself. 198 C, F, uneasy.

Ld. *Fop.* Ha! ha! Lady *Easy*, I ask Ten thousand Pardons, I'm afraid I am rude all this While.

L. *Ea.* O not at all, my Lord, you are always good Company, when you Please; Not but in some things, Indeed, you are apt to be like other Fine Gentlemen, A little too loose in your Principles.

L. *Fop.* O, Madam, never to the Offence of the Ladies, I agree in any Community with them; No Body is a more Constant Churchman, when the Fine Women are there.

L. *Ea.* O Fy, my Lord, you ought not to go for their sakes at all And I wonder, you that are for being such a Good Husband of your Vertues, are not afraid of bringing your Prudence into a Lampoon or a Play?

L. *Bett.* Lampoons and Plays, Madam, are only Things to be laugh'd at.

Ld. *Mo.* Plays now indeed one need not be so much afraid of, for since the late short-sighted View of 'em, Vice may go on and Prosper, the Stage dares hardly shew a Vicious Person speaking like himself, for fear of being call'd Prophane for Exposing him.

L. *Ea.* 'Tis Hard, indeed, when People won't Distinguish between what's Meant for Contempt, and what for Example.

L. *Fop.* Od so! Ladies, the Court's coming home, I see, shall not we go make our Bows?

L. *Bett.* O! by all means.

L. *Ea.* Lady *Betty* I must leave you: For I'm oblig'd to write Letters, and I know you won't give me Time after Supper.

L. *Bett.* Well, my Dear, I'll make a short Visit and be with you. Pray what's become of my Lady *Graveairs?*

(Ex. Lady Easy.

Ld. *Mo.* I believe she's gone home, Madam, she seem'd not to be very well.

Ld. *Fop.* And where's Sir *Charles,* my Lord?

Ld. *Mo.* I left him at his own Lodgings.

L. *Bett.* He's upon some Ramble I'm afraid.

199 F, Ld. *Fop.* I ask. 205 L. *Fop.* P, p. 53. B, D, E, Offense. 208 C, E, fie. 209 P, Husband o your. C, E, F, Virtues. 212 P, into f Lampoon. B, D, E, or Play. 222 C, F, omit go. 228 C, Oh! I believe.

L. *Fop*. Nay, as for that Matter, a Man may Ramble at Home sometimes! But here come the Chaises, we must make a little more Haste, Madam. *(Exeunt.*

The Scene changes to Sir Charles's *Lodgings.*
Enter Lady Easy, *and a Servant.*

L. *Ea*. Is your Master come home?

Servan. Yes, Madam.

L. *Ea*. Where is he?

Servan. I believe, Madam, he's laid down to Sleep.

L. *Ea*. Where's *Edging,*—Bid her get me some Wax and Paper—stay, it's no matter, now I think on it, there's some above upon my Toilet. *(Exeunt severally.*

The Scene Opens, and Discovers Sir Charles *without his Periwig,* and Edging *by him, both asleep in two Easy-Chairs.*

And then Enter Lady Easy *who Starts and Trembles, some time, unable to speak.*

L. *Ea*. Ha!
Protect me Virtue! Patience! Reason!
Teach me to Bear this Killing sight, or let
Me think my Dreaming Senses are Deceiv'd!
For sure a Sight like This might raise the Arm
Of Duty, even to the Breast of Love! At least
I'll throw this Visor of my Patience off:
Now wake him in his Guilt,
And Barefac'd Front him with my Wrongs.
I'll talk to him till he Blushes, nay, till he—
—Frowns on me, perhaps,—and then
I'm lost again—The Ease of a Few Tears
Is all that's left to me—
And Duty too forbids me to Insult,
Where I have vow'd Obedience—Perhaps
The Fault's in me, and Nature has not Form'd
Me with the Thousand little Requisites
That Warm the Heart to Love—

242 B, D, E, me Wax. 245 *The Scene*. P, p. 54. 255 F, Vizor. 263 F, When I.

Somewhere there is a Fault—
But Heav'n best knows what Both of us deserve:
Ha! Bare-headed, and in so sound a Sleep!
Who knows, while thus Expos'd to the unwholsome Air,
But Heav'n offended may o'ertake his Crime,
And in some languishing Distemper, leave him
A severe Example of his violated Laws—
Forbid it Mercy, and forbid it Love.

This may prevent it. *(Takes her Steinkirk from her Neck, and lays it gently over his Head.)*

And if he shou'd wake offended at my too Busy Care, let my Heart-breaking Patience, Duty, and Fond Affection plead my Pardon. *(Exit.*

(After she has been out some time, a Bell rings; at which the Maid waking starts, and stirs Sir Charles.

Edg. Oh!

Sir *Cha.* How now, what's the Matter?

Edg. O! Bless my Soul, my Lady's come home.

Sir *Cha.* Go, go, then.

Edg. O lud! my Head's in such a Condition too—*(She Runs to the Glass. Bell rings.)*—I am coming, Madam—O lud! here's no Powder neither—Here Madam. *(Exit.*

Sir *Cha.* How now! *(Feeling the Steinkirk upon his Head.* What's this? How came it here?—Did not I see my Wife wear this to Day?—Death! she can't have been here sure! It cou'd not be Jealousie that Brought her home—for my coming was Accidental—so too, I fear, might hers.—How careless have I been?—Not to secure the Door neither—'Twas Foolish—It must be so! She certainly has seen me here Sleeping with her Woman —If so, How Low an Hypocrite to her must that sight have Prov'd me? the thought has made me Despicable ev'n to my self—How mean a Vice is Lying? And how often have these Empty Pleasures lull'd my Honour and my Conscience to a Lethargy, while I grosly have abus'd her, Poorly Skulking behind

270 C, unwholesome. F, th'unwholsom. 273 C, E, F, of its. 275 D, E. F, off her neck. C, on his. 278 A, F, and my Fond. 280, 281 C, E, F, *rings; Edging wakes, and stirs Sir Charles.* 285 Sir *Cha.* P, p. 55. 286 P, prints stage-direction on line 285. 291 F, could. C, F, Jealousy.

a Thousand Falshoods?—Now I reflect, this has not been the first of her Discoveries—How Contemptible a Figure must I have made to her!—A Crowd of Recollected Circumstances confirm me now, she has been long acquainted with my Follies, and yet with what amazing Prudence has she born the secret Pangs of Injur'd Love, and wore an everlasting Smile to me?—This asks a little Thinking—something should be done—I'll see her Instantly, and be resolv'd from her Behaviour. *(Exit.*

The Scene Changes To Another Room.

Enter Lady Easy, *and* Edging.

L. *Ea.* Where have you been, *Edging*?

Edg. Been, Madam! I—I—I—came as soon as I heard you Ring, Madam.

L. *Ea.* How Guilt confounds her—but she's below my Thought. Fetch my last new Scarf hither—I have a Mind to alter it a little—make haste.

Edg. Yes, Madam—I see she does not suspect any thing. *(Exit.*

L. *Ea.* *(sitting down.)* Heigh ho!—I had forgot—but I'm unfit for Writing now—Twas an hard Conflict—yet it's a Joy to think it over: A secret Pride, to tell my Heart my Conduct has been Just—How low are Vicious Minds, that Offer Injuries, how much superior Innocence that Bears 'em?—Still there's a Pleasure ev'n in the Melancholy of a Quiet Conscience—Away my Tears, it is not yet Impossible: For while his Humane Nature is not quite shook off, I ought not to Despair.

Re-enter Edging, *with a Scarf.*

Edg. Here's the Scarf, Madam.

L. *Ea.* So, sit down there, and, let me see—here—Rip off all that Silver.

Edg. Indeed, I always thought it wou'd become your Ladyship better without it, but now suppose, Madam, you carried another

[303] E, F, confirms. [314] C, Thought. *(aside)* Fetch. [322] a Pleasure. P, p. 56. [324] E, F, Human. [330] F, would. [331] A, carri'd. C, E, F, carry'd.

Row of Gold round those Scollops, and then you take and lay this Silver Plain all along the Gathers, and your Ladyship will perfectly see, it will give the Thing Ten Thousand times another Air.

L. *Ea.* Prithee don't be impertinent, do as I bid you.

Edg. Nay, Madam, with all my Heart, your Ladyship may do as you please.

L. *Ea.* This Creature grows so Confident, and I dare not Part with her least He shou'd think it Jealousy. *(Aside.*

Enter Sir Charles.

Sir *Cha.* So, my Dear, what, at Work! How are you employ'd, pray?

L. *Ea.* I was thinking to alter this Scarf, here.

Sir *Cha.* What's amiss; methinks its very pretty.

Edg. Yes, Sir, it's pretty enough for that Matter—but my Lady has a Mind it shou'd be Proper too.

Sir *Cha.* Indeed!

L. *Ea.* I Fancy Plain Gold and Black wou'd become me better.

Sir *Cha.* That's a Grave Thought, my Dear.

Edg. O Dear Sir, not at all, my Lady's much in the Right, I am sure; as it is, it's fit for Nothing but a Girl.

Sir *Cha.* Leave the Room.

Edg. Lard Sir! I can't stir, I must stay to—

Sir *Cha.* Go!— *(Angrily.*

Edg. *(Throwing down the Scarf Hastily, and Crying aside.)* If ever I speak to him again I'll be Burn'd. *Exit* Edging.

Sir *Cha.* Sit still, my Dear,—I came to Talk with you, and which you well may wonder at; what I have to say is of Importance too, but 'tis in order to my Hereafter always talking Kindly to you.

L. *Ea.* Your Words were never Disobliging, nor can I charge you with a Look that ever had the Appearance of Unkind.

Sir *Cha.* The perpetual Spring of your Good Humour lets me draw no Merit from what I have Appear'd to be, which makes me Curious now to know your Thoughts of what I really am:

333 B, Ladiship. 336 F, Pr'ythee. 340 D, F, should. D, E, Jealousie. 345 C, D, E, F, it's. 347 D, F, should. 349 C, F, would. P, sure, as. 355 P, Go. 364 Sir Cha. P, p. 57.

And never having ask'd you this before it puzzles me; nor can I (that strange Negligence consider'd) Reconcile to Reason your first Thoughts of venturing upon Marriage with me.

L. *Ea.* I never thought it such an Hazard.

Sir *Cha.* How cou'd a Woman of your Restraint in Principles, Sedateness, Sense, and Tender Disposition, Propose to see an Happy Life with One (now I reflect) that Hardly took an Hour's Pains, ev'n before Marriage, to appear but what I am, A loose Unheeding Wretch, Absent in all I do, Civil, and as often Rude without Design, Unseasonably thoughtful, Easy to a Fault, and in my Best of Praise but carelesly Good-Natur'd; How shall I reconcile your Temper with having made so strange a Choice?

L. *Ea.* Your own Words may Answer you—Your having never seem'd to Be, but what you really were; and through that carelesness of Temper, there still shone forth to me an Undesigning Honesty, I always Doubted of in smoother Faces: Thus, while I saw you took least Pains to win me, You pleas'd, and Woed me most: Nay, I have often thought that such a Temper cou'd never be Deliberately Unkind: Or, at the worst, I knew, that Errors from want of Thinking might be Born; at least, when Probably one Moment's serious Thought wou'd End 'em: These were my worst of Fears, and These when weigh'd by Growing Love against my solid Hopes were Nothing.

Sir *Cha.* My Dear, Your Understanding startles me, and justly calls my own in Question: I Blush to think I've worn so Bright a Jewel in my Bosom, and till this Hour, have scarce been Curious once to look upon its Lustre.

L. *Ea.* You set too High a Value on the common Qualities of an Easy Wife.

Sir *Cha.* Virtues, like Benefits, are Double when Conceal'd: And I confess I yet suspect you of an Higher value far, than I have spoke you.

L. *Ea.* I understand you not.

Sir *Cha.* I'll speak more Plainly to you—Be free, and tell me—Where did you leave this Handkerchief?

L. *Ea.* Hah!

368 C, my strange. 373 A, Hours. 377 B, D, E, F, carelessly. 384 F, I have thought. 395 D, E, easie.

Sir *Cha.* What is't you start at? You hear the Question.

L. *Ea.* What shall I say? my Fears confound me.

Sir *Cha.* Be not Concern'd, my Dear, be Easy in the Truth, and tell me.

L. *Ea.* I cannot speak—and I cou'd wish you'd not Oblige me to it—'tis the only Thing I ever yet refus'd You—and tho' I want a Reason for my Will, let me not Answer You.

Sir *Cha.* Your Will then be a Reason, and since I see you are so Generously Tender of Reproaching me, 'tis fit I should be Easy in my Gratitude, and make what ought to be my Shame, my Joy; let me therefore, Pleas'd to tell you Now, your Wondrous Conduct has wak'd me to a sense of your Disquiet Past, and Resolution never to Disturb it more—And (not that I offer it as a Merit, but yet in Blind Compliance to my Will) let me Beg you wou'd Immediately Discharge your Woman.

L. *Ea.* Alas! I think not of her—O, my Dear, Distract me not with this Excess of Goodness. *(Weeping.*

Sir *Cha.* Nay, Praise me not, lest I reflect how little I have deserv'd it—I see you are in Pain to give me this Confusion—Come, I will not Shock your Softness, by my untimely Blush for what is Past, but rather sooth you to a Pleasure at my sense of Joy for my Recover'd Happiness to come: Give then to my new-born Love, what Name you Please, it cannot, shall not be too Kind: O! it cannot be too soft for what my Soul swells up with Emulation to deserve—Receive me then Intire at last, and take what yet no Woman ever truly Had, my Conquer'd Heart.

L. *Ea.* O the soft Treasure! O the Dear Reward of long Desiring Love—Now I am Blest indeed to see you Kind without th'Expence of Pain in being so, to make you mine with Easiness. Thus! thus to have you mine is something more than Happiness, 'tis Double Life, and Madness of Abounding Joy. But 'twas a Pain Intollerable to give you a Confusion.

Sir *Cha.* O thou Engaging Virtue! But I'm too slow in doing Justice to thy Love: I know thy softness will refuse me; but

405 Sir Cha. P, p. 58. E, easie. 408 P, only Thng. 412 D, E, easie. 413 P, therefore Pleas'd. F, let me be therefore Pleas'd. 417 F, would. 419 P has a comma after Goodness. 420 P, A, B, C, D, E, least. 431 P, omits stop. C, D, F, Easiness: Thus! thus to have. 434 C, E, F, Intolerable.

remember I insist upon it—let thy Woman be Discharg'd this Minute.

L. *Ea.* No, my Dear, think me not so low in Faith, to fear that, after what you've said, 'twill be in her Power to do me future Injury: When I can conveniently Provide for her I'll think on't: But to Discharge her Now might let her Guess at the Occasion; and methinks I wou'd have all our Differences, like our Endearments, be Equally a Secret to our Servants.

Sir *Cha.* Still my Superior every way—be it as you have better thought—well, my Dear, now I'll confess a thing that was not in your Power to Accuse me of; to be short, I own this Creature is not the only one I have been to Blame with.

L. *Ea.* I know she is not, and was always less concern'd to find it so, for Constancy in Errors might have been Fatal to me.

Sir *Cha.* What is't you know, My Dear? *(Surpriz'd.*

L. *Ea.* Come, I am not afraid to accuse you Now—my Lady *Graveairs*—Your Carelesness, my Dear, let all the World know it, and it wou'd have been Hard indeed, had it been only to me a Secret.

Sir *Cha.* My Dear, I'll Ask no more Questions, for fear of being more Ridiculous: I do confess I thought my Discretion there had been a Masterpiece—How Contemptible must I have look'd all this while?

L. *Ea.* You shan't say so.

Sir *Cha.* Well, to let you see I had some Shame, as well as Nature in me, I had writ this to my Lady *Graveairs,* upon my first discovering that you knew I had wrong'd you; Read it.

L. *Ea. (Reads.)* "Something has happen'd that Prevents the "Visit I intended you; and I could gladly wish, You never "wou'd Reproach me, if I tell you, 'tis utterly Inconvenient "that I shou'd ever see you more.

This indeed was more than I had merited.

Enter a Servant.

Sir *Cha.* Who's there? Here—step with this to my Lady *Graveairs.* *(Seals the Letter, and gives it to the Servant.*

[437] B, Discharged. [440] A, F, 'twill ever. [441] F, Provide for her, but to Discharge her now. [445] Sir Cha. P, p. 59. [467] P, omits stop.

Serv. Yes, Sir,—Madam, my Lady *Betty*'s come.

L. *Ea.* I'll wait on her.

Sir *Cha.* My Dear, I'm thinking there may be other things my Negligence may have wrong'd you in; but be assur'd, as I discover 'em, all shall be Corrected: Is there any Part or Circumstance in your fortune that I can change, or yet make Easier to you?

L. *Ea.* None, my Dear, your Good Nature never stinted me in that; and now, methinks I have less Occasion there than ever.

Re-enter Servant.

Serv. Sir, my Lord *Morelove*'s come.

Sir *Cha* I am coming—I think I told you of the Design we had laid against Lady *Betty*.

L. *Ea.* You did, and I shou'd be pleas'd to be my self concern'd in it.

Sir *Cha.* I believe we may Employ you: I know he waits me with Impatience. But, my Dear, won't you think me tastless to the Joy you've given me, to suffer at this time any Concern but You t'employ my Thoughts.

L. *Ea.* Seasons must be Obey'd; and since I know your Friends Happiness Depending, I cou'd not taste my own, shou'd you neglect it.

Sir *Cha.* Thou Easie Sweetness—O! what a waste on thy Neglected Love, has my Unthinking Brain committed: But Time and Future Thrift of Tenderness shall yet repair it all: The Hours will Come when this soft Gliding Stream that swells my Heart, uninterupted shall Renew its Course,

And like the Ocean after Ebb, shall move
With Constant Force of Due Returning Love. *(Exeunt.*

The Scence Changes to another Room,

And then Re-enter Lady Easy *and Lady* Betty.

L. *Bett.* You've been in Tears my Dear, and yet you look Pleas'd too.

[485] L. Ea. P, p.60. [487] F, he waits for me. [488] C, E, F, tasteless. [491] F, Friend's. [492] P, own shou'd. [494] A, wast. [495] B, comited. [498] C, uninterrupted.

L. *Ea.* You'll Pardon me, if I can't yet let you into Circumstances: But be satisfied, Sir *Charles* has made me Happy ev'n to a Pain of Joy.

L. *Bett.* Indeed I am truly Glad of it: tho' I am sorry to find that any One who has Generosity enough to do you Justice shou'd unprovok'd be so great an Enemy to me.

L. *Ea.* Sir *Charles* your Enemy!

L. *Bett.* My Dear you'll Pardon me, if I always thought him so. But now I am convinc'd of it.

L. *Ea.* In what, 'Pray?' I can't think you'll find him so.

L. *Bett.* O! Madam, it has been his whole Business of late to make an utter Breach between my Lord *Morelove* and me.

L. *Ea.* That may be owing to your Usage of my Lord, perhaps he thought it wou'd not Disoblige you: I am Confident you are Mistaken in him.

L. *Bett.* O! I don't use to be out in things of this Nature, I can see well Enough: But I shall be Able to tell you more, when I have talkt with my Lord, ha! ha! ha!

L. *Ea.* Here he comes; and because you shall Talk with him—No Excuses—for Positively I will leave you together.

L. *Bett.* Indeed, my Dear, I desire you wou'd stay then; for, I know you think now, that I have a Mind to—to—

L. *Ea.* To—to— ha! ha! ha! *(Going.*

L. *Bett.* Well! remember This.

Enter Lord Morelove.

Ld. *Mo.* I hope I don't fright you away, Madam.

L. *Ea.* Not at all, my Lord; but I must beg your Pardon for a Moment, I'll wait upon you immediately.

L. *Bett.* My Lady *Easy* gone?

L. *Mo.* Perhaps, Madam, in Friendship to you, she thinks I may have deserv'd the Coldness you of late have shewn me; and was willing to give you this Opportunity to Convince me, you have not done it without Just Grounds and Reason.

L. *Bett.* How Hansomely does he Reproach me? But I can't

505 F, if I can't let. 508 F, I'm. 511 F, Sir Charles. 512 B, you'l. 513 F, so, but now. 522 C, E, F, talk'd. 522 E, ha! ha! ha! omitted. 524 C, I'll. 525 L. Bett. P, p. 61. 525 C, would. 538 B, Handsomely. C, Handsomly. A, Hansomely.

bear that he shou'd think I know it— *(Aside)* My Lord, whatever has Pass'd between you and me, I dare swear that cou'd not be her Thought at this time: For when two People have appear'd profess'd Enemies, she can't but think one will as little care to give, as t'other to receive a Justification of their Actions.

Ld. *Mo.* Passion indeed often does repented Injuries on both sides; but I don't remember in my Heat of Error, I ever yet profess'd my self your Enemy.

L. *Bett.* My Lord, I shall be very free with you—I confess I do think now I have not a greater Enemy in the World.

Ld. *Mo.* If having long lov'd you, to my own Disquiet, be Injurious, I am contented then to stand the foremost of your Enemies.

L. *Bett.* O, my Lord, there's no great Fear of your being my Enemy that way, I dare say—

Ld. *Mo.* There is no other way my Heart can Bear to Offend you Now, and I foresee in that it will persist to my Undoing.

L. *Bett.* Fy, fy, my Lord, we know where your Heart is well Enough.

Ld. *Mo.* My conduct has indeed Deserv'd this Scorn; and therefore 'tis but Just I shou'd submit to your Resentment, and beg, tho' I'm assur'd in vain, for Pardon. *(Kneels.*

Enter Sir Charles.

Sir *Cha.* How, my Lord! *(Ld* Mo. *rises.*

L. *Bett.* Ha! he here? This was Unlucky. *(Aside.*

Ld. *Mo.* O Pity my Confusion! *(To L.* Betty.

Sir *Cha.* I am sorry to see you can so soon forget your self; methinks the Insults you have born from that Lady, by this Time, shou'd have warn'd you into a Disgust of her Regardless Principles.

Ld. *Mo* Hold, Sir *Charles!* While you and I are Friends, I desire you wou'd speak with Honour of this Lady: 'Tis sufficient I have no Complaint against her, and—

L. *Bett.* My Lord—I beg you wou'd resent this thing no

589 P, omits comma. 541 C, toughts. 544 F, repeated Injuries. 554 F, There's. 556 C, D, E, F, fie, fie. 559 F, should. 560 C, tho 'I am assur'd. F, tho' I'm assured in vain. 564 Ld. Mo. P, p. 62. 570 F, would. 570 C, 'T is. 572 C, would.

farther: An Injury like this is better Punisht with our Contempt; Apparent Malice only shou'd be laught at—

Sir *Cha.* Ha! ha! the Old Recourse, Offers of any Hopes to delude him from his Resentment; and then as the *Grand Monarch* did with *Cavalier,* you are sure to keep your Word with him.

L. *Bett.* Sir *Charles,* to let you know how far I am above your little Spleen, my Lord, your Hand, from this Hour—

Sir *Cha.* 'Pshah! 'Pshah! All Design! all Pique! meer Artifice, and Disappointed Woman.

L. *Bett.* Look you, Sir, not that I doubt my Lord's Opinion of me; yet—

Sir *Cha.* Look you, Madam, in short your word has been too often taken to let you make up Quarrels, as you us'd to do with a soft Look, and a fair Promise you never Intended to Keep.

L. *Bett.* Was ever such an Insolence, he won't give me leave to speak.

Ld. *Mo.* Sir *Charles!*

L. *Bett.* No 'Pray', my Lord, have Patience; and since his Malice seems to grow Particular, I dare his worst, and urge him to the Proof ont: 'Pray', Sir, wherein can you Charge me with Breach of Promise to my Lord?

Sir *Cha.* 'Death, you won't deny it? How often, to piece up a Quarrel have you Appointed him to Visit you alone; and tho' you have promis'd to see no other Company the whole Day, when he has come, he has found you among the laugh of Noisy Fops, Coquettes, and Coxcombs, Dissolutely Gay, while your Full Eyes ran o'er with Transport of their Flattery, and your own vain Power of Pleasing? How often, I say, have you been known to throw away at least four hours of your good Humour upon such Wretches; and the Minute they were gone, grew only Dull to him, sunk into a Distastful Spleen, complain'd you had talk'd your self into the Head-ach, and then Indulg'd upon the Dear Delight of seeing him in Pain: And by that time you

[573] C, D, F, punish'd. [574] C, laugh'd. D, only should be laugh'd at. F, shou'd only be laugh'd at. [576] B, Resentement. [580] Pshaw! Pshaw! [585] C, F, used. [592] C, F, on't. [594] F, How often to. [598] C, F, Coquets. E, noisie Fops, Coquets. [603] F, Distasteful. [605] C, Pain? [605], [606] C, you had stretcht. D, you had stretch't. F, you had stretch'd.

stretcht, and Gap'd him Heartily out of Patience, of a sudden most importantly remember you had out-sate your Appointment with my Lady Fiddle-faddle; and immediately order your Coach to the Park.

L. *Bett.* Yet, Sir, have you done?

Sir *Cha.* No— tho' this might serve to shew the Nature of your Principles: But the Noble Conquest you have Gain'd at last over Defeated Sense of Reputation too, has made your Fame Immortal.

Ld. *Mo.* How, Sir?

L. *Bett.* My Reputation!

Sir *Cha.* Ay, Madam, your Reputation—my Lord, if I advance a Falshood, then Resent it—I say, your Reputation—'t has been your Life's whole Pride of late to be the Common Toast of every Publick Table, Vain ev'n in the Infamous Addresses of a Married Man, my Lord *Foppington*; Let that be reconcil'd with Reputation, I'll now shake Hands with Shame, and Bow me to the low Contempt which you deserve from him; not but I suppose you'll yet Endeavour to recover him: Now you find your self by Ill Usage in Danger of losing your Conquest, 'tis Possible you'll stop at Nothing to preserve it.

L. *Bett.* Sir *Charles—* *(Walks disorder'd, and he after her.*

Sir *Cha.* I know your Vanity is so Voracious, 'twill ev'n wound it self to feed it self; Offer him a Blank, perhaps, to fill up with Hopes of what Nature he Pleases, and Part with ev'n your Pride to keep him.

L. *Bett.* Sir *Charles,* I have not deserv'd this of you. *(Bursting into Tears.*

Sir *Cha.* Ah! True Woman, drop him a soft Dissembling Tear, and then his Just Resentment must be Husht of Course.

Ld. *Mo.* O, *Charles!* I can bear no more, those Tears are too Reproaching.

Sir *Cha.* Hist for your Life! *(Aside, and then aloud.*

My lord if you believe her, you're undone; the very next sight of my Lord *Foppington* wou'd make her yet forswear all that she can Promise.

607 out-sate. P, p. 63. 621 A, Marri'd. C, D, F, Marry'd. 624 P, D, F, you find Ill Usage. 639 F, would.

L. *Bett.* My Lord *Foppington!* Is that the mighty Crime that must Condemn me then? You know I us'd him but as a Tool of my Resentment, which you your self, by a Pretended Friendship to us Both, most Artfully Provokt me to—

Ld. *Mo.* Hold, I conjure you, Madam, I want not this Conviction.

L. *Bett.* Send for him this Minute, and You and He shall Both be Witnesses of the Contempt, and Detestation I have for any Forward Hopes his Vanity may have given him, or your Malice wou'd Insinuate.

Sir *Cha.* Death! You wou'd as soon eat Fire, as soon Part with your Luxurious Tast of Folly, as Dare to own the Half of this Before his Face, or any one, that wou'd make you Blush to deny it to—Here comes my Wife, Now we shall see—Ha! and my Lord *Foppington* with her—Now! Now, we shall see this mighty Proof of your Sincerity— Now, my Lord, you'll have a Warning sure, and henceforth know me for your Friend Indeed.

Enter Lady Easy *and Lord* Foppington.

L. *Ea.* In Tears, my Dear, what's the Matter!

L. *Bett.* O, my Dear, all I told you's true: Sir *Charles* has shewn himself so inveterately my Enemy, that if I believ'd I deserv'd but Half his Hate, 'twou'd make me Hate my self.

L. *Fop.* Hark you, *Charles,* 'Prithee what is this Business?

Sir *Cha.* Why yours, my Lord, for ought I know—I have made such a Breach betwixt'em—I can't promise much for the Courage of a Woman; but if hers holds, I am sure it's wide enough, you may Enter Ten a Breast, my Lord.

Ld. *Fop.* Say'st thou so, *Charles;* then I hold Six to Four I am the first Man in the Town.

L. *Ea.* Sure there must be some Mistake in this; I hope he has not made my Lord your Enemy.

L. *Bett.* I know not what he has done.

Ld. *Mo.* Far be that Thought! Alas! I am too much in Fear my self, that what I have this Day Committed, Advis'd by his Mistaken Friendship, may have done, my Love Irreparable Prejudice.

L. *Bett.* No, my Lord, since I perceive his little Arts have not

644 A, E, F, provok'd. 648 -ward. P, p. 64. 649 C, F, would. 651 F, Taste. 652 F, would. 655 D, have Warning. 661 F, 'twould. 662 P, Business.

prevail'd upon your Good Nature to my Prejudice, I am bound in Gratitude, in Duty to my self, and to the Confession you have made, my Lord, to acknowledge Now, I have been to Blame too.

Ld. *Mo.* Ha! Is't Possible, can you own so much? O my Transported Heart!

L. *Bett.* He says, I have taken Pleasure in seeing you Uneasy—I own it—but 'twas when that Uneasiness I thought Proceeded from your Love; and if you did love—'twill not be much to Pardon it.

Ld. *Mo.* O let my Soul, thus Bending to your Power, adore this soft Descending Goodness.

L. *Bett.* And since the Giddy Woman's Slights I have shewn you too often have been Publick, 'tis fit at last th' Amends and Reparation shou'd be so: Therefore what I offer'd to Sir *Charles,* I now Repeat before this Company, my Utter Detestation of any Past or Future Gallantry, that has, or shall be offer'd me to Your Uneasiness.

Ld. *Mo.* O be less Generous, or teach me to deserve it—Now Blush, Sir *Charles,* at your Injurious Accusation.

Ld. *Fop.* Hah! *Pardi voilà quelque Chose D'Extraordinaire!* *(Aside.*

L. *Bett.* As for my Lord *Foppington,* I owe him thanks for having been so Friendly an Instrument of our Reconciliation; for tho' in the little outward Gallantry I received from him, I did not immediately trust him with my Design in it; yet I have a better Opinion of his Understanding, than to suppose he cou'd Mistake it.

L. *Fop.* I am struck Dumb with the Deliberation of her Assurance; and do not Positively remember, that the *Non Challence* of my Temper ever had so Bright an Occasion to shew it self before.

L. *Bett.* My Lord, I hope you'll Pardon the Freedom I have taken with you.

Ld. *Fop.* O, Madam, don't be under the Confusion of an Apology upon my Account; for in Cases of this Nature I am never Disappointed, but when I find a Lady of the same Mind two

[681] D, Uneasie. [685] Ld. Mo. P, p. 65. [688] C, often, have been made Publick. [689] C, should. [699] F, Galantry. F, that has or shall. [698] F, Galantry I receiv'd. [703] C, D, F, Non-chalence.

hours together—Madam, I have lost a thousand Fine Women in my time; but never had the Ill Manners to be out of Humour with any one for refusing me since I was Born.

L. *Bett.* My Lord, that's a very Prudent Temper.

Ld. *Fop.* Madam, to Convince you, that I am in a Universal Peace with Mankind, since you own I have so far Contributed to your Happiness, give me leave to have the Honour of Compleating it, by Joyning your Hand where you have already offer'd up your Inclination.

L. *Bett.* My Lord, that's a Favour I can't refuse you.

Ld. *Mo.* Generous indeed, My Lord.

Ld. Fop. *Joins their hands.*

L. *Fop.* And stap my Breath, if ever I was better Pleas'd since my first Entrance into Human Nature.

Sir *Cha.* How now, my Lord! What! throw up your Cards before you have lost the Game?

Ed. *Fop.* Look you, *Charles,* 'tis true, I did design to have Play'd with her alone: But he that will keep well with the Ladies, must sometimes be content to make one at a Pool with 'em: And since I know I must engage her in my Turn, I don't see any great Odds in letting him take the first Game with her.

Sir *Cha.* Wisely Consider'd, my Lord.

L. *Bett.* And Now, Sir *Charles*—

Sir *Cha.* And Now, Madam, I'll save you the Trouble of a long Speech; and, in one Word, Confess that every thing I have done in Regard to you this Day was purely Artificial—I saw there was no way to secure you to my Lord *Morelove,* but by Allarming your Pride with the Danger of losing him: And since the Success must have by this time Convinc'd you, that in Love nothing is more Ridiculous, than an over-acted Aversion; I am sure you won't take it Ill, if we at last Congratulate your good Nature, by Heartily laughing at the Fright we had put you in. Ha! ha! ha!

L. *Ea.* Ha! ha! ha!

L. *Bett.* Why—well, I declare it now, I hate you worse than ever.

711 C, F, an Universal. 717 F, Joining. 723 C, the Cairds. 726 A, Plai'd. 727 sometimes. P, p. 66. 727 A, D, F, Poole. 736 F, Alarming.

Sir *Cha.* Ha! ha! ha! and was it afraid they wou'd take its Love from it—Poor Lady *Betty!* ha! ha!

L. *Ea.* My Dear, I beg your Pardon; but 'tis impossible not to laugh when one's so heartily pleas'd.

L. *Fop.* Really, Madam, I am afraid the good Humour of the Company will draw me into your Displeasure too; but if I were to expire this Moment, my last Breath wou'd Positively go out in a laugh. Ha! ha! ha!

L. *Bett.* Nay, I have deserv'd it all, that's the Truth on't—but I hope, my Lord, You were not in this Design against me.

Ld. *Mo.* As a Proof, Madam, I am inclin'd never to Deceive you more—I do confess—I had my share in't.

L. *Bett.* You do, my Lord!—then I declare 'twas a Design, one or other—the best Carry'd on, that ever I knew in my life; and (to my shame I own it) for ought I know, the only thing that cou'd have prevail'd upon my Temper: 'Twas a Foolish Pride, that has Cost me many a Bitter Lip to support it—I wish we don't both repent, my Lord.

Ld. *Mo.* Don't you Repent without me, and we never shall.

Sir *Cha.* Well, Madam, now the worst that the World can say of your Past Conduct, is, that my Lord had Constancy, and you have try'd it.

Enter a Servant to Lord Morelove.

Serv. My Lord, Mr. le *Fevre*'s below, and desires to know what time your Lordship will Please to have the Musick begin.

Ld. *Mo.* Sir *Charles,* what say you? will you give me leave to bring 'em Hither?

Sir *Cha.* As the Ladies think fit, my Lord.

L. *Bett.* O! by all means, 'twill be better here, unless we cou'd have the Terrace to our selves.

Ld. *Mo.* Then Pray Desire 'em to come all hither Immediately.

Serv. Yes, my Lord. *(Exit Servant.*

Enter Lady Graveairs.

Sir *Cha.* Lady *Graveairs!*

745 F, take away its Love. 748 A, ones. 749 F, the Humour. 751 C, would. 754 C, against me. 758 E, F, carried. 761 C, E, F, bitten. 765 F, is that. 767 Enter. P, p. 67. 768 F, Mr. le Fev're's. 774 E, F, Terras.

L. *Gra.* Yes! you may well start! But don't suppose I am now come like a Poor Tame Fool to upbraid your Guilt; but if I cou'd, to Blast you with a Look.

Sir *Cha.* Come, come, you yet have sense—Don't Expose your self, you are unhappy, and I own my self the Cause—The only Satisfaction I can offer you, is to Protest, No New Engagement takes me from you: But a sincere Reflection of the long Neglect, and Injuries I've done the Best of Wives, for whose Amends, and only sake I now must Part with You, and all the Inconvenient Pleasures of my Life.

L. *Gra.* Have you then fallen into the Low Contempt of Exposing me, and to your Wife too?

Sir *Cha.* 'Twas Impossible, without it, I cou'd ever be sincere in my Conversion.

L. *Gra.* Despicable!

Sir *Cha.* Do not think it so—for my sake I know she'll not reproach you, nor by her Carriage ever let the World perceive you've wrong'd her—my Dear.

L. *Ea.* Lady *Graveairs,* I hope you'll Sup with us?

L. *Gra.* I can't refuse so much Good Company, Madam.

Sir *Cha.* You see the Worst of her Resentment—in the mean time don't Endeavour to be her Friend, and she'll never be your Enemy.

L. *Gra.* I am Unfortunate—'tis what my Folly has deserv'd, and I submit to it.

Ld. *Mo.* So! here's the Musick.

L. *Ea.* Come, Ladies, shall we sit?

After the Musick, a SONG.

Sabina *with an Angel's Face,*
By Love Ordain'd for Joy,
Seems of the Syren's *Cruel Race,*
To Charm, and then Destroy:

With all the Arts of Look, and Dress,
She Fanns the Fatal Fire,

[779] F, Ye! [781] P, cou'd to. [782] C, F, You have Sense. [785] F, Reflexion. [786] F, Amends and. [791] F, could. [796] C, her. My Dear. [806] After. P, p. 68. [809] F, Sirens. [812] A, C, D, E, F, fans.

Trough Pride, Mistaken oft for Grace,
She Bids the Swain Expire.

The God of Love Enrag'd to see
The Nymph Defy his Flame,
Pronounc'd this Merciless Decree
Against the Haughty Dame.

Let Age with Double Speed o'ertake her,
Let Love the Room of Pride supply;
And when the Lovers all forsake her,
A Spotless Virgin let her Dye.

Sir Charles *comes forward, with Lady* Easy.

Sir *Cha.* Now, my Dear, I find my Happiness grow fast upon me; in all my Past Experience of the Sex, I found ev'n among the Better sort so much of Folly, Pride, Malice, Passion, and Irresolute Desire, that I concluded Thee but of the foremost Rank, and therefore scarce worthy my Concern; but thou hast stirr'd me with so severe a Proof of thy Exalted Virtue, it gives me Wonder Equal to my Love—If then the Unkindly Thought of what I have been hereafter shou'd intrude upon thy growing Quiet, let this Reflection teach thee to be Easy:

Thy Wrongs when Greatest Most thy Vertue Prov'd,
And from that Vertue Found, I Blusht, and Truly Lov'd.

816 D, defie. 822 C, E, Die. 833 and. 834 C, D, E, F, virtue.

APPENDIX I

The Theatre during the Commonwealth

On the second of September 1642 the theatres were closed, as appears from the following *Order of the Lords and Commons concerning Stage-playes:*

"Whereas the distressed Estate of Ireland, steeped in her own Blood, and the distracted Estate of England, threatned with a Cloud of Blood, by a Civill Warre, call for all possible meanes to appease and avert the Wrath of God appearing in these Judgements; amongst which, Fasting and Prayer having bin often tryed to be very effectuall, have bin lately, and are still enjoyned; and whereas publike Sports doe not well agree with publike Calamities, nor publike stageplayes with the Seasons of Humiliations, this being an Exercise of sad and pious solemnity, and the other being Spectacles of pleasure, too commonly expressing lacivious mirth and Levitie: It is therefore thought fit, and Ordeined by the Lords and Commons in this Parliament Assembled, that while these sad Causes and set times of Humiliation doe continue, publike stage Playes shall cease, and bee forborne. Instead of which, are recommended to the people of this land, the profitable and seasonable Considerations of Repentance, Reconciliation, and peace with God, which probably may produce outward peace and prosperity, and bring againe Times of Joy and Gladnesse to these Nations.

Die Veneris, Septemb. 2. 1642.

Ordered by the Lords and Commons in Parliament, that this Order be forthwith Printed and published.

John Browne Cler. Parl."

This order had to be repeated several times, but there is sufficient evidence to show that it was never absolutely enforced. For some time it was the custom to bribe the officer, in command of the guard at Whitehall, who then connived at the acting of plays at the Red Bull, for a few days. When the Civil War was over, the actors, who had been Royalists almost to a man, returned to London; the remnants of the various companies amalgamated and tried to make a living by carrying on their old profession. In the winter before the execution of Charles I, in 1648, they performed for some days at The Cockpit. During Cromwell's government they generally acted at some private house a few miles out of London and were paid out of the contributions of the noblemen and gentry who came to hear them.[1] That Davenant continued to give performances of some sort during the Commonwealth is well-known.

It is interesting to note that the history of other public amusements which had been forbidden runs parallel to that of the theatre. In a recent article on *"Bear gardens and bear baiting during the Commonwealth"*,[2] it was proved that the Bear-garden remained one of the most popular and uninterrupted amusements of London during the Interregnum. A Parliament Newsbook for Dec. 29th to Jan 5th. 1655, contains the notice: "Yesterday a man was killed by a bull at the Bear-Garden". At a public garden *(The Hope)* the bears were shot by a company of soldiers on Feb. 9th, 1655. Bear baiting was continued, however, at private gardens.

[1] *Historia Histrionica,* p. 16.
[2] Publ. Mod. Lang. Ass. of America XI, No. 2, p. 281.

APPENDIX II

CIBBER'S ATTITUDE WITH RESPECT TO COLLIER'S "SHORT VIEW"

As was to be expected, Cibber's protests against Collier's "Short View", were distinguished from most of the others by their extreme moderation, because Cibber did not introduce into his plays several elements, that were considered objectionable by Collier. In the dedication to the first edition of *Love Makes a Man,* he writes as follows:[1] "But suppose the stage may have taken too loose a liberty? Is there nothing to be said for it? Have not all sciences been guilty? Was it to be expected in a reign of pleasure, peace and madness, that the poets should not be merry? Did not the court then lead up the dance? And did not the whole nation join in it? Was it not mere Joan Sanderson, and did not the lawnsleeves, cuffs, and cassocks fill up the measure? But since those dancing days are over, I hope our enemies will give us leave to grow wise and sober, as well as the rest of our neighbours: Why shall we not have the liberty to reform as well as the clergy, and lawyers? I believe upon a fair examination we may find, that prophaneness, cruelty, and passive obedience, are now less than ever the business of the Stage, the bench or the pulpit; and I doubt not, but we can produce examples of new plays, lawyers and pastors that have met with success without being obliged to immorality, bribery, or politics.

Now if the stage must needs down, because 't is possible it may seduce, as instruct; the same rule of policy might forbid the use of physic, because not only their patients, but physicians themselves die of common diseases; or call in the milled crowns, because they are but so many patterns for coiners to counterfeit by, or might as well suppress the Courts of Just Judicature, because some persons have suffered for what a succeeding reign has made a new law, that makes that law, that sentenced them illegal: The same conclusion might discountenance our religion, because we sometimes find pride, hypocrisy, avarice, and ignorance in its teachers. So that if our zealous reformers do not stick fairly to their method we may in time hope to see our nation flourish without either wit, health, money, law, conscience, or religion....

But this sort of reformation, I hope will never be thoroughly wrought, while the King, and the Established Church have any friend: The stage I am sure was never heartily oppressed but by the enemies of both."

[1] Quoted in full by De Witt Croissant because it was omitted in all editions except the first.

No doubt this comparison of the stage with the pulpit and the Law-court must have seemed irreverent to Collier, but in the views expressed above, Cibber did not stand alone.[1]

In the Dedication to *The Lady's Last Stake,* we read: "If I would have been less instructive, I might have met with a louder, tho' not a more valuable Applause. But I shall always prefer a fixt and general Attention before the noisy Roars of the Gallery. A Play without a just Moral, is a poor and trivial Undertaking; and 't is from the Success of such Pieces, that Mr. Collier was furnish'd with an advantageous Pretence of laying his unmerciful Axe at the Root of the Stage".

Throughout his *Apology* we find the same sentiments expressed, but as most of these passages have been referred to before, it is unnecessary to quote them again, with the exception of the following: "However just his (Collier's) charge against the authors that then wrote for it (the stage) might be, I cannot but think his sentence against the Stage itself is unequal: reformation he thinks too mild a treatment for it, and is therefore for laying his axe to the root of it; if this were to be a rule of judgment for offences of the same nature, what might become of the pulpit, where many a seditious and corrupted teacher has been known to cover the most pernicious doctrine with the mask of religion?"

.... "My first play of *The Fool in Fashion,* too, being then in a course of success; perhaps for that reason only, this severe author thought himself obliged to attack it: in which I hope, he has shewn more zeal than justice, his greatest charge against it is that it sometimes uses the word Faith! as an oath, in the dialogue: but if Faith may as well signify our given word, or credit, as our religious belief, why might not his charity have taken it in the less criminal sense?"

In the prologue to *Xerxes,* he very neatly turns the tables on Collier:

"Thus ev'n sage Collier too might be accus'd,
If what h'as writ, thro' ignorance abus'd:
Girls may read him, not for the truth, he says,
But to be pointed to the bawdy plays".

[1] In *Some Cursory Remarks,* Steele says: "I think a good company of Comedians as necessary in a well-govern'd City as any one Thing beside. I don't know but we may owe more to the Theatre than the Pulpit, in the Reformation of many Vices of the Age; and I'm certain, a Line of Satyr has more efficacy than some whole Volumes of Moral Discourses; and I must confess, to my Shame, that I have often been so sensibly touch'd by Things I have seen in Plays, that I have found my Folly and reform'd."

APPENDIX III.

CIBBER AND POPE.

We had occasion before to point out the disparaging tone in which references to Cibber are usually worded in most of the handbooks of literature, when he is mentioned at all, and in the preceding pages we have tried to point out that this is doing him an injustice. This peculiar attitude towards Cibber is based in the first place on a very superficial acquaintance with his works and then on too implicit a reliance on the opinion of some of his contemporaries, especially on that of Dennis and Pope.

Cibber was highly successful and so it was perhaps natural that a great many of those, who considered themselves the equals of this selfmade man, should envy him and try to do everything in their power to bring him down to their own level. One of these anonymous enemies[1] wrote as follows about his *Apology:* "I may be allowed to say of this voluminous Performance: Sunt bona sunt quaedam mediocria, sunt mala plura;

There are some good Things in thy Book, old Colley,
But all the rest is, self-sufficient Folley."

And again: "I now come to the fifteenth and (thank Heaven) the last chapter of this long, heavy, dull, pert, injudicious laughing History; the work of a most undaunted Scribler".

Another sample[2] in the same style may be given here: "The ingenious and modest Mr. Colley Cibber has outdone Montaign, and not only talked a great deal of himself, but has set so great a value on himself, that after being so long known, he will not let any one know what he really is, under a less consideration than a Guinea." (At the bottom of the page there is a note to this effect: "Since this was wrote, the Apology is sold for 2 s. 8 d. in Dublin").

The author then makes a few remarks about Cibber's *Apology,* and concludes with: "Videri Pauper vult, et est Pauper",

"When humble Cinna cries,—I'm poor and low,
"You may believe him,—he is really so.

"I shall give the Latin Line a different turn"

"The Cibbers both themselves dull Rogues declare.
"But what they say in Jest, in Truth they are."

The quotations given here are particularly interesting, because they show

1 *The Laureat: or the Right Side of Colley Cibber, Esq.,* London 1740.
2 *An Apology for the Life of Mr. The' Cibber,* Dublin 1741

that the anonymous authors discovered Cibber's dulness while reading his *Apology,* the only one of his works to find grace in the eyes of nearly all critics.

In his birthday-odes and even in his plays, he is more vulnerable and most of the attacks to which he was exposed were aimed at these, but the final reputation of dulness he owes to Pope, who enthroned him in the *Dunciad.*

Though nearly all who have written on this subject and taken the trouble to know who and what Cibber really was, have come to the conclusion [1] that the "Homer of Twickenham" never came so near to qualifying for a place in his own *Dunciad,* as when he substituted Cibber for Theobald, *King Colley* to many students of literature remains nothing but the hero of the *Dunciad* and consequently a dunce.

In this matter Pope lost sight of reason and decency. He merely indulged in personal pique, as Cibber fully explains in his *Apology* [2], to which ought to be added the expression of his political and religious indignation at the *Non-Juror.* Cibber's protests against the treatment he received at Pope's hands are in his best prose-style and that is saying a great deal.

His first *Letter from Mr. Cibber to Mr. Pope, inquiring into the Motives that might induce him in his satyrical works to be so frequently fond of Mr. Cibber's Name* [3] is written in a very kind and reserved way. It is only in his reference to the lines from Pope's *Epistle to Dr. Arbuthnot:*

"Whom have I hurt, has Poet yet or Peer,
"Left the arch't Eye-brow, or Parnassian Sneer?
"And has not Colley too his Lord and Whore,"

that Cibber abandons his usual reserve and turns on Pope by describing an escapade Pope was once guilty of. [4]

By way of illustration a few passages will here be quoted in full: "As you have for several Years past (particularly in your Poetical Works) mentioned my Name without my desiring it; give me leave at last to make my due Compliments to yours in Prose....

[1] See e.g. Walpole's Letters, passim; Birkbeck Hill II, p. 92; *The Age of Pope,* p. 196; *Biographia Dramatica,* p. 120; *Hazlitt's Lectures,* p. 353 and so on, ad infinitum.

[2] On one occasion Cibber performed Bayes in the *Rehearsal,* while Pope was among the audience. It was then the custom to restore the zest of that old satyre by introducing allusions to recent theatrical events, and this time Cibber referred to an absurd incident in *Three Hours after Marriage,* a comedy by Pope, Gay and Arbuthnot, that had proved a complete failure. The plot of this silly piece hinged on the contrivance of two lovers getting access to the wife of a virtuoso, one curiously swathed up like an Egyptian Mummy, and the other slily covered in the pasteboard skin of a crocodile and it was this that provided Cibber with the subject of his joke. After the performance was over, Pope came behind the scenes and in a trembling voice called Cibber to account and ordered him to leave out the allusion referred to. Cibber refused to comply and intimated his intention to repeat the jest as long as the public approved of it.

[3] The Third Edition, Glasgow (undated). [4] Pages 49 ff.

If I have lain so long stoically silent or unmindful of your Satyrical Favours, it was not so much for Want of a Proper Reply, as that I thought they never needed a Publick one....

But since the Publication of your last new Dunciad (where you still seem to enjoy your so often repeated Glory of being bright upon my Dulness) my Friends now insist, that it will be thought Dulness indeed, or a plain Confession of my being Bankrupt in wit if I don't immediately answer those Bills of Discredit, for, say they, your dealing with him, like a gentleman, in your Apology for your own Life you see, has had no sensible Effect upon him.... You have drawn upon me. They desired I would enter the Lists with you; notwithstanding I am under the Disadvantage of having only the blunt and weak weapon of Prose to oppose you.

While I am conscious you can say nothing truly of me, that ought to put an honest Man to the Blush, what in God's Name, can I have to fear from you?"

With respect to his poetry, he remarks: "I wrote more to be fed, than be famous, and since my Writings still give me a Dinner, do you rhyme me out of my Stomach if you can."

And again, writing about himself he continues:[1] "How comes it then that in your works you have so often treated him as a Dunce or an Enemy? Did he at all intrench upon your Sovereignty in Verse, because he had now and then written a Comedy that succeeded? Or could you not bear, that any kind of Poetry, but that, to which you chiefly pretended, should meet with Applause? Or was it that he had an equal Reputation for Acting his own Characters as for Writing them, or that with such inferior Talents he was admitted to as good Company as you, with your superior, could get into?"

Referring to the charge of dulness, Cibber says:[2] "I will leave it to your own Conscience, to declare whether you really think I am so guilty of it, as to deserve the Name of the dull Fellow you make of me. Now if the Reader will call upon my Conscience to speak the Question, I do from my Heart solemnly declare, that I don't believe you do think so of me."

Later on he mentions Pope's statement that he, Cibber, was unsuccessful as an actor of tragedy and smartly defends himself by saying:[3]

"But if I have made so many crowded Theatres laugh, and in the right Place too, for above forty Years together, am I to make up the number of your Dunces, because I have not the equal Talent of making them cry too? Make it your own Case: Is what you have excelled in at all the worse for your having so dismally dabbled (as I before observ'd) in the Farce of *Three Hours after Marriage?* Non omnia possumus omnes, is an allow'd Excuse for the Insufficiences of Mankind; and if, as you see, you too must sometimes be forc'd to take Shelter under it, as well as myself, what mighty Reason will the World have to laugh at my Weakness in Tragedy, more than at yours in Comedy?"

Thus much for Cibber's first letter to Pope, the quiet argumentative

[1] Page 10. [2] Page 12. [3] Page 16.

tone and the keen, though reserved, raillery of which were well calculated to infuriate that poet, not because of any excesses in his style, but because of the ease with which Cibber in this document demonstrated his own superiority to Pope, in this respect at least.

What strikes an attentive reader most in all his references to Pope as an artist, in this letter as well as in his *Apology,* is the respect that speaks from them. Cibber knew and admitted in so many words that his opponent was by far the greater artist, but at the same time he proved himself to be his superior in another respect. This was a thing Pope, "our little Homer of Twickenham", as Cibber called him, could not bear, though he pretended that Cibber's letter merely amused him.[1] Pope retaliated and thus provoked Cibber into writing his second letter, the tone of which is deservedly more severe and sarcastic than that of the first.

The very motto gives us an idea of what is coming:

"Remember Sawney's Fate!

"Banged by the Blockhead, whom he strove to beat.

After an introduction in which he once more goes over the whole dispute he says that Pope's nature "seems to be incurable: for tho' in my first Letter, without regard to your Quality, I had honestly taken the Whip and the Bell to you and (as evry Body tells me) made you as uneasy as a Rat in a hot Kettle for Twelve-month together, I still find that bitter Pug is at his old Tricks again, and as silly a Devil as ever;....

This, you will say, is Language not fit to be used to a Gentleman: I grant it, but like other general Rules, this too may have its exceptions; I cannot therefore allow it unfit for so particular a Gentleman: it is at least as gentle as what your Oyster-mouth'd Muse has bestowed upon your humble Servant; And though yours 'tis true is charmingly chim'd in Verse, I still find that the plain Words *Brazen, Brainless, Coxcomb, Blockhead, Impudent,* with that burthen of your Song, *Dull* upon *Dull* for ever, whether in Verse or Prose, have just the same Signification. Nor can I conceive why Rhyme should have a more unlimited Licence than Reason! Is the Filth in the one of a sweeter Smell than in the Other? If therefore you think you have a right to lay your satyrical Tail at my Door, whenever your Muse has a Looseness, have not I an equal Right to rub your Nose in it?

These I confess again are most unsavoury Similies: but I have the classical Authority of your Dunciad to plead for them, where we occasionally find your filthy slut of a Muse emptying her Jordan, Toast and all, into the Street. A delicate Nosegay it is indeed! Smell it Reader—

"Full in the middle Way, there stood a Lake,
"Which Curl's Corinna chanc'd that Morn to make;
"(Such was her Wont, at early Dawn to drop
"Her Ev'ning Cates before his Neighbour's Shop) *Dun.* B. 2. l. 69.

Now, Sir, if you, who say you have copy'd these vile Ideas from Homer, and Virgil, will either own that you have belied these Authors, or that a

[1] Page 15.

Stink will be a Stink, let who will make it: then I say (provided you will eat your words) I will give up mine, as equally unfit to come into civil Company".

Once more Pope pretended to be amused by Cibber's letter, but he did not succeed in keeping up the pretence.[1] Particularly did Cibber's relation of some tavern episode, in which he had prevented Pope from committing a serious indiscretion, sting the poet to the quick, and call forth a hot denial from Pope. And this was aggravated when in his second letter, Cibber followed it up with that terribly personal allusion: "When crawling in thy dangerous deed of darkness, I gently, with a finger and a thumb, picked off thy small round body by thy long legs, like a spider making love in a cobweb."

Cibber's overtures of peace had been refused and, therefore, urged on by his friends, he showed his teeth and chastised Pope by means of sarcasm that was unanswerable, but, generally speaking, the actor's attitude to his opponent is best summed up in that well-known paragraph in the first volume of his *Apology*:[2]

"Not our great imitator of Horace himself can have more pleasure in writing his verses than I have in reading them, though I sometimes find myself there (as Shakespeare terms it) dispraisingly spoken of: If he is a little free with me, I am generally in good company; he is as blunt with my betters; so that even here I might laugh in my turn. My superiors, perhaps, may be mended by him; but, for my part, I own myself incorrigible; I look upon my follies as the best part of my fortune, & am more concerned to be a good husband of them than of that. And, if I don't mistake, I am supported in my way of thinking by Horace himself, who, in excuse of a loose writer, says:

Praetulerim scriptor delirus, inersque videri,
Dum mea delectent, mala me, aut denique fallant,
Quam sapere, et ringi —"

Notwithstanding the fact that most writers at the present day agree that it was absurd on the part of Pope to hold up Cibber as an example of dulness, attempts are still occasionally made to prove the contrary, attempts which invariably necessitate a good deal of juggling with the word "dulness".

In Elwin and Courthope's edition of Pope's works,[3] for example, the

[1] Cf. *Works of Samuel Johnson,* Vol. XI, p. 142:
"Cibber, according to his engagement, repaid *Dunciad* with another pamphlet, which, Pope said, "would be as good as a dose of hartshorn to him", but his tongue and his heart were at variance. I have heard Mr. Richardson relate that he attended his father, the painter, on a visit, when one of Cibber's pamphlets came into the hands of Pope, who said, "These things are my diversion". They sat by him while he perused it, and saw his features writhing with anguish; and young Richardson said to his father, when they returned, that he hoped to be preserved from such diversion as had been that day the lot of Pope."

[2] Page 12.

[3] Vol. IV, Introduction to the Dunciad, p. 29.

editors say: "Warton and Bowles have blamed Pope for replacing Theobald by Cibber, on the ground that the character of the latter disqualified him for the throne of Dulness. This objection is not very well founded. It is true that Cibber, as his lively *Apology* shows, was not a Dunce of the same kind as Theobald. But in the word 'Dulness', Pope meant to include every sort of rebellion against right reason and good taste: the pert Templars are as much the subjects of the Goddess as the pedantic critics:

Laborious, heavy, busy, bold and blind,
She rules in native anarchy the mind.

Cibber is chosen as the type of pertness and impudence, and Pope's judgment on him was not simply arbitrary. As a writer he had openly proclaimed his slender acquaintance with literature; as a theatrical manager he had sanctioned exhibitions which lowered the character of the stage: and, as a laureate, he was allowed to be the worst that ever wrote a birthday ode. Besides, the notoriety of his character and his public position, qualified him better than Theobald to be the hero of a poem which had been considerably increased in moral weight by the addition of the Fourth Book."

This, to be sure, is a good example of the specious argumentation and incoherent accumulation of unconvincing and contradictory statements, typical of a critic, eager to whitewash the character of the author whose works he is editing.

Every attempt to prove that Cibber was dull, is bound to be a failure, for it is incredible that anybody, acquainted with his life and works, should be so lacking in artistic and literary taste as to persist in the attempt in the face of such evidence as may be gathered from *Love's Last Shift, The Careless Husband,* and several others of his plays and especially from his *Apology*.

Cibber himself felt he could rely on the intrinsic value of his work to be a sufficient refutation of the criticisms of Pope and others, as appears from the quotation with which he concludes the second chapter of his *Apology,* the last few pages of which are entirely devoted to Pope's attacks on him:

"Time is the judge; time has nor friend, nor foe;
False fame will wither, and the true will grow;
Armed with this truth, all critics I defy,
For, if I fall, by my own pen I die.
While snarlers strive with proud but fruitless pain,
To wound immortals, or to slay the slain."

LIST OF BOOKS AND ARTICLES CONSULTED

Addison and Steele. The Spectator.

An Apology for the Life of Mr The' Cibber, Comedian, being a Proper Sequel 'to the Apology for the Life of Mr. Colley Cibber, Comedian, with an Historical View of the Stage to the Present Year. Supposed to be written by Himself in the Style and Manner of the Poet Laureat. Dublin 1741.

A. Aston. A brief Supplement to Colley Cibber Esq., his Lives of the Late Famous Actors and Actresses. By Anthony, vulgo, Tony Aston. Printed for the Author. *(Undated; in the Catalogue of the British Museum it is queried for 1747).*

Thomas Baker. The Humour of the Age. A Comedy. As it is Acted at the Theatre Royal in Drury-Lane by His Majesty's Servants. London 1701.

Thomas Baker. An act at Oxford. A Comedy. London 1704.

F. W. Bateson. The Double Gallant of Colley Cibber, The Review of English Studies, Vol. I, No. 3.

A. Beljame. Le Public et les Hommes de Lettres en Angleterre au dix-huitième siècle (1660—1744). Paris 1897.

E. Bernbaum. The Drama of Sensibility. A Sketch of the History of English Sentimental Comedy and Domestic Tragedy (1696—1780). Boston and London 1915.

R. Besser. Colley Cibber's *The Double Gallant* und seine Quellen. Halle 1903.

G. Birkbeck Hill. Boswell's Life of Johnson. Oxford 1887.

The Cambridge History of English Literature. Cambridge 1909.

H. S. Canby. Congreve as a Romanticist. Publications of the Modern Language Association of America, Vol. XXXI, I.

C. Cibber. Plays. London 1721.

C. Cibber. The Dramatic Works. London 1760.

C. Cibber. The Dramatic Works. London 1777.

C. Cibber. The Careless Husband. The First Edition. London 1705.

C. Cibber. The Careless Husband. The second Edition. London 1705.
Another Edition. London 1710.
The Sixth Edition. Dublin 1723.
The Seventh Edition. London 1731.
Another Edition. London 1735.
Another Edition. Dublin 1752.
The Eighth Edition. Dublin 1760.
Another Edition. London 1771.

C. Cibber. An Apology for the Life of Colley Cibber, Comedian, and late Patentee of the Theatre Royal. The Golden Cockerel Press, 1925.

W. J. Courthope. A History of English Poetry. London 1911.

P. Cunningham. The Letters of Horace Walpole, fourth Earl of Oxford. Edinburgh 1906.

E. Curll. The Life of That Eminent Comedian Robert Wilks, Esq. London 1733.

Thomas Davies. Dramatic Miscellanies. London 1785.

John Dennis. The Stage defended, from Scripture, Reason, Experience and the Common Sense of Mankind for Two Thousand Years. London 1726.

J. Dennis. The Age of Pope. London 1921.

R. Dohse. Colley Cibber's Bühnenbearbeitung von Shakespeare's Richard III. Bonner Beiträge zur Anglistik, Heft 2, 1899.

W. Egerton. Faithful Memoirs of the Life, Amours and Performances of That Justly Celebrated and most Eminent Actress of her Time, Mrs. Anne Oldfield. Interspersed with several other Dramatical Memoirs. London 1731.

W. Elwin and W. J. Courthope. The works of Alexander Pope. With Introduction and Notes. London 1889.

Joseph Gay. A Compleat Key to The Non-Juror, Explaining the Characters in that Play, with Observations thereon. The Third Edition. London. Printed for E. Curll, 1718.

Genest. Some account of the English Stage, from the Restoration in 1660 to 1830. Bath 1832.

H. Glicksman. The Stage History of Colley Cibber's: "The Careless Husband". Publ. Mod. Lang. Ass. of America, Vol. XXXVI, 1921.

E. Gosse. A History of Eighteenth Century Literature (1660—1780). London 1889.

J. R. Green. Short History of the English People. London 1916.

Antoine Hamilton. Mémoires du Comte de Grammont. Histoire Amoureuse de la cour d'Angleterre sous Charles II. Réimpression conforme à l'édition princeps (1713). Paris 1876.

Haslewood. Dramatic Tracts and Papers, collected by Mr. Haslewood.

William Hazlitt. Lectures in the English Comic Writers. Third Edition. Edited by his son. London 1840.

W. Heldt. A Chronological and Critical Review of the appreciation and condemnation of the comic Dramatists of the Restoration and Orange Periods. Neophilologus VIII, 1 & 2.

A Hymn to the New Laureate by a Native of Grubstreet. London 1731.

I. d'Israeli. Miscellanies of Literature. London 1840.

Stephen Jones. Biographia Dramatica. Originally compiled to the year 1764 by *David Erskine Baker.* Continued thence to 1782, by *Isaac Reed* F. A. S. Brought down to the end of Nov. 1811 by *Stephen Jones.* London 1812.

J. Knight. John Downes. Roscius Anglicanus, or, an Historical Review of the Stage from 1660 to 1706. A fac-simile Reprint of the Rare Original of 1708. With an Historical Preface. London 1886.

K. Köppe. Das Verhältnis von Cibber's "Papal Tyranny in the Reign of King John" zu Shakespeare's "King John". Halle 1901.

W. Krüger. Das Verhältnis von Colley Cibber's Lustspiel "The Comical Lovers" zu John Drydens "Marriage à la Mode" und "Secret Love, or, The Maiden Queen". Halle 1902.

J. W. Krutch. Comedy and Conscience after the Restoration. New York 1924.

Gustave Lanson. Histoire Illustrée de la Littérature Française. Paris 1923.

A Lash for the Laureat; or an Address by way of Satyr; Most Humbly Inscribed to the Unparallel'd Mr. Rowe, on Occasion of a late Insolent Prologue to the Non-Juror. London 1718.

The Laureat; or the Right Side of Colley Cibber, Esq; containing Explanations, Amendments, and Observations, on a Book intituled, An Apology for the Life of Colley Cibber. With some anecdotes which he (thro' modesty) omitted. To which is added the History of the Life, Manners and Writings of Aesopus. London 1740.

W. D. H. Lecky. A History of England in the Eighteenth Century. London 1882.

J. R. Lowell. My Study Windows. The Scott Library. London. Boston and London 1871.

Macaulay. The Comic Dramatists of the Restoration. Tauchnitz-Edition. Vol. 188.

Jeannette Marks. English Pastoral Drama, 1660-1798. London 1908.

B. Matthews. The Dramatic Essays of Charles Lamb. London 1891.

The London Medley; containing the exercises spoken by Several Young Noblemen and Gentlemen, at the Annual Meeting of the Westminster Scholars, on the 28th of Jan. 1730-1, at Westminster School; London: Printed for J. Roberts, near the Oxford Arms in Warwick-Lane.

L. Melville. Life and Letters of John Gay London 1921.

E. Michels. Quellenstudien zu Colley Cibber's Lustpiel The Careless Husband. Marburg 1908.

A. Murphy. The Works of Samuel Johnson, with an Essay on his Life and Genius. London 1824.

Allardyce Nicoll. A History of the British Drama. London 1925.

Allardyce Nicoll. A History of Early Eighteenth Century Drama, 1700-1750. Cambridge 1925.

Allardyce Nicoll. A History of Restoration Drama, 1660-1700. Cambridge 1923.

John Nichols. "The Theatre" by Sir Richard Steele; to which are added "The Anti-Theatre"; "The Character of Sir John Edgar"; Steele's Case with the Lord Chamberlain &c. &c. Illustrated with Literary and Historical Anecdotes. London 1791.

G. Ost. Das Verhältnis von Cibber's Lustspiel "Love makes a Man" zu Fletcher's Dramen "The Elder Brother" und "The Custom of the Country". Halle 1897.

J. Palmer. The Comedy of Manners. London 1913.

Rapp. Studien über das Englische Theater. Tübingen 1862.

Remarks on 'Squire Ayre's Memoirs of the Life and Writings of Mr. Pope in a letter to Mr. Edmund Curl, Bookseller. London 1745.

G. Saintsbury. The Peace of the Augustans. London 1916.

G. Saintsbury. The Best Plays of John Dryden. The Mermaid Series.

G. Saintsbury. The Best Plays of Thomas Shadwell. The Mermaid Series.

Sawney and Colley, a Poetical Dialogue occasioned by a Late Letter from The Laureat of St. James to the Homer of Twickenham. Something in the Manner of Dr. Swift. London *(Undated)*.

F. E. Schelling. English Drama. Channels of English Literature. London 1914.

G. M. Scheurer. An Early Sentimental Comedy. Anglia XXXVII, 1913.

W. Schneider. Das Verhältnis von Colley Cibber's Lustspiel "The Non-Juror" zu Molière's Tartuffe. Halle 1903.

Henry Steele. Some Cursory Remarks on the Play call'd "The Non-Juror", Written by Mr. Cibber. London 1718.

Leslie Stephen. History of English Thought. London 1902.

W. M. Stoye. Das Verhältnis von Cibber's Tragödie "Caesar in Egypt" zu Fletchers "The False One". Halle 1897.

Montague Summers. The Works of Aphra Behn. London 1915.

H. Taine. Histoire de la Littérature Anglaise. Paris 1905.

P. Toynbee. Supplement to the Letters of Horace Walpole, fourth Earl of Oxford. Oxford 1918.

H. D. Traill. Social England; A Record of the People. By Various Writers. Edited by H. D. Traill. London 1895.

A. W. Ward. The London Merchant. Belles Lettres Series. Boston & London.

A. W. Ward. A. History of English Dramatic Literature to the Death of Queen Anne. London 1875.

A. W. Ward. The Poetical Works of Alexander Pope. The Globe Edition. London 1908.

O. Waterhouse. The Development of English Sentimental Comedy in the Eighteenth Century. Anglia XXX, 1907.

T. Whincop. Scanderbeg or Love and Liberty. To which are added a List of all the Dramatic Authors, with some Account of their Lives; and of all the Dramatic Pieces ever published in the English Language, to the year 1747. London 1747.

T. Wilks. A General View of the Stage. London 1759.

De Witt C. Croissant. Studies in the works of Colley Cibber. Humanistische Studien. Vol. I, No. I, 1912.

James Wright? Historia Histrionica: An Historical Account of the English Stage, shewing the Ancient Use, Improvement, and Perfection of Dramatick Representations, in this Nation. In a Dialogue of Plays and Players. London 1699.

STELLINGEN

I

De invloed van Collier's *Short View of the Immorality and Profaneness of the English Stage,* wordt in de geschiedenis der Engelsche litteratuur gewoonlijk schromelijk overdreven.

II

Op bladz. 161 van zijn werk *Early Eighteenth Century Drama,* zegt professor Allardyce Nicoll: "The general atmosphere of *The Careless Husband* is immoral."

Dit oordeel is oppervlakkig en dus onjuist.

III

Elke poging om aan te toonen dat Pope terecht Cibber maakte tot den held van *The Dunciad,* is tot mislukking gedoemd.

IV

Ten onrechte meent Dr. Kruisinga, dat in het Engelsch, in "declarative sentences", de hulpwerkwoorden van den toekomenden tijd, "assume the character of enclitic particles added to the subject."

(A Handbook of Present-Day English II, bldz. 26 § 60.)

V

In den zin: "Clara also had passed most of the day there, with a few intervals at her own home; but now Clara *was gone* and Janet too *had gone,"* die volgens dr. Kruisinga, met betrekking tot de cursieve vormen, "seems to show that there is no difference at all," kan een duidelijk verschil tusschen bedoelde constructies worden aangetoond.

(A Handbook of Present-Day English II, bldz. 43 § III, c.)

VI

Ten onrechte beweert professor Clark, dat de, in het geschrift Περὶ ὕψους, cap. X, aangehaalde ode van Sappho, geen kwaliteiten zou bezitten, behoorende tot dezelfde categorie als "Elevation, dignity, grandeur."

(A. F. B. Clark, Boileau and the French Classical Critics in England. Paris 1925, bldz. 373).

VII

De vertaling van den titel Περὶ ὕψους, *"Concerning Effectiveness or Distinction in Literary Style,"* door denzelfden geleerde aanbevolen als "more comprehensive than any yet presented," is èn onvolledig, èn, wat het laatste gedeelte betreft, onjuist.

VIII

De zoogenaamde directe methode van onderwijs in de moderne talen, op orthodoxe wijze toegepast, is niet zoo voortreffelijk, als de voorstanders het doen voorkomen.

IX

Voor de juistheid van de verbetering: *"Quid tu moraris,"* voor: *"Quod tumeraris"* (Marlowe, *The Tragical History of Doctor Faustus,* scene III, v. 20. The Mermaid Series), kunnen bewijsgronden worden aangevoerd, niet aan den tekst ontleend.

X

De critiek van Ruskin op Coleridge's hanteering van het begrip „Vrijheid", in zijn *Ode to France,* berust op een verkeerde basis. (*The Seven Lamps of Architecture* in the New Universal Library, blz. 209 en bldz. 230).

XI

De vrijwel algemeen aanvaarde interpretatie van den titel van Shelley's gedicht E p i p s y c h i d i o n als diminutief van een door hem zelf gemaakt e p i p s y c h e ('a soul upon a soul'), is onjuist.

XII

Ten onrechte laten de commentatoren van Shelley's *Epipsychidion,* v. 304:
"The wandering hopes of one abandoned mother," onbesproken.

XIII

De meening, dat het bij het onderwijs in de vreemde talen van meer belang is dat de leerlingen de stemming van een gedicht voelen en de karakters van een drama begrijpen, dan dat zij de woorden ervan kunnen vertalen, is onjuist en berust niet op een logische gedachtengang.

XIV

Elke maatregel, die er toe zou leiden, dat tusschen de toelating van een leerling tot de middelbare school en de financiëele positie zijner ouders, een nauwer verband wordt gelegd dan thans reeds bestaat, is strijdig met het landsbelang.